CAN HER GLOR
A life of Ma

*To Juliet
Enjoy
Jay Magrave.*

Also by Jay Margrave

The Gawain Quest

Luther's Ambassadors

The Nine Lives of Kit Marlowe

Love and Loyalty

CAN HER GLORY EVER FADE?

A life of Mary Seacole

Jay Margrave

Goldenford Publishers Ltd
Guildford
www.goldenford.co.uk

First published in Great Britain in 2016 by
Goldenford Publishers Limited
The Old Post Office
130 Epsom Road Guildford
Surrey GU1 2PX
Tel: 01483 563307
Fax: 01483 604222
www.goldenford.co.uk

© Jay Margrave 2016

The right of Jay Margrave to be identified as the author of the work has been asserted by her in accordance with the Copyright, Designs and Patents Act 1988.

All rights reserved. No part of this publication may be reproduced, stored in or introduced into a retrieval system, or transmitted, in any form or by any means (electronic, mechanical, photocopying, recording or otherwise), without the prior written permission of both the copyright owner and the publisher of this book.

This book is sold subject to the condition that it shall not, by way of trade or otherwise, be lent, re-sold, hired out or otherwise circulated in any form of binding or cover other than that in which it is published and without a similar condition including this condition being imposed on the subsequent purchaser.

Cover design by Namie King

Printed and bound by CPI Group (UK) Ltd, Croydon, CR0 4YY

ISBN 978-0-9559415-9-7

AUTHOR'S NOTE

It should be pointed out that this is historical fiction and is faithful to the mores and beliefs of the Victorian era. Some readers might find the descriptions of differently coloured peoples embarrassing now. For instance, Mary Seacole describes those of a darker hue than her as *blackies* and describes herself as *yaller*. She calls a servant *Jew Johnny* because all the servants employed by the British in Constantinople were called *Johnnys* (their Turkish names could not be pronounced by the British), but Mary decides to differentiate him as 'Jew'. Whether he was or not we do not know.

I hope that by being faithful to the way Mary saw her world, I have written a novel that will transport the reader back into those times.

CONTENTS

Chapter 1: Herbs and good humour	1
Chapter 2: Ginger tea	7
Chapter 3: Lemon grass for fever	12
Chapter 4: A cure for ignorance.	24
Chapter 5: Curing cholera for one	29
Chapter 6: Mustard and calomel	34
Chapter 7: Raspberry vinegar	38
Chapter 8: Emetics to purge	46
Chapter 9: Cod liver oil	49
Chapter 10: Apple juice	61
Chapter 11: English brewed tea	66
Chapter 12: Sour sorrel	79
Chapter 13: Crates of sherry and champagne	82
Chapter 14: Lavender bags	102
Chapter 15: Wormwood	110
Chapter 16: Warmth, nourishment and fresh air	124
Chapter 17: Lemonade and cake	128
Chapter 18: Lignum vitae	141
Chapter 19: Fig-tree sap	146
Chapter 20: Plantain juice and mercury rubs	151
Chapter 21: Sauces and stews for sustenance	165
Chapter 22: Peruvian bark mixed in brandy and water	172
Chapter 23: Opium	176
Chapter 24: Blistering the patient	180
Chapter 25: Dock leaf to cure the sting	189
Chapter 26: Preserves and guava jelly	202
Chapter 27: Claret, water, lemon peel, sugar, and nutmeg	206
Chapter 28: Kind nursing and attention	215
Chapter 29: Cloves	218
Chapter 30: Porter and pies	223
Chapter 31: Peppermint tea	229
Chapter 32: Incense	243

Chapter 33: Simples and sympathy	251
Chapter 34: Camomile tea compresses	261
Chapter 35: Jelly and sweetmeats	281
Chapter 36: Dandelion and burdock tincture	286
Chapter 37: Finale	304
References	306
Historical note	307

Chapter 1: Herbs and good humour

'You follow dat Mary Seacole and you have nottink' but trouble, all you long life, you ma'k ma words, girl. Nottink but trouble, just trouble. Ya stay home here and be safe.'

Those words echo in my ears, even now, half a century on. My mother was right, but I don't regret one minute of the times I spent travelling, always moving on to the next adventure, with Mother Seacole, far away from my home in Jamaica.

'She might be good with dem herbs, and she don cure you dadda of his aches, but why don' she stop home? Look yah, why don' she just stay with her mother and sister, and keep that Blundells Hotel from goin' bust, and keep you and de others in de wuk?'

My mistress was preparing to leave Jamaica once again, leaving her family and friends, for a place so far away that it would take days and days to get there.

I begged and begged to be let to go – I might've been a pinkney skivvy, but I knew my mind – I didn't want to stay in the heat of Jamaica which made my black skin shiny with sweat as I laboured at my duties.

'Why does a big ooman like her wanna go wey from yah, when she makin' big money out of dem whiteys who like her ackee and curried chicken, hey?'

I didn't listen, or rather I did, and all that my mother said made me want to go even more.

Of course I went, who wouldn't? I was a ten-year-old servant, with half a dozen siblings poking in my meagre belongings, in the wood'n'thatch hut that we called home, and throwing their arms over me as we slept, so I was shot awake of a sudden. My mistress was kind to her servants and it was good to sleep at the hotel, some nights when the cook needed extra help to get the oven going in the mornings. And even though she was my mistress, and so much older than me, she always addressed me as if we were equals. But she was a whole generation of class, if I can put it like that, distant.

Her father was a white soldier, mine a black labourer who had been a slave; *her mother ran her own hotel for white folks;* my parents owned nothing except many children to be fed.

But our lives were to be intertwined from that moment I stood before her and asked, 'Can I go with you, Ma-am? My Madda, she don' says I can.'

She'd looked up from the letter she was laboriously writing, and stared at me. I was supposed to be packing but I judged her to be in a good mood so I'd gone in and asked. I held the folded clothes close to me, as if to hide the lie, instead of putting them in her large portmanteau. It was also to soften the blow against a negative reply.

'You know I'm going to where there are strange men, searching for gold, and they can be rough with women, do you know what that means?'

''Course,' I said, cockily, 'but if you's a-going, then I's a-be safe, you keep a-me safe, safe.'

She smiled, and it was a sad smile. 'We will go where men are cruel to each other and will take what they want from anyone. If we're good to them and lucky, they'll pay well for it, do you understand?'

I could feel the blush darken my skin even more and I twisted the cotton under-garment so that it was like a ball. The palms of my hands were damp and I could see dark marks spreading on the material and tried to twist the clothing even more to hide them. Of course I understood, I'd seen what the boat boys did to their girls on the beach in the twilight, and had felt a rush of something I didn't understand in the depth of my belly and knew it was to do with babies being made.

Mary gave her deep laugh that I knew so well, at my embarrassment, 'Mary, not like that. I mean I will travel as a doctress, and hotel keeper, and supply the men with good food and warm blankets, and cure their ills. And, if my luck holds, I'll be well paid for my ministrations to them. I'll leave such pleasures to others.'

She came towards me and took the clothes that I held so tight that they were well and truly crumpled, and placed them on top of the other items in the trunk.

'I will ask your mother, of course,' I opened my mouth to protest but she continued. 'And you must be kitted out. You'll need more than just that simple shift. I have travelled in other Caribbean islands and also to England, where sometimes it is so cold that you can see your breath freezing – imagine a cool Jamaica night and then imagine it ten times as cold.'

I shivered as she spoke, even though I couldn't imagine it being that cold, but nodded, and replied, 'Ma-am I don't care, I want to go and madda, she seys I can, I'se already asked.'

Now that my hands were free I twisted one of my tight braids in excitement and also to hide the lie – a habit I would never lose. I felt it was my fate, to follow a mistress with the same name as mine.

Mother said no of course, and I got a beating for lying.

Mary was kinder and tried to explain. 'I must respect your family's views and if they say no, then it's no. Anyway, you're too young. Wait for my next trip and I promise you can come. In the meantime, you can still help out here, working for my sister Louisa. You're too keen to slope off, and need to learn more about looking after guests. Lousia might also teach you about the use of herbs, and perhaps cooking. Then you will be useful to me.'

I knew she was trying to comfort me, but there was no way I was going to stay with Louisa. She was younger than Mary and for some reason hadn't learnt kind ways. She was a sourpuss who carried out her duties with a stiff back and made sure everyone around her knew she was suffering as she worked. Both Mary and her mother had run their family hotel in a relaxed manner but Louisa was stricter, as if she had to prove she was as good as her older sister.

What grown ups didn't know was that my tiny frame could hide in all sorts of places, and it was when I'd hid in her portmanteau before, that I'd heard about her exploits in the great mother country, England. She'd returned home, and, before she'd even emptied her trunks, she'd been in the kitchen ordering people about, so she could relax with a good blend of tea, and sit down and tell her mother about her journey. I grabbed the opportunity, knowing she and her mother would sit on the veranda, surrounded by her unpacked trunks and packages, so I could eavesdrop, I was that curious. As I listened, although her voice was muffled through the thickness of the portmanteau, I was fired by a longing to go with her if she went off again.

So it wasn't difficult to get away with her by slipping into that large portmanteau, making a sort of nest on one side and hiding under her bodices and petticoats. I had some qualms as Louisa came into the room, moaning about having to do everything, and pulled the other side of the portmanteau onto where I was hiding, and snapped shut the catch.

I'd taken a bag full of water bottles, mangoes I picked off the tree in their garden, and some sugar cane that I'd filched from a market stall and a chicken pie from the kitchen. I also placed a potty underneath Mammy's smalls, hoping I could sneak out and empty this when Mammy was asleep. When, a few days later, I felt the land swell beneath me, so that I felt sick, and was forced out of hiding by hunger and thirst, I pushed open the trunk and found myself in my mistress's cabin.

Of course she was mighty angry when she first saw me emerge and pulled my pigtails in a ferocious manner, holding my arm so I couldn't wriggle free.

'What am I going to do with you? I can't send you back, and look how my clothes are all ruffled.'

'No, I can iron them for you, Mammy.'

She couldn't help smiling at my cheekiness and shrugged. She still held on to me, as she thought what to do.

I got to call her Mammy because everyone else called her Mother Seacole. She earned the nickname from the way she looked after the British soldiers at Up-park Camp. Sometimes they'd be sick even before they got to the island. I never did have much respect for them 'cos they seem feeble to me but Mammy was kind and careful with them, as I seen.

Eventually she loosened her grip on my arm, and looked into the portmanteau where she could see the little nest I had made for myself with her clothes neatly piled around it. What she don't know is that I ditched some of her undergarments to make sure I fitted. I hope she won't notice because I'll be the one doing the laundry and I think that if I can wash them more often she won't notice some are missing.

When she let go of me, I backed away, waiting for the next onslaught of anger but suddenly she's laughing and looking at me.

'Surely you are the naughtiest girl I ever did know. I can't send you back on your own, so you'll have to stick by me now and I hope you don't regret it. You are going to work harder than ever, because as I warned you, where we're going is just not civilised.'

One of her traits is that she don't hold anger too long – she might shout and be forceful for a while but she calms down quicker'n lightning and that's one reason why I wanted to go with her.

'But I can't keep on calling you Mary; that's my name and I'm mighty proud of it but if someone's calling me and you're there too, who is they calling?'

I didn't say anything, but sometimes her sister Louisa, who is as bossy as Mary but not with her charm, would just call out 'girl' and I always knew she meant me. But I didn't like it and might linger a little too long so she would have to call again.

After a pause, she raised her hands and exclaimed, 'I know. I'm going to call you Horatia after someone who was dear to me, so you will always remind me of him. And I hope that the name will make you as goodhearted and helpful as he was. One day I might tell you all about your namesake.'

So that was who I became and over time, with the bustle of our life together, I became 'Ratia' and I didn't mind at all, 'cos Mammy don't yell at me, but calls calmly with a smile in her deep voice.

Chapter 2: Ginger tea

Here I am then, everyone knowing me as Ratia now, sitting by the side of a dirty harbour in a place called Navy Bay, surrounded by crowds, who take no notice of me as I sit patiently on top of those portmanteaux which have become so familiar to me.

Mammy and me travelled in a steam boat and I never did see such black smoke belching and so much noise as that engine made and shuddering of the planks beneath my feet, so that I was glad when we landed on the coast of Panama, where Mammy is going to seek out her brother. She reckons that she can find him upriver, where they're searching for gold, and she's left me with the luggage so she can search out how we get to go upriver.

I'm back to back with Mammy's other servant. I don't know him that well yet but he's black like me and has a smiley face and he reminds me of my Dadda, who smiles a sad smile, so I did like him right away when I see him loping after Mammy.

When she left me to look after the boxes and cases I'd had a hard time of it, having to run round and scream at the thieves who buzzed round me, worse than the no-see-ums we have at home, darting at me, and trying to swipe a bag or case, while white men laughed and pointed. It's raining and I'm wet through and my hair is so tight frizzed that it hurts my head.

I'm not going to say I regret the travelling but it wasn't like I thought it would be. I spent a deal of time being sick on the boat journey, until Mammy dragged me on deck and told me to look at the sea. She also gave me some ginger tea, assuring me it would settle my stomach. On deck, after another puke, I leant on the rail and looked and it was beautiful with gold and silver flecks and *moving* all the time. I never could have imagined that – I thought it would be like the harbour I knew at home, with gentle blue waves, broken sometimes when a fish comes to the surface, but here it was rolling up into crests like mountains, and down into valleys and the vessel we were on was riding these mountains. I know I'd seen the sea crashing on the beach at home but I thought that was because it was hitting our island.

After a while, as I watched and wondered I forgot about the sea sickness. When Mammy could see I was well, she explained about the tides and how the seas in the world were constantly being pulled one way and another by the moon. I'd been working so hard as a skivvy, falling asleep as soon as my work was finished that I'd not had time to learn these things, and no-one had ever bothered to tell me anything except what I needed to know, to help out at the hotel. Except Mammy had explained, back home, about the medicines she used, as she got me grinding and pounding, and I learnt quick. And that was another reason why it was good to be with Mammy. But now I am cold and wet and it doesn't seem such a good idea.

'It's not fair, leaving us here like this to be stared at by all these strangers.'

Mac, who she had hired in Gatun, laughed and pats me on the shoulder.

'You lucky, young lady, and you moaning? What else you gonna do? You can't bargain with the boatmen and she can, 'cos she's got the authority.'

I don't answer. I know he's right, but that little devil in me starts again when a white man stares at me like I'm dirt. I stare him out as I moan, 'But she could have left us with the umbrella, to keep dry. And anyway, all her goods are getting wet as well.'

The white man sneers at me and I rile but look away. I've seen white men before coming to the hotel, and sometimes they're kind and sometimes they ignore us servants, but they don't sneer and I wonder why he does that.

Mac's kind and his white teeth gleam as he smiles at me.

He's wearing a funny rubbery overcoat which is keeping him dry but now he stands and takes it off and wraps it round me.

'All right, little lady, it's true you'n not yet toughened up so I'se a let you have my coat, for now, and I'm sure Mrs Seacole will be back soon. Oy, you! Just you put that back.'

He takes a swipe at a vagabond who sneaks up behind us, and is about to take one of the packages spread around us, as he's helping me on with the coat. We're then very vigilant because the porters are surrounding us, eager to help – if it can be called that – but Mammy has warned us they'll filch anything if we're not careful. We know that if we let our guard down just one second they'll be off with one of the bags.

I'm a bit more comfortable now I'm not being soaked, so I start to enjoy watching the passers-by while Mammy's off searching for a way to navigate the river on the next stage to her brother. That was the reason Mammy gave to her sister, who didn't want to be left alone and in charge of the *establishment* as she described it. We've travelled to a place called Panama and it's wild and there's ugly shanty towns that we've passed on the coast. Even though the raincoat gives me some protection, the golden clay is being splashed up my ankles as horses and carts go by.

Mac tells me why the passers-by are staring at us.

Oh, missy, you not be anywheres, 'ave you? Look yah, we're two black servants without a master, and where I come from, that looks like we're slaves and should be chained with a slavemaster over us. They prob'bly think we're escaped slaves.'

Slave, me? My Fada and Madda, they'm mighty proud that they no longer slaves, though we're poor and we all us chillun have to work, so I hold my head high.

I take pride in protecting Mammy's goods. I know I have to stop the thieves from making off with the medicine chest, or Mammy's special bag with her hats in it. I know that the medicine bag is the magic that means she earns money and she loves her hats, does Mammy and I know I'd get a telling off if they go. So I stay vigilant, and thankfully so does Mac. And then, as I wait, I see the most gorgeous lady approaching us, her sedate walk, head in air, making the crowd step aside for her. She's holding a gaily coloured umbrella and somehow the rain doesn't seem to touch her.

Despite the downpour, she's exquisitely dressed in a shimmering outfit of white lace, her waist pinched tight with a gleaming silvery belt and a white lace veil held in place with a flowery tiara. The veil shadows her face and she walks towards us with such determined strides I'm sure we will have to get out of her way, but my mistress comes across the road and her stride is also determined so that she reaches the raised pathway before the lady and hides her from view. Eventually both women meet, and they edge around each other, careful not to touch or step off into the mud. The apparition glides on her way without a backward glance. I gape and turn to watch her go. Mammy grabs one of my braids and murmurs, 'Don't stare – she's a bad woman. That type follow the men to the gold, take what they can and then abandon them when there's no more gold. They're as bad as them girls back home who hung around Up-Park Camp.'

I know what she means but this lady was dressed so much more pretty than those back home. And she didn't hide her shame like the whores – there, I've said the word – who earn their living by giving their bodies to the soldiers for coin.

Mammy chivvies us along to the harbour, where she's found a boat and I daydream about the beautiful tiara as I struggle with the two cases I've been entrusted with, which are as heavy as lead, even though I'm not in one of them. We board this mean little boat with one hammock and Mammy watches as Mac and I stow her boxes and paraphernalia evenly.

'We don't want to rock the boat, now do we?' she laughs as she settles her large carpet bag onto the hammock and dives into the bag to fetch out a mirror – of all things – to settle her hair.

Her hair is tight and curly but not as frizzed as mine, but she primps and perms it so it looks straight so she could look more white than she is. She was never cruel to us but always aware of
her higher status as a Creole.
'You two sleep under the hammock and it'll be dry there. This rain is the heaviest I did see in my life but if we can bear this in our travels, we can bear anything, can't we?'

Mac and I look at each other and I can see in his eye what I call the old slave look, which I learned from my parents; don't say anything but we know what the master means. But I turn away because Mammy would never be as bad as the old slave masters, even though she is better'n us.

With the mackintosh – Mac has told me what it's called now – and I think it's called that because it belongs to him - over me, and the hammock above me, it's not so bad and Mac sleeps head to toe with me but I'm tiny enough to fit in the small of his back, so's we're back to back, and I sleep well.

And the next day it's still raining.

Chapter 3: Lemon grass for fever

It's still raining days later, when we reach Cruces, after we've walked through jungle, navigated a narrow river where we'd only had guavas to eat and trekked through jungle where I'd been startled by a huge snake dropping from the tree just in front of my face. We had passed small shanty towns along the way where Mammy had purchased rancid meat that had tasted nasty even after hours of cooking. Mammy had even sprinkled it with precious herbs but it still took real hunger to eat it.

'Don't worry, when we reach my dear brother's house, all will be well.' Mammy's voice was soothing but it couldn't penetrate the misery of always being wet, despite the *mackintosh*.

'We'll have hot baths and good food, he assures me all is well and he is looking forward to welcoming us.'

I knew that she had set out on a whim, after a letter had arrived, months late, from brother Edward, who I remembered as a scrawny sickly man, the opposite to his sisters 'cos both Mammy and her sister Louisa have straight backs and are well upholstered, showing what strong women they are.

He'd written and told how he'd used her remedies to make himself well after a bout of fever, but that he was still weak. That was when she'd hurriedly packed those cases which I knew so well by now, even though they were battered and misshapen.

So we land at Cruces and Mammy, Mac and me watch as the porters carry our baggage onto the wet landing slip – a few rough boards that are hardly connected together with black tar. And there's Edward waiting for us, smiling broadly and I think he's laughing at Mammy's appearance, 'cos after our rough journey she don't look like no lady. Her ballooning skirts are caked with dry mud and her hair is all ratty-tailed and she smells, but that ain't her fault. You would think that with all that rain we travelled through we would be kept clean but I learnt soon that it don't work like that.

I watch as they hug, and notice that Edward is still scrawny, as Mammy seems to squash him in her arms, and his face is a soft yellow colour. Edward struggles free and points upwards and so we follow him as he makes his way into the main town. It is a rough place of hovels made of what seems to me to be flotsam and jetsam; planks of wood joined together without any finesse or design. There's no verandas or fancy trellis-work here, to shade from the sun, even if they have sun in this place. A gap in a wall here and there I guess is where a window should be, but there's no window frame, and most of the holes are covered with rough material, which flaps in the breeze.

I keep close to Mammy because they're talking in low tones and I don't like the way Mammy's reacting.

'I hope you won't be disappointed with my place. I warn you it's not like mother's hotel in Jamaica – here it's rough and ready, I'm afraid.'

She's leaning on his arm now, and I hear her reply,

'Brother, all I need is a good bath and a stint in the laundry house for Ratia here, after she's had a bath as well of course. If I can get out of these clothes and put on some decent clean ones, your hotel will be luxury.'

He doesn't reply but gestures up the hill where we can see that the 'town' peters out and there's jagged trees. Some of the palms don't have leaves and I notice that the hovels have roofs of dried leaves, instead of the neat shingles of the houses in East Street, Kingston that I'm used to. There's a large stream of muddy water on either side of what might be a road, it's pitted where the wagons roll slowly along and it's edged either side by boardwalks outside the buildings which are raised a little. Some of the buildings don't have any boardwalks outside them so we have to constantly step up and down and I swear that each time we step down there's a huge puddle and the murky water splashes us even more. We make our way through this morass until we get to the end where the jungle starts again. It's as if the men have taken great scythes and cut a straight line, and there's jagged tree-trunks which are sprouting just below where they've been spliced down.

And there's Edward's place. It's just like the others and I begin to fear that we won't have hot water for that bath.

'It's a good place to be when it rains, at the top of the slope,' he explains with a laugh and Mammy laughs too, although I can tell from her slumping shoulders that she's thinking like me. He adds, 'the real rains come twice a year and the rest of the town is under water but it doesn't reach up here.'

I truly hope we're not here when the real rains come because this rain is sheeting down and I can't imagine anything worse.

As we approach I realise there's a lot of people and mules and horsemen milling around waiting, at the end of the road, and Edward rushes forward.

'Mary, I have to go. The mule trains have arrived from the goldfields.' He turns then and splays out his arms in a funny shrug. 'And I surely don't know where I'm going to put you and your servants because I'm going to be full tonight – even having sleepers in the dining room, I can tell.'

Mary doesn't answer but carries on walking and pushes past him to enter the building he'd indicated is his hotel, and he follows sheepishly after. I step up onto a sort of veranda where at least it's not raining on me, and wait. I don't look at the others leaning on the walls, men who look rough and unshaven, smoking bits of cigar and not talking. Mac catches up with me and we dump our packages and sit down.

Mac, who I learnt can be quite funny sometimes, dances around me and then stops, his face close to mine.

'Come on, little maid, and what's worrying you with a face so down, now that we've arrived?'

I start to cry. I'm dead weary with it all.

'I – I wish I was home with mah madda and fadda,' I sob. He stops joking and looks serious.

'No you don't, just you wait. We've had fun on the way haven't we? Seeing all those weird creatures – when the parrots started to move, you just done gone and stared at their bright colours that you never saw before, and remember the log in the water that moved and you screamed, and come on, it's been fun.'

I'm still crying but I defend myself. 'Well I never did see an alligator before did I?'

'No, but what's upset you now?'

'I done heard them talking and they's no room for us 'cos of all the gold men coming, and he said that we can't even sleep in the dining room. I never slept in a dining room in my life.'

Mac stands in front of me and I know I've got his attention now. 'Well, that's rum, but I know one thing. Your Mammy is in there right now sorting something. If I ain't learnt nothing in the last few weeks, it's that your Mrs Seacole is resourceful and can manage anything; you just wait.'

I cheer up. I should have known. He was right, Mammy would sort it.

Mammy comes out and she looks angry.

'Ratia, Mac, come on in here and bring the best packages with you. We got work to do.'

I gather up some bags eagerly. I can tell Mammy's not angry with us.

I walk past all the men on the veranda, keeping my head down. Those who are smoking cigars blow the smoke my way, and I know they're trying to make me look up. One of them, a darkie dressed in a suit with braces, holds out his hand to me as if I should give him something, or maybe shake it, but I manage to get past him. He eyes the other men and they all laugh, a rude loud mocking laugh, and I scuttle inside.

I follow Mary and find myself in a long low hut, and I can see gaps in the walls that are badly filled with mud and bamboo, with no distemper on them to keep them clean. It's a long room and someone's tried to make it look festive with stripes of red and white calico hung on the walls but it's obvious they've been up a long time. They're all cobwebby and dust settles in the pleats. I can see cracks in the ceiling.

'That's where the bedrooms are,' explains Edward as he sees me looking up. 'They're all taken, Mary, I don't have room for you, as I said. I've even rented out my own room,' He gestures to three smart ladies who are pottering about in a corner, one of them trying to tie a dirty piece of muslin across the entrance.

'What am I to do? Why did you ever bring me here? See what a state I'm in – cold, hungry and wretched.'

I'd never heard my mistress so upset and I try to hide in the gloom, not knowing what would happen. But her brother just shrugs his shoulders. I don't like him.

Mary strides around the hut, and eventually stops in a corner of the room, arms akimbo as if measuring. She calls to me, 'Ratia, find that large muslin curtain we stowed away – yes, in that large portmanteau.'

I hurry 'cos I can tell she's got that anger in her and, after rummaging in the trunk, I hold up the piece.

'Yes, that's it. Mac, come here. Pin that up across this corner. This is our home for now, young Ratia. Mac you'll have to take your chances with the men. Edward, this is my quarters.'

She's laughing now – see how she changes when things are on the up.

Edward doesn't reply, but turns on his heel and strides away. Mammy gestures to me to follow and she starts to poke around in the bar and we then go through a door, and found ourselves in a kitchen. There's something steaming and smelling rancid, on a rough stove that looks like it's made out of old bits of iron from a ship – I recognise the shape from the one we came over on. There's chicken feathers stuck to the greasy floor, which is a dark brown colour, not from the earth that's been beaten down but I reckon from spilt gravy and other spillings. I reckon no-one ain't taken a broom to this place since it was built.

In the corner a boy about my age is curled up half asleep, desite the hub-bub.

I wouldn't want to eat anything that is cooked here and Mammy also looks horrified, 'Edward,' she calls and soon he comes scuttling and I know Mammy's got the better of him for now. 'What's this? Didn't we teach you anything at the old hotel? You know that a place for cooking has to be kept clean – get those chickens out and put them in a coop, Ratia. She strides around, and reaches the boy I spotted, and pokes him so that he jumps awake. 'And you, boy, scrub this table before you start chopping those greens.'

Edward says nothing as his servant look at him and then looks at Mammy. I grin behind my hand as I run towards a chicken and grab it by the legs and hold it up triumphantly showing Mammy. She's smiling at me and I see behind her that there's more servants who have come running in, and they're obeying her – moving quickly and running round, and I reckon they think she'll hit them with the umbrella she still holds if they don't get that kitchen sparkling soon.

'I don't know what makes you stay in this God-forsaken spot, I really don't.' Mammy grumbled at her brother.

He shrugs as he watches the bustle, and explains. 'Since they discovered gold in California, about eighteen months ago – I reckon it was early 1848, Mary – there's a constant stream of people coming and going, and we can demand prices which they have to pay. The men who come through here are rough. All they want is a bed for the night and something to fill their bellies. There's good profits, here.'

Mammy doesn't say anything, but it's not long before she's stirring the pot and adding some herbs from her own supplies and the cloying smell disappears to be replaced by Mammy's special savoury odour that I recognise from home and I begin to feel much more comfortable.

And that night we eat well and so does everyone else and the rough men eat greedily, some with their hands and others cutting their food with daggers they keep on their belts. Even the Americans and local whites are eating as if their hunger could not be satisfied. Mammy says nothing but observes, her arms folded in front of her. I watch my manners in front of Mammy even though I'm as hungry as everyone else, if not hungrier.

And the night is a riot. Edward won't allow gambling in his place which pleases Mammy, but the men only travel a few buildings down to drink and gamble and there's a lot of noise. The local women dance and I watch them for a while and tap my feet to the staccato rhythm of their music. I wish I could join them and move the way they're moving which gives me that strange feeling in my belly. Mammy watches too and I know she don't approve so I try to hide in the shadows and watch her, still tapping my feet to the wild rhythm.

I can see she's thinking and I sure hope she's thinking that this is no place for us and we should hot foot it back home.

But that isn't at all what's on her mind, as I soon find out the next morning after we've helped with the breakfasts and the visitors move on, some to get down to Panama to take the boat out of the country, and others joining mule trains on the way to the goldfields of California, and I sure don't know which group is the saddest. The newcomers are anxious in a sort of civilised way but the ones coming from the goldfields are wild either with too much gold or through the lack of it.

'I can't stay here, Edward, but I reckon there's enough trade for both of us,' she says when she returns from what she describes as 'reconnoitring' – 'I've found something across the way that I'm going to work on.'

'But, Sis, you were going to help me,' says Edward but it sounds faint. I'm still grinning because I know he's no match for his elder sister.

I also gather from his lack of welcome that he'd forgotten

how bossy his elder sister could be. Maybe he's regretting her coming now.

'Sure I'll help – by getting a restaurant set up opposite – no beds for the night – so these travellers can eat well and then sleep l at your place, how does that sound?'

He doesn't answer 'cos he knows he's beat but I'm not sure I like this because it sounds like a mighty lot of hard work.

'Come, Ratia, let's sort this place out before the next group of travellers pass by.'

I grab my bag and look at Mac who is already gathering up other parcels and we follow – to find she's settled herself just across the road, in a cabin not unlike her brother's but even more cobwebby and with plants already growing out of the floor where it had been abandoned. We set to work. She gets me scrubbing and washing and polishing before Mac is shown how to pin up the multi-coloured ribbons and bows and banners that Mary produces from her many portmanteaux and I then open up the muslin sheets. Our muslin covers are clean and I proudly display them to Mac who touches them gingerly before helping me to spread them over the trestle table that he's set up. It's all made of rough wood and old stuff that people have thrown away but after we're finished it looks just like Mammy's place back in Jamaica and my homesickness starts to fade.

Soon she calls us to look at what we've done, and she's been working as well so I can't complain. There's a long wooden bench in the middle of the room, and it's scrubbed so clean you can see the inner grain under the thin muslin cloth.

The rest of the place is the same – she's somehow managed to find a range which is spotless and there's food galore being delivered.

And Mary doesn't miss a trick. I see her leaning against her umbrella watching an argument between her brother and a darkie.

I creep up behind her and listen.

Edward's saying, 'No, I don't want your services. No room here. Go away, go on. Stop bothering me.' He's shooing the man off his steps so that he nearly falls backwards.

The man's got a leather parcel under his arm, like its gotknives and other sharp equipment in it as I seen back home. Mary saunters over and I just about hear her talking to the men.

'Now, what's the matter, Edward, didn't mama tell you always to be kind and polite to people. Why're you being so rude to this man?'

'He thinks he can ply his trade here, and I don't want him bothering my guests.'

'And what is your trade, man?'

'I'm a barber, ma'am, thinking I can pay my way to the goldfields and make my fortune where I don't have to barber no more to the rich white men who are always rude to me.'

I see her smiling at him and she puts her hand on his arm to guide him away from her brother who puts one arm akimbo and the other to his forehead in a gesture which says, *now what is she up to?*

'Come, making fortunes out of gold is a pipe dream. You've got a skill and you should use it to make your living and I'm going to help you do that. What's your name?'

'José, Ma-am,'

'Well, José, you can set up here, on my veranda, and have as many hot towels as you need, and paying me one shilling per towel and you can ply your trade here so long as my British Hotel is here. How does that sound?'

He nods and I run inside and get a good chair and a small table, a bowl and a jug of water, guessing that is what he needs from what I'd seen at home and Mammy pats me on the head and congratulates me.

So we are all set up and we wait for our first customers coming through.

And they do come – all in a rush and they all expect to be

fed and housed and shaved, and José is busy and I'm dashing around with laundry and food and everything is noisy and busy.

Our place is a haven of order compared to what happens outside, with wicked ladies leaning on Edward's veranda – Mammy shooshes them away from our place – and gambling tables set up, and Spanish singers and dancers who Mammy says look cheap and tawdry. but I like their wild singing which makes me want to tap my feet to the hard rhythm before Mammy gently pulls me away and points at the washing up that is piling up behind me.

I seen guns and daggers drawn at them gambling tables and Mammy warns me never to get involved, even though there's other women gambling with the men and swearing and hollering just like them. There's even a makeshift racecourse set up just in front of Mammy and Edward's place and Mammy and me set to making pies and her special lemon drink and she's mighty pleased with the money she makes that day.

The mule trains move on and the people disappear and that's what Edward hasn't told us – that in between there's nothing and no-one comes through. So all is boom or bust, but Mammy as ever is not one to be put off.

'Ratia, here's what we do. We cut up these here and make more towels – we'll have more'n anyone can ever want so that when there's a queue for José's services he don't have to wait for anything – and that'll keep us busy when we're waiting.'

See, she always is busy and so am I and I like it that way.

On another day she goes wandering in the forest and comes back with armloads of strange fruit which she boils up and makes chutneys and jams, somehow finding the jars to store it.

I gonna tell you now how some of them men is good and some is bad and Mammy spots it soon – the Americans are brash and some are happy to throw their money and gold around but some of them are just plain mean and Mammy spot one that is so plain mean that she decides to get her own back. The way it works is this. Chickens and eggs are in short supply so Mammy charges special for them – eightpence an egg and you show her the eggshells at the end of the meal and she charges you per eggshell. But one of them Amerikays, well we can *see* him eating and eating but when he comes to pay he shows two eggshells.

I say nothing but I can see Mammy's eyes creasing in that way that shows she's a-thinking and the next night, when he comes in all smug and strutting out his big belly even though he's as thin as a polecat that hasn't eaten for months, she whispers to me, 'Ratia, climb under the table near him and count what he throws down and then mark his coat tail with this chalk.'

I'm still small so nobody notices when I dive down and crawl under the table. I recognise the man by his trousers which are tight and stretch over his skinny thighs. His shoes ain't polished either.

And Mammy's right 'cos I watch him drop eight eggshells – *eight* – how can a man eat that many and still stand up at the end of the meal? But it's even worse because he hands Mammy two eggshells as normal but before he gets out two shillings I am standing next to him holding up his coat tails with the chalk mark on it.

'I don't think so, sir,' says Mammy, 'Not sixteen pence but eighty pence please, for your dinner, for my little maid here has got you all found out.' She says it jokingly and loudly pointing at the chalk mark on his coat tails, so his colleagues turn and listen and they are laughing as well as Mammy.

But our quarry is furious and he bangs down the money in front of Mammy and storms out, almost falling over a chair leg as he goes. The room is in uproar as the story is relayed to those who didn't hear and everyone is slapping each other and laughing. Bet we don't see him again.

And betting is what everyone gets up to in this place but

Mammy don't allow any of it in her British Hotel, but she watches as Edward sets up tables on his veranda, just across the road and tuts as she comes in and I hear her muttering,
  'I'll have to tell him, it's not how we were taught.'
The next thing I see she's strutting across the road – I know I am supposed to be mixing the dough for that day's bread – and I see her pointing and shrugging and I can just guess what she's saying, but Edward is just staring at her, one arm on his hip, the other at his forehead as if she's hurting him with her words.

And I reckon she is, because when Mammy speaks bad to you, it's really bad. But then it don't last long and you can see her shoulders drooping and she steps inside as he gestures and I reckon she's going to take a drink with him before our real cooking starts for the dinner we give our guests. I turn and pound into the dough.

Chapter 4: A cure for ignorance.

One night Mammy comes back from Chagres where she orders supplies for the hotel, really tired and she don't ask for nothing but her bed, and I stash away a few of the packages she's brought in, but I'm tired too, even though, while she was away, I had a good afternoon nap. So now I can't sleep and then I hear it, the scraping of the roof, which is more than the old mules munching the thatch and the next moment I see moonlight coming through and a couple of legs appearing. I scream but at first Mammy don't wake up and nor does Mac come. I jump up and go to wake Mammy but the intruder's following me so I hide under the bed, which shakes so much because Mammy is wide awake now.

She's seen him and she's screaming too now, real loud – as I say, Mammy's got a strong voice on her and it sounds like the whole town is going to wake up.

Despite that, the man's grabbed her dress which is hanging on the bottom of the bed. I know that's where she keeps her money so I try to stop him by pulling it towards me, down under the bed with me. It's then that I see the glint of a knife and I beetle it back under the bed, but I still hold tight to the skirts and I'm praying it don't tear. But Mammy is brave – or so mad she don't care what she's gonna do and she's suddenly in view, and she's holding the old rusty pistol that brother of her's gave her and she's pointing at the man, and screaming, 'you let that go, or I'll shoot.'

I'm so scared that I let go of the dress and the robber falls backwards, holding it still, but he catches his balance and then he runs and I don't blame him.

Mammy chases him but she's got too much weight to catch him and she comes back.

'Ratia, where are you?'

I creep out from my hiding place and run to her and we hug each other in fear. Her doggone brother doesn't come until the morning. I settle at the bottom of her bed and, as dawn comes up, I fall asleep.

I'm woken by Mammy bustling about and she calls, 'awake at last, come we've work to do. I found my purse and dress, outside and everything's fine. He must've dropped it in his fright to get away.' She's saying it gaily, and I can see that, now it's day, she's looking on it as just another adventure. 'The mule train'll be here soon, so let's get cooking.'

Despite her light-heartedness, I can see she's rattled because she drops stirring spoons and asks me to find tins of tea or flour. I'm hoping maybe she'll think about going because this place is getting me down.

When the rainy season comes again and the visitors dry up Mammy begins to look around for something to occupy her and I have an idea. I know my numbers up to twenty – I could count how many eggs that doggone Yankee had eaten – and I have some idea of the alphabet but I can't really read and when it comes to the addings and the takings away that Mammy does in her little notebook I don't know none of it.

So I sidle up to her when she's sitting on the veranda, picking over some dry goods that are no longer dry and trying to save some, and I stand in front of her, wondering how to start. I twist my braid around until she notices me.

'Yes, Ratia, what is it?' she says softly, somehow knowing that I'se a mite embarrassed.

'Mammy, will you teach me to read, proper, and to do those sums you do?'

She puts down the pack of flour that's all damp at the bottom where the rain's come in and gestures to me to get nearer to her.

'How old are you, now?'

'I'm not sure Mammy, with all the travelling and all.'

'Well, I reckon you are eleven, nearly twelve now and it

25

might be time to teach you a thing or two, what do you say?'

I nod and add, 'I'se finished all my work for the day.'

She says, 'I know a cure for ignorance. Go fetch some charcoal, and some lemons and mango, and we'll start your learning now.

I rush off and find what she wants, a bit of charcoaly wood which I had seen her scrape out from the fire before, to make notes with.

Come, let's start.'

She lines up the lemons and then puts the mangoes in gaps between them, then she asks how many lemons before the first mango and I know that answer; then she asks me to add up the lemons between that first mango and the next, which I manage, but as she asks me to go beyond twenty, when I go for more fruit, I can't do it so we start on the counting and the adding, and the taking away.

Each day, I rush through my work so I can be with her and learn more, and, after a few weeks, she says to me, 'Ratia, you're a natural. We'll start on the reading soon.'

My chores are not many because there's no guests and we don't have the large cooking pots going, so Mammy has plenty of time to show me the letters and how they join together to make words and them words make sentences and then I can write all this down to tell the world wonderful things, like Mammy does, when she's story telling.

And it's fun and she doesn't tell me off when I put my 'b's the wrong way round so they look like 'p's, but corrects me, her great laugh echoing around the room.

It don't last long, that quiet time. There's fear and whisperings – cholera has arrived and my lessons stop.

Mammy makes me work even harder, pressing and chopping and stirring the herbs we've been gathering in the forest.

'Come, bring the medicines,' she orders, but I'm reluctant to go with her where there's terrible groanings from the people who lie on rough pallets, sweating and smelling and with constant diarrhoea. At home my mother always told me to stay away when anybody got sick like that so I hide but she grabs my arm, not so it really hurts and looks me in the eyes, with that look she gave me when she first found me in her luggage.

'These people are ill, they need our help. How would you feel if you were lying there with a big black crow of a man waving a cross in front of your face and chanting, but doing nothing to stop the pain?'

I knew what she was talking about – the priests. We'd seen them striding along the main street, their dark robes flying, to reach the lost souls before they die, to make sure they get to heaven. Mammy had had no truck with that, although I'd seen her pray and she goes to church like we all do, but she is more practical. So I pick up the heavy bag of potions and follow her.

We reach an outpost where there's a whole lot of men all lying in one room, some of them soaked in their own yellow bile, and Mammy moves from one to the other, bathing their foreheads and asking for different medicines which I hand to her. She uses crushed garlic steeped in a ginger concoction but mostly the men sick it up as soon as she gives it to them.

I take the sweaty rags she's using and put them in another bag, and I know I'll have to scrub them clean when we get home for the next batch of patients. I'm feeling queasy but Mammy isn't taking any notice of me. She just keeps prodding me when I'm not quick enough with the medicines so I concentrate on what I'm doing and soon the queasiness goes as I work, just because I have to concentrate on what I'm doing.

I realise that the men are murmuring their thanks and one of them takes my hand as I go by and shakes it and croaks, 'Thank you, little one, thank you so much,' before he sinks back and his eyes close.

I look at him horrified. Even though it's gloomy in this hut I can see he's turning blue black and he's curled up like a baby, but it's agonising to watch him because he's been lashing and kicking as if he's been fighting off the cholera like it's a big man straddling him.

I call Mammy and she looks down at the man, but shakes her head and I can see there's a tear in her eye so I don't call her any more to the ones who are dying. I learn quickly which they are.

I follow her as she continues to work the room with her medicines, and we're there for many hours. When we leave we're both exhausted.

The cholera rages for some time and both Mammy and me are out all times of the day and night, until a disaster occurs and I don't know what to do.

Mammy gets sick, and she don't get out of bed.

Chapter 5: Curing cholera for one

She's sweating and moaning like I see in all the others that we visited. She whispers to me, 'Ratia, stew up them herbs we did for the others and give it to me, wipe my brow, as I've taught you. Quick, now.'

I'm panicking and my brain won't work, and I wish I'd paid more attention when we were nursing the others. I burn my hand on the hot water and suck the palm to try to kill the pain. Mac is watching from the door, hopping from foot to foot trying not to show he's in a panic as well. The room seems full of heady scents from the drying herbs Mammy was always collecting and hanging, or pounding, but it seems to send me in a swoon. Mac comes towards me and says, 'Look, you've watched her using herbs. Try these.'

And he cuts down some dried leaves that hang from the roof. They're dried nettle leaves and I remember Mammy boiling these and mashing them into a deep green soupy liquid.

I look at Mac and he says, 'Go on, you can do it.'

So I concentrate, and then I can see Mammy doing it, as if she's standing in the room with me and perhaps she is, as a ghost. That thought frightens me so I think even harder and as I watch the water come to the boil, I forget my own troubles and just think of Mammy who might be dying. I drop the leaves into the pot and stir and mash and boil it until it becomes thick, and I can hear Mammy murmuring in my ear, 'get it to the right consistency.'

I pour some into a beaker and blow on it to cool it as I go to Mammy, who is thrashing about now, and I wonder if she'll hit out and spill the precious brew and I'll have to start all over again. Mac comes and holds her arms and says firmly, like I've never heard him speak before.

'Now Mammy Seacole, you just calm yourself, calm yourself, and drink. Ratia has done good.'

She must have heard him, because she opens her eyes wide and it's as if there's a window to her soul and she sits up and sips at the upturned beaker that I hold so tight, to stop it spilling. After I make her drink which is mighty hard because she starts thrashing again, and Mac has to hold her head while I spoon in the rest of the liquid and it takes a time.

I call her brother Edward. It's only right, I am thinking, that he should see her afore she dies, and then he might take me and Mac into his hotel. But I don't respect him. Like the ninny he is, he stands by the door, handkerchief to his nose, and asks Mammy how she is, but she's muttering now, nonsense, and I push him away. I go back to Mammy and her eyes are rolling but she gestures for me to come close.

'Ratia, keep them away from me, just give me the brew,' Her voice is rasping and she's got that look on her face like the others, as if the whole of her insides is eating her up. I do as she says, bathing her with cool towels and washing away the yellow bile that she brings up, like it's exploding from her. She's that ill for over a week and Mac and me watch and keep on with the bathing of her face and arms, the same as she done to all those others.

The news soon gets out. And I come to understand that it's not only me that calls her Mammy, for all those she's helped call her respectfully, *Mammy* or *Mother Seacole* and they all come and ask me, their hushed tones asking, 'How's Mammy? Pray she don't die for we won't know what to do when the river fever comes again. She's the only one that knows how to cure it.' and I say she's getting better but don't let them see her.

Even the priest tries to get in, but she'll have none of it and turns away from him and I ask him to leave in a serious voice like I heard Mammy talk.

I remember what we did for the others, and found more herbs, ginger and thistle seeds and I chop and stew and hold her head which is all hot and sweaty, as I help her to drink. I'm scared, what will happen to me and Mac if she dies? This doubles my efforts and I give her drinks so often that she pushes me away, but I keep on insisting.

After more'n week of this, I'm not counting, I'm exhausted and Mac is helping me, but suddenly, as we're forcing her to drink, she sinks back and falls into a deep sleep but her body still writhes in her sleep. She sleeps all day and I watch her all night but I must have dozed off because I suddenly realise it's dawn and Mammy is sitting up, watching me.

'Ratia, I need a bath, I'm smelly.'

I laugh and dance around the room in relief and total joy until she says, in a weak voice, but the authority's still in it, 'Ratia, stop that, and run me a bath.'

I don't care how horrible she sounds, all stern, I am so pleased I run out the room and scream for Mac.

'She's won, she's won. She beat the sickness. Quick, help me with the water.'

As he brings the water from the well and I stoke the range, and get out the greatest saucepan I can find to heat it, I tell Mac, 'Of course I knew she'd be all right.'

I can feel a new authority about me, as if I had fought a battle as well.

He says nothing but looks at me in that way he has, which I know says, *yes, of course, I'm not going to upset you by arguing with you.* But he pats me on the shoulder and smiles. He knows that inside I'm so mighty relieved that I could sing and dance all down that muddy main road the same as in Mammy's room, not caring who saw me.

Mammy takes her time to get better but then, as if she's been bit by a flea, she jumps out of bed and calls me.

'Come, we've got work to do, the next mule train will be coming through any day now.'

So the old routine starts again, as well as the thieving and lying. I watch as Mammy does her tallying up and her brow creases as she sucks the pencil. She starts again but stops and sighs. I know something's wrong.

'What is it, Mammy?'

'Ratia, you're old enough to be told. No matter how I play with these figures it sure does not add up and this hotel will be the breaking of me. Somehow, we just don't make ends meet. I think it's time to move on.'

She stops and looks at me and I know she can see I've grown while she was ill. She's treating me with respect.

'You know, my dear, if it wasn't for Edward I'd up and go now. I'll have to talk to him, make him see that this is a hand to mouth existence and there's no money to be had to put away for another day, and we might as well go.'

Then she stands up and looks her old excited self and I know something's coming.

'But before we go back to Jamaica, Ratia, we're going to see something of this country. We're going to see what all the fuss is about.'

I sigh. I remember the alligators and the rain and the mud that comes up to my ankles and all I can see is trouble but somehow I know I'll go with her. What else can I do?

'But first I need to speak to Edward. He can't stay in this disease-ridden place with his weak constitution. I won't be long, but you and Mac can start packing.'

She's not long and I know when she's back because the old wooden door is nearly knocked off its hinges as she hurries into the dining hall where Mac and I have already dismantled the trestle table.

She booms at us, 'Well, you will not believe this! The town is closing down anyway because the river won't be navigable soon. You'd think my brother would tell me this? Oh no, he's making hay while the sun shines and is organising dinners for the departing hotel owners.'

'Mammy, you were right then to think about going,' I point out.

She slumps onto the pile of struts for the table and looks at me and the grin shines up her face.

'Yes, Ratia, that's true.' Then she jumps up again, always impatient to be on the move, and adds, 'but they've invited me to the dinner tonight which is for the Yankees. Apparently it's to celebrate their day of landing and they call it Thanksgiving. Press my red dress with the blue ribbons, Ratia, I might as well leave a good impression in the souls of these men.'

Chapter 6: Mustard and calomel

Now's I going to tell you something that will shock you because Mammy is the kindest and most helpfullest – and, now I know my words, I know that isn't a word in the dictionary but it just sounds right to me – person in the world.

If there's sickness in a house, she's there a-brewing and a-steaming up her potions and we're hurrying to the place, with me loping behind as I've already described. But some people just don't respect her *because she's black.* That's how they see it. When there's yellow fever among them Yankees in Cruces and Gorgona, we're there and she nurses them, even when one of them tries to rise up and asks "what's a goddam nigger" doing, touching him. She just shushes him and smiles and cures him.

By the time she is fully recovered, and she agrees I am grown up now, even though I am still small, her fame has spread all over that region and many a man and woman comes to her door, even though its rough and crude, to seek her help and she gives it, whether they pay or not and whether they be black or white or in between, she don't care and she's not easy taking money or charging for the nursing services.

I watch and work out those who can afford the treatment and, holding back a bit behind her, I tell them out of earshot how much they owe for her ministrations. I keep the money in a velvet purse I found one day, and it swells real good. One day soon I'm going to surprise Mammy with the largest gift of money she ever did see.

So when I hear how those Amerikays treat her, I can't but help think they're a right wicked race, and I think of that egg-shells deceit again That evening, she's dressed in her best satin and she twirls in front of me, and she's buzzing with excitement. Mammy did always like a good dinner and conversation with friends, and I'm not criticising her by saying she did like the men, not that there was any messing with her.

As she preens in front of me, I nod approvingly. It is true that the deep blue and red ribbons set off her soft dark-cream complexion.

She tells me, proudly, 'And them Americans are paying, and Edward's supplying champagne and the best food he can get. You can have a quiet night yourself, Ratia.'

But I wait up for her. Somehow I feel she needs watching and looking after, especially since her illness. I feel responsible for her now. I can hear the laughter and speeches coming from the Independence Hotel across the way, but they're too far away to make out the meaning.

It's late when she wanders across the road and I can tell the champagne's hit her head hard, so I open the door, quiet like, hiding behind it, so she don't really notice that she needs help, and I take her arm and lead her to her bedroom. She's humming to herself and I can't make out whether she's happy or sad.

When she's sat there a while, having loosened her stays and pulled off her stockings, she says, 'They made a speech about me, Ratia, but I was so riled I didn't thank them properly, and I still don't know whether I've done right or not.'

'Why, Mammy, what happened?'

'There were a lot of toasts and one of them mentioned me especially, and I will always remember them words, Ratia, always.

'He says, with all due dignity; *Let's drink a toast to Aunty Seacole, Gentlemen, we can't do less for her, after what she done for us when the cholera was among us.*

See I swelled up with pride, Ratia, and I should know pride comes before a fall, so he carries on.

So I say, God bless the best yaller woman He ever made from Jamaica. And gentlemen, I expect there are only two things we're vexed for and the first is, that she ain't an American citizen,- and Ratia I thank the Lord I am not as I would be enslaved there if I was, but he went on, *and that providence made her a yaller woman. I calculate that we're all vexed that she's so many shades removed from being wholly white....*

'I won't tell you any more Ratia, it was too upsetting. Except to say they offered to *bleach me!* I ask you. But I gave as good as I got, even though Edward, always mindful of his profit as I now understand, tried to stop me.'

She pauses for breath and I can see she is still tipsy from the champagne she's drunk. As she slowly unbuttons the bodice of her dress, she takes a deep breath and continues, 'So I answered them, "I return your best thanks in drinking my health. As for what I have done in Cruces, Providence evidently made me to be useful, I can't help it,"'

I nod and say, 'That's true, Mammy, how true.'

She looks at me and her eyes narrow, 'Now don't interrupt Ratia or I shall lose my thread.'

I look down and let her go on.

'I says to that man, "I don't altogether appreciate your kind wishes with regard to my complexion. If it had been as dark as any nigger's I should have been just as happy and as useful and as much respected by those respect I value and as to the offer of bleaching me, I should, even if it were practicable, decline it without any thanks." And then, Ratia, I tells them what I think of their slave driven country and hope that they will learn good manners. And I then sat down without thanking them for my dinner.'

'And how did they take it, Mammy?'

'Well I could see they were embarrassed but they laughed at it good-natured like. So you see, Ratia, we should be off soon, as we're done here one way and another. And I sure don't like the Yankees, and wouldn't want to treat them again if there's another outbreak.'

She goes all quiet then and adds, 'They're just not gentlemen, like the British. But I still think I should have thanked them for making me guest of honour at their

Thanksgiving party, even though they was so rude. I tell you Ratia, the men in the British Army at Up-Park Camp were gracious and kind but strict. Discipline, that's what's missing from these gold diggers. I truly wish we were back with our British soldiers.'

And so I can tell she's made her decision and we'll be back in Jamaica and home as soon as a boat can take us, I reckon.

She tries to persuade Edward to go with her but he's adamant he's staying and I know why. Since I's been travelling, I'se understood and I don't know why Mammy don't know it too but maybe she just gone and shut her eyes to her brother's lady who has his babies, even though she's a native, not even yaller like Edward and Mammy, but a dusky brown with straight hair. So we leave Edward, who looks even more sickly than when we arrived but I don't care because I never liked him. There was something *dishonest* about him.

Chapter 7: Raspberry vinegar

It did us no good us delaying for when we get to the next town, Gorgona, there's nothing to be had and I hope we move on. It's got the same atmosphere as Cruces, with greedy men travelling up to the gold mines and disappointed men coming back. There's the same hangers on, women and gamblers and thieves. But we don't move on. Mammy is determined to open an establishment – as she calls it – to nurse those who get sick on the way to the goldmines.

Her good deeds help her now because an American, who admits he heard about the dinner and was mighty embarrassed about the so-called toast, lends his boat so we can travel to the other side of the river and gather the materials to build. Mammy explains to me, 'Y'see, Ratia, there's good and bad in all lands, and when you've travelled as much as I have, you'll learn this yourself. You carry yourself with good grace, polite but firm, and you can't go wrong.'

I don't remind her what she said, in her drunken disappointed state, about Americans, but I take note of what she says about mankind now, and I hide Mammy's words away in my soul. She has no hesitation in accepting the offered help and soon we have a sturdy hut similar to the one in Cruces and we're working hard again. Mammy confides in me that she still hopes her brother will leave and return home with her.

But it's not good; there's a lot of thieving from the natives even though if they're caught the punishment is very severe; that's what Mammy thinks, but I reckon that if they're taking our bread out of our mouths without working then they should have their hands cut off and sometimes that's what happens but sometimes they're taken to a prison off the coast where there's no way to escape and no fun either.

But as Mammy says some men are bad and some are good and she tells me, 'I'm mighty impressed by the blackies here who are hard-working and kind. That's what happens when you give people freedom. They who are free take responsibility for their lives.'

I don't take it hard that Mammy calls the locals, *blackies*, even though I am as black as them because I know she don't really notice what colour you are once she gets to know you, and her kind ways and ministrations are not reserved for the white men but are spread right through the local blackies as well as the high-up whites from all parts. On one occasion she sews back a blackie's ear, when it's shot off in a gunfight, making no comment nor asking how it happened; she can see well enough. When she's talking about the local blackies, she's comparing them with the slaves of the Yankees who come through. Most of them are surly and slow and I don't blame them 'cos they were often beaten and kept hungry. I reckon I'd be beaten down nasty if I was treated that way.

On one terrible occasion I tries to help one of them. I meet her at the landing post where she's taking up some huge parcels that are for her mistress. She can't carry them all no matter how she tries to tuck some under each arm, and some on her head and then holds some, one of those parcels always falls. I've only got a bag of fruit so I offer to help. She's scared and shakes her head but I can see she wants help so I take a few of the parcels and we share one big bag between us. As we walk up the road I ask her name. 'I'm Sarah and I'm fourteen.' She says it to try to show she's grown up and can manage, I can tell, but still I'm surprised.

'You can't be fourteen, you're the same size as me and I'm nearly thirteen, so my mistress says.'

But she's vehement and then adds quietly, 'And I got a baby – with the master.'

I'm shocked but don't say nothing. 'Course I know about babies, especially working for Mammy, but I reckon I'm too young to do anything about them, if you know what I mean. And even if I could do *it* I sure as sure wouldn't get pregnant without being respectable like Mammy. I know that Mammy has helped some young girls back in Jamaica with her potions but I won't think on that now and I certainly wasn't going to upset my new friend Sarah by telling her what can be done.

Her mistress is staying at the Yankee hotel that is set up by Doctor Casey where there's a gambling room and there's a lot of cheating, so says Mammy.

'I have to go now, my mistress was ill but she's getting better and we'll be away soon.'

She starts to struggle up to the veranda and I say, 'Come, I'll help you in with them,' but she shakes her head.

'Ok, I'll sit on these ones, and keep an eye on them while you take the ones you carrying in, 'cos you can't take all of them, can you? And there's thieves that are just watching you now to see what pickings they can get.'

She looks around and sure enough there's loafers leaning against the veranda rails and cheekily grinning at us, just as when I entered Edward's hotel in Cruces. She realises there's sense in what I say, so she takes the biggest parcel and I sit there until all have gone in. She gives me a smile and she's gone but I make a point that I'll look out for her at the market.

A few nights later there's terrible screams and Mammy comes to me and says, 'get the medicine bag, something awful's happening, it sounds like a child.'

We rush to Doctor Casey's where all are awake and someone's banging on a door upstairs. Mammy pushes forward and says, 'If you don't let me in to help that poor soul who's in so much agony I'll get this door bashed down.'

It is opened and there stands a horrible sight. She's a tall thin white woman and she's got a whip help high and in the candlelight it looks like its nine feet long.

'How dare you interrupt me?'

'We want to know what's going on.'

Mammy forces herself into the room and we all see. I gasp. There's my friend Sarah, with nothing on, tied to the bedpost, her back is all red with wheals and her head is hung down but I can see she's crying. Mammy quickly rushes to my friend, and, as she approaches her, she unties her cloak and wraps Sarah in it. The white woman is trying to pull her away but Mammy is strong and angrily shakes her off as she struggles with the knots of the rope. As she loosens them, Sarah collapses onto the floor, but Mammy helps her up and, holding Sarah close to her, she turns to the white woman, and her eyes are coal black and you can see by the way her eyes have closed into slits she's mighty angry. But the white woman is not fazed.

'She's my slave. She disobeyed me and she deserves to be whipped,' says the white woman so calm I can't quite believe my ears.

'We'll see about that,' says Mammy, walking towards the gaping group at the door, still holding the child tight to her body. 'In front of the governor, tomorrow morning.'

'How dare you?' The woman tries to stop Mammy but I can't help smiling because Mammy, like a big ship dashing a rowing boat, just keeps going. 'She's my property and if you take her away you'll have to pay me for her.'

Mammy ignores her. 'Come to the governor's tomorrow.'

The next morning there's a huge crowd around the big house where the governor lives but Mammy walks through it all, and I think she still looks like a great ship pushing through waves. Sarah's dressed in one of my robes and we've cleaned her up and washed her hair and dressed it nice.

I don't follow all the arguments that go on and my head starts to buzz but when I hear a great cheer going up, I know that governor man has freed my friend Sarah, but then she wails, and I think I know why. I understand what the white woman is saying.

'Well, Sarah you think you've got your freedom but you

won't never see your baby again.'

Mammy stands up, and leaning on that umbrella she always carries in this damp place, says, 'Baby! A young girl like this has a baby?'

'She's a slave,' says the white woman scornfully, 'My brother had her, to get more slaves without paying for them.'

I was shocked. I know Mac has told me how Amerikays treat their slaves but this woman just thought it *normal* that a white man could have sex with his slave to get more slaves! Mammy's forehead creases again, and I know the anger is coming. She approaches the woman but walks past her and sweeps Sarah into her lap where she cries as if nothing, not even Mammy, can console her.

Mammy looks over the head of Sarah and her face is set hard. 'We'll buy the baby from you; it can't be worth much to you if it's still a babe.'

The white woman laughs and names a price and then she and Mammy are haggling but I know Mammy will win because I can tell the white woman don't really care, and Mammy does.

'The baby's back in the plantation and it'll take a while to fetch her, and I don't have a slave to do things for me now.'

Mammy goes right up to that white woman and says, 'You just do it, and make sure that baby is delivered to my hotel soon, it's not right that a baby's separated from her mother.'

Sarah stays with us until her baby arrives and we get to be good friends and she's really willing and hardworking, so I like having her around. It's a picture to see the way she holds that babe, which is struggling and wriggling in joy.

But that white woman is causing trouble and her compatriots are complaining that the locals can't interfere with Yankee property. One night there's another break in but we stop that by Mammy firing the gun that she keeps cocked all the time now

After that, she is not so complacent about the place, and she worries about us and I know that, if it weren't for the problem of what to do about Sarah, we would be gone.

'I'm going to find Sarah a job inland so they can't find her. Ratia! Mac! You keep care now while I go and sort something out with the governor.'

She's gone all day. I see her striding from the governor's house up the road to someplace else as I throw the slops out into the road, but she don't see me. As we work, Sarah tells me about her life, how she lives in a long hut with other Negro women and the men live in another and they're locked in at night and the overseers make sure they don't have time for anything but work during the day. She teaches me a song which I remember to this day, and although she says they sing it to put their babies to sleep, the words make me cry every time:

Oh the world's going on without me
'cos I stuck in this hell plantation
Oh the world's going on without me
But I know I'm the Lord's creation
And He'll take me to heaven sometime

Those massers think that they own me
'cos I stuck in this hell plantation
Those massers think that they own me
But I know I'm the Lord's creation
And He'll take me to heaven sometime.

My massers think they own me
But my soul belongs to the Lord.

She whispers to me what happened when the master spotted her.

'My mam had tried to keep me away, she could see I was mighty pretty and warned me that it might happen one time, like it had to her and to most of the women. She told me to keep it secret when I started bleeding but it's mighty hard. And you know what, Ratia? It was one of my own what told the master I was ready; big Hannah, the nanny of the white children. She sees me cramping up with the period pains and asks me all sympathetic like if I'm a woman now and all I can do is nod. And it's the next week that the master calls for me and as I go into the big house for the first time through the kitchen you understand, I see Hannah standing on the stairs, leaning over the banisters, grinning at me. It's the first time I've seen inside the big house, and the room he takes me to is all velvet curtains and dark, even though it's day and even though I'm trembling he takes me and it hurts real bad. After that Hannah keeps asking me if I'm budding with child and soon she can see. But you know what, Ratia, when that baby comes out, and the pain goes, it's like a big light has come shining into my life and I just couldn't let her go.'

And I agree with her, because her baby's with her and she's beautiful, and I wonder if I'll ever marry and have babies. If only Mammy will stay still long enough for me to meet someone.

But I also wonder about my mother and father who were slaves before they were freed. They never talk about it. Were they whipped? How did they meet? Was it on a plantation? I make a point to ask them when I see them again.

Shortly after that, Sarah leaves and we cry in each other's arms. She's going to live in a big house and be nanny to the owner's children and be paid, like I'm paid, with an allowance for clothes. Will I ever see her again?

Soon after that, Mammy is in pensive mood, which is a strange thing to see. She's sitting on one of the rickety chairs on our veranda, staring into space, but it's not for long and she's jumping up and sorting the tins of food with me. I can tell something's brewing and she then bursts out, 'God sure is telling me something, Ratia, and I am mighty tired of this.'

And I don't blame Mammy because we've had to contend with floods and watching our neighbours' properties being swept away, while Mammy's place, chosen as she usually does, high up, escaped. And then there was a fire that gobbled up the remaining places, as if to dry out the floods, but being greedy couldn't stop. 'If Edward won't come, he can have this place and we'll take the next boat back to Jamaica.'

Chapter 8: Emetics to purge

So we travel back to the coast of Panama which Mammy assures me is only twenty miles but it seems like a hundred as we move slow on the river, in hole-ridden vessels and I look out for those alligators this time, and Mac doesn't tease me. Sometimes we use donkeys but I flatly refuse to ride one because I've seen how they dig in their heels and throw their riders if they want to be stubborn, and I'm fit enough to keep up with the group on foot.

When we reach Navy Bay, something happens that makes me think real hard. I'd always look up to Mammy and respect her and other people do too, and if they don't she makes a joke of it, like those rude Americans who *patronised*, as Mammy said, her at the dinner in Cruces. This time though, she is well and truly put down and I am cruelly treated as well.

We've made our way to the harbour to board the steamer that Mammy's booked, which was an American one, because it was the one leaving soonest. Mammy's always the same; once she decides on something, well, it happens, without any waiting, if she's got anything to do with it.

Mac helps us on and Mammy leaves me to settle into our cabin while she goes exploring. When I'm done, which don't take long, I go to find her and she's sitting in the saloon with two ladies, dressed in wide pastel shaded crinolines which shows just how uppity they are, not thinking of their slaves' work, when they choose the colours of their clothes. I can imagine the hard work to keep them clean. Oh, no, they're light coloured with pure white lace at wrists and necks, and I can see they have no idea how their slaves work on keeping them spotless.

They're obviously American from the designs, and they're talking to Mammy and you can see by the way she holds her head that she don't like what they're saying.

I head for her and she's answering them, polite like, but I can tell she's in defiant mood.

'I booked my passage, and I'm going to Kingston on this vessel.'

And then one of the ladies says, all high and mighty, so I'm shocked, 'Don't be impertinent, yaller woman, you are not allowed in here.'

Mammy don't move but before I can hear any more, a *young gentleman,* who is not polite, pulls me away by one of my braids.

'And what is this nigger doing in this here saloon, which is for whites?'

I turn to him but he's got a group of boys and girls with him and they all lunge at me, pinching and pulling towards the door. 'You get outta here now, nigger,' they're saying. They're not much younger than me. One of them spits at my face and it's then I get mad.

'I'm not one of your slaves,' I lash at them with both fists, 'I'm a free servant, of my mistress Mary Seacole, the famous doctress.'

But that makes them snigger and they push me again, so I'm tripping backwards out of the door and if I don't move quick I can see me falling on the deck, not far from the railing and them all climbing on me. Would they be so cruel as to see me fall overboard?

I can see my mistress talking to the stewardess and I lunge through my tormentors and manage to reach Mammy and wrap my arms around her skirts, even though I'm nearly as tall as her now. She holds my hand firm and I feel safe.

The white ladies call over the stewardess to them, and she leaves Mammy. She acts placatingly to them, nodding and smiling and then returns to us. When I hear her speak, she's also American so naturally she takes their side. She speaks sternly.

'You can't expect to stay with white people in the saloon and this is the only place. I advise you to get your money back and leave, and go on a Britisher ship if they're so friendly as to put up with blacks.'

Mammy's creasing her eyes in that angry way but she says nothing and leads me away. We get to the cabin without speaking but I can see Mammy is trying hard not to explode.

'Mac, get our things together, we won't stay on this vile vessel with these wicked people.'

Then she bends down and looks me in the face, the same as when she found me in the luggage, 'Ratia, just remember not all white men are like that. There are others in the world who do not worry about what colour you are, such as my late husband's countrymen who are respectful and kind, just remember that.'

I nod, but I'm shaking, and say nothing but turn away and gather up some of our bags, not wanting Mammy to see I am embarrassed at her humiliation.

But, when we're away, with her refund and walking back to our lodgings, she bellows that great laugh, and says, 'Hey, I never did like those Yankees, and we sure won't mix with them again, don't you think, Ratia?'

I laugh with her, and hope that I can live my days with such a happy outlook.

We have to wait only two days for the English steamer *the Eagle,* and we are soon heading for Jamaica and home. I say goodbye to Mac, and I'm crying but he says, 'You no longer a little chile, and I mighty proud of you. But I got my family here, so I'm staying.'

Chapter 9: Cod liver oil

You might think it was a great welcome that we receive when we land at the Port Royal harbour, but it was not to be. We walk straight into a yellow fever epidemic. I had barely time to greet my mother. As I remove my bonnet, she exclaims, 'Hey look at yo, with you' hair all wound round and up in de bun, you look so grown up.'

And I knew I was. I was filling out into a woman and felt I could hold up my head with dignity, remembering how I had nursed my mistress through her fever.

Now I saw our home through grown-up eyes, it seemed dismal, mother had shrunk and her ways seemed coarse after seeing how Mammy, with her courtesy and gentle ways, treated people.

I don't stay long. I don't even have time to ask my parents about their slave background and as I depart, I realise I don't want to know. That was all in the past and I was looking forward.

I was pleased when I was summoned by Mammy to help her with the poor whiteys, some of them coming straight off the ships, struck down with the yellow disease.

'As soon as the news spread I had returned, people came to ask for my healing potions, Ratia, and now Doctor Henderson as called for me to help because he can't cope. He's waiting for new doctors to arrive, so we must go, Ratia.'

We climb the hill to the camp, passing near the race-course on the way and cutting across the stream. When we reach it, I'm surprised. It's not at all impressive. All I can see is a group of single storey buildings, surrounded by park land.

We're soon inside, and I hid my horror at the look of the patients in the dormitories, which are not much more than wooden huts. The smell of unwashed men, and vomit also assails me. I'd seen sights in the Panama but I expect an English army camp to have some cleanliness in it and that is why I'm so shocked.

I begin to think we can never work miracles in such a place. And I'm partly right. Despite our ministrations, most of them die, and Mammy doesn't know why, even though she works tirelessly, and I can see how the British are grateful in a humble way, so unlike the Yankees. It's the softness and gentleness they like, and a few do recover, but are very weak.

One day as we work, a new young surgeon enters the hut. At first he merely nods and starts his round, pretending he knows it all and Mammy doesn't interfere as he bleeds some of the men and gives others cod liver oil to make them vomit, thinking that would eviscerate what was causing the sickness, and he's puzzled when his cures don't work. He takes to following us around as Mammy administers the thistle seeds and fig tree sap which she always uses for yellow fever.

Eventually, he greets us courteously, 'I understand you're Mrs Seacole, and Ratia?'

It is the first time one of the medical staff has addressed me by name and Mammy smiles, her huge warm smile. 'Why, yes, young man, that's who we are.'

'I'm Dr Charles Macworth Smith. I'd welcome your help as I'm new out here, and I can't fathom this illness at all.'

He's come with his innocent knowledge and black leather bag like all of them but instead of the others, I discover from this that he isn't arrogant.

'We can work together,' says Mammy, taking his arm, 'You must observe the patient and try to counteract the symptoms you see. If they're vomiting, you must give them something to stop that; if they're hot you have to cool the fever.'

He's got a shock of blond hair and the bluest eyes you ever did see and Mammy treats him like the child he is, but not in a condescending way. He learns from Mammy and is tireless in treating the soldiers and their families, as we are too. We only go back to Mammy's kitchen at Blundells to brew more potions to use on the sick.

She says, after a few days, when his puzzlement at the lack of success, even after using the same remedies as us, is screwing up his forehead like the bark of the holy wood, 'You can't fight it, you know, the yellow fever will have its way and all we can do is make the sufferers comfortable.'

'But I have studied hard to cure people, Mrs Seacole, and it is not good to find on my first posting that I'm being defeated. It seems that you have more success than I do.'

He looks so tired, I can see that, and Mammy says, 'Come, I'll give you some of my ginger tea which should relax you, and we can talk about how we can help each other with these poor sick people.'

He looks very pale and I could see Mammy inspecting him in the way she does sometimes with sick people. As we leave the dormitory he staggers. Mammy and I exchange looks but say nothing.

'Come, Ratia, we need more herbs. Sir, I think you should rest, you're tired out.'

Before we arrive back at Blundells a message is delivered, followed shortly by Dr Macworth-Smith lying on a stretcher. Mammy led the sad party into the front parlour which is light and airy, facing east where it was coolest during the day, with the sea breezes wafting in from the veranda outside.

'Go and ask Louisa for pillows, blankets and heat up some kettles so we can bathe him.'

Louisa is none too pleased to have another dying guest, but she doesn't say anything as we work together. When I get back to the sick room, Mammy is holding her hand to his forehead.

'I thought as much,' she mutters to me, and I know what she means. I visit the kitchen to fetch the thistle seed potion that we use sometimes to cure diarrhoea and Mammy holds his head as she tries to force it down the burning and delirious doctor.

'Get me some of the fig-tree sap dilution as well, that will cool his stomach.' I nod. For the rest of the day, Mammy tries other remedies but the Doctor became ever more delirious, and as she held his head in her lap, he called out.

'Mother, mother, take away the pain,' and he sounds so much like an infant with his first earache, that my heart goes out to him, and I can see, as Mammy bathes his forehead, she too has tears in her eyes, as she speaks to him soothingly. We both know he isn't seeing her, Mother Seacole of Kingston, Jamaica, but his real mother who, in his delirium, is as solid a figure as Mammy, even though she is miles away.

When he dies we dress him and call the commander, who organises the funeral.

Afterward, Mammy says, 'I know the Army will notify the family but I'll also write to his mother and tell her what a brave soul he was. You know, Ratia, in that short time, I learned to be so fond of that young man, he was so conscientious and I could see that, with more experience, he would have made a fine doctor. I felt like he was the son I'll never have, and I'll tell his mother so, and pray that will comfort her.'

Because Mammy is so well-known as a doctress, when I deliver the letter to the post-ship, instead of to the post office, the captain takes it and hides it in his breast pocket.

'It will go with tonight's sailing,' he tells me, so I believe it will reach the mother in England before the cold official letter she is sure to receive eventually.

Some weeks' later Mammy receives a letter from the mother. When she opens the envelope, out falls a small token. Mammy is mighty proud that the mother should respond to her, and she reads it aloud to her sister Louisa, and later to me.

My dear Madam, will you do me the favour to accept the enclosed trifle, in remembrance of my dear son whose last moments were soothed by your kindness, and as a mark of my gratitude.

Signed Mrs Macworth Smith

Mammy shows me the enclosure, a little gold brooch with a curl of the surgeon's hair in it and I marvel at how a mother could give up such a memorial of her dead son.

For the next few months it is a boring slog of nursing the men at Up-Park Camp and I see that Mammy is loved by these Britishers. The doctors who are sent from the mother country – who quite often succumb to the fever themselves, like our young doctor, especially if they are new to Jamaica - respect her and by association, me, and we are well rewarded. Mammy doesn't like to take money, so as I follow her. I make it plain, by opening my little purse, that they should place their coin in that, and not say anything further.

It is about this time that Mammy does something that really shocks me but it will certainly prove helpful in our future work. It is a chaotic time, you understand, with parents dying and leaving sick babies, and nobody to care for them except us. There was one babe that we try so hard to save that, when she died, we both cried. But Mammy's tears dry first and she whispers to me, 'This babe shall not die in vain, it will help us. Come, bring it and a lamp, out into the clearing where we gather herbs.'

It is growing into night-time and I wonder what we are going to do but I obey, as I trust my mistress. When we reach a secluded spot, outside the town, Mammy says, 'Give me the babe, and hold up the oil lamp above me, so I can see what I'm doing.

Before I can do anything she cuts into the tiny body as if she is slicing a giant watermelon and starts poking about inside. I am so shocked the lamp wavers but she looks sharply at me so that I calm myself.

At first I am so horrified I want to look away, but then a sort of fascination overcomes me and I look closer. She points with the knife at a dark shape and explains. 'Look, here is the liver, all dried up, and the kidneys – the same. It seems to me Ratia, that this fever takes the liquid out of the body somehow. So what do you think we should do?'

'Make sure they drink a lot, Mammy?'

She laughs but it is a grim sound she made. 'Yes, we must make sure they drink a lot and it should be good clean water, perhaps with sugar or other goodness in it so they keep their strength. This poor little one never stood a chance.'

After she finishes poking about, she replaces the organs, gently, and then sews up the gap, and we dress the body so that the scar does not show. We allow the priest to bury the baby properly, without telling him what we had done, and he insisted on carrying out the full burial rites, even though the babe can't know about it, so that it could go to heaven. And I am sure that baby did get into heaven, for helping Mammy in her future work.

Her reputation grows after that, when some of those she nurses recover, slowly, but they got well, sure enough, and so they spread the word as living examples of her skills. Like most epidemics, after several months, there's less people to nurse and I, as Mammy pounds her potions, her actions become more positive, and I guess she is becoming restless.

When Mammy says she intends to go back to Panama, to settle her affairs there, I at first refuse to go.

'You can stay here, your reputation is such that you'll never want for anything, and I could stay as well. We're settled here.'

She recoils as if what I had said was so shocking that a good woman could not be tainted with it.

'Stay here? When there's a whole world out there to discover?'

She is twirling this globe thing that's a feature in her drawing room. I know what it is because she'd explained about it when she first started on her journeys some years back. I remembered she had gone away when I was very young and knew that our Panama adventures were not the first journey she had undertaken. I learned, as we travelled together, that she had been to England as a young woman.

'Look, there's Great Britain for a start, don't you want to see our mother country? One day I'll take you there.'

I try another tactic. 'I could stay here, and look after the poor sick men, while you're away, Mammy.'

But no, she explains. 'Ratia, you've turned into my right hand and I can't do without you now, I'm sure of that. It'll only be for a few months and then we'll be back.'

Then she trys another crafty ploy.

'Surely that cheeky little girl who climbed into my trunk hasn't lost the spirit of adventure? I cannot believe it. You must have been bewitched.'

I blush, not only to be reminded of my naughty ways, but perhaps I had been touched. Truth is I'd fallen in love with young Robert, a plain soldier from England. He was so confident and good at his job I was sure he'd get promotion and we would have a good life together. I would sneak out the back when Mammy was busy with one of her patients and meet him in the forest in the hills above town, not far from Up-Park Camp where he is stationed. It was not that far away and he would walk me back through the fields when we only had the moon for light. We learned to love, and he never forced himself on me, because I was as willing as him in our lovemaking. And I'd learned some herbal remedies, not from Mammy I am quick to say, so I didn't have babies. He promised me a home where I wanted, even Jamaica, and he would care for me and I knew that he meant it. I'd seen enough of men in our travels to know who I could trust, and I knew Robert was true so I looked forward to the day when we could be married and have babies like I knew I wanted, after seeing Sarah and her baby together.

Truth is, I think I am cured of my wanderlust by the terrible times we'd had in Panama, although I did like being with Mammy, and she is still teaching me the English and proper accounting so I know I should stay by her side.

I didn't tell Mammy all this, though, because I love her and don't want her to think I'll desert her.

I tell Mammy I'll think about it further and decide to meet

with Robert and see what he thinks. I'm hoping that he'll say we can get married now and that will be the best excuse to stay.

Robert asks, when I manage to creep out to him soon after that conversation with Mammy, 'You don't think she's guessed about us? Maybe it's her way of protecting you, to take you away from temptation. I know she's a good and wise soul.'

I am surprised at this and it makes me love Robert even more but I doubt if Mammy is that devious. 'No, she's too straightforward. She'd come right out and say what she's thinking. I want to stay with you here.'

His next words surprise me even more. He encourages me to go. 'Horatia, you and I are too young to be married, because I want to provide for you properly, and you are a temptation to a man, so if you go with Mrs Seacole, I know you'll be safe and I will wait for you.'

He kisses me, so passionately, but then holds me at arm's length and looks at me so lovingly, without wanting the baby-making activity, that I can see he's sincere, so I agree to go, and Mammy and me set off back to Navy Bay, on the first step to where her brother was still living.

I won't dwell on that journey – except to say I was surprised that Mammy got caught by the gold mining bug and, passing through Cruces, we collect her brother Edward and travel to Panama. I know Mammy is still hoping to persuade him to leave that damp and foetid country and return home to Jamaica, but even on this intimate trip, just a few of us travelling alone, she cannot make him agree to leave. Mammy didn't seem to notice he had a woman with him. As I now know, the love between a man and woman, even if they are different colours or come from different parts of the world, is much stronger than common sense. And he has a son by his woman, as I discover, but I don't tell Mammy.

It was on this trip that Mammy met Mr Day – another man like Edward who I didn't take to. He was more cunning than

Edward and hides his greed and deviousness very well and I could not say a word against him. I truly regret that now, even though I would have raised that frown on her face and knew she would get angry. I know I should have said something, because meeting that man led to her greatest disaster as I will tell later on. We met him in New Granada where he was putting himself out as a merchant but I could see he was buying from the poor and selling to the rich with a vast margin for himself in between. If that's what merchants are then I didn't like it.

Yes, Mammy bought and sold, but never with such a margin and then she'd always use her excess money to help those who couldn't afford proper doctors or pay her. Mammy would never be rich; she bought and sold to the rich to help the poor.

It was while we are travelling in Panama that Mammy hears that her regiments – as she had come to know them – are on the move in a real war. Even those in Jamaica are being mobilised and I hear that Robert's regiment, the 97th, has been called away too. I fear for my Robert and wonder if I would ever see him again.

'I have to go, and you can come, too. We're needed, Ratia, and cannot refuse to help our boys.'

Of course I did not need any persuading, if I was going to be near my Robert.

Mammy explains that we are going to a place called the *crime eya*, (like a cry of the wild birds in the forest) and I thought it was to do with murders and wicked things – I was later to find out it was both of those but not in the way my still immature mind imagined it. Although I was confident in what I did with and for Mammy, I was still young enough to worry about the future that she described to me.

I was eager to learn, so, as Mammy explained it all to me, I wrote it down in my exercise book, savouring the new words such as *mobilising* and *Crimea,* after she explained that this was the name of a piece of land shaped like a diamond in the Black

Sea, miles and miles away.

Although there were British garrisons all over the world, there had not been any insurrections or real battles since 1815, so Mammy told me, which to me seemed a lifetime away, when my parents were still slaves. Now the British were mobilising – this was the proper military term to use Mammy said – against the Russians in this place called the Crimea.

Mammy consulted her globe and studied the maps in the magazines that arrived so late after they had been published, and taught me about different lands.

She told me about the war and how it had started. It all seemed silly to me, how men decided what a boundary was and then fought over it – I kept thinking of the poor peasants who farmed the land, they don't care who governs them when soldiers march over their fields ripening with corn and tell them they are conquered and they are no longer one nation but another. Or one nation decides another shouldn't be allowed to get rich with trade through shipping. The Crimea seemed a petty slip of land to me, jutting out into the Black Sea, not even a real sea like the huge one in which Jamaica sits.

'Mammy, why do these great men fight? So far away, as well.'

Mammy laughed, and picked up the news sheet and read to me. It seems that this piece of land belongs to Russia, which was a vast country that bordered the Ottoman Empire.

I interrupted, 'But why do the British have to go there?'

Before answering, Mammy read the Times and explained, 'The Russians are getting powerful and if they come through the Black Sea down the Bosporus, passing Constantinople' – and she pointed out a thin line of sea that looks as if a riverboat couldn't get down it – 'then the Mediterranean trade routes will be threatened.' She added, as if in wonder, 'This time, things are so serious that the British are being joined by the French and they are traditionally enemies. The great Nelson lost his life fighting the French.'

'So, all those people are joining together to fight. Surely they're bound to beat the Russians, aren't they?'

'I hope so, Ratia, but there's going to be bloodshed and we need to be there, to do our duty, for our mother country.'

I was so scared, and forgot about Robert, and protested, 'Oh, no, I can't travel all that way, it's miles and miles.' I didn't like the sound of *bloodshed.*

Mammy laughed, 'Of course, you can, Ratia, it's just like we've been doing, the travelling, only it will take longer. And instead of diseases we'll see wounds that we can dress, just like that poor Negro who had his ear shot off.' She paused, and then added, slyly, as if she knew about my secret love. 'Of course, we might meet up with some of our friends who've been stationed in Jamaica.'

She didn't look at me as she said it. *Did she know about Robert?* I thought our secret meetings out back had been missed by her but now I wasn't so sure. It was the way she said it, so persuasively. I knew I would go with her. She was right, if I went, I might find my Robert. At least I wouldn't be stuck at home, wondering whether he was alive or dead.

She was always good at persuading people to do what she wanted. It was just her family, like Edward, or Louisa, who disapproved of all her travelling, who could see through her and resist her.

She continued, as if what she had said was not enough for me. 'And we will stop at London which is a marvel in itself. You know I've already been there, and we can lodge a while with my dear deceased husband's family.'

'Deceased husband? Mammy you never mention your husband.'

'Ratia, come with me, and I'll tell you about him, as we travel,'

I was that curious, it was the same as the first time when I crept into her luggage, I couldn't resist. Not only was it the prospect of finding Robert, but I looked forward to hearing my mistress tell me stories, she had that way with her. So once more I packed my bags and followed Mary Seacole and listened to her tale.

Chapter 10: Apple juice

Before we left, Mammy set to work, to make sure her arrival at the Crimea would be known about. Mammy knew how to do this. Firstly, we visited Dr Munro, who Mammy greeted familiarly. I vaguely recognised him as one of the men Mammy had helped in Cruces when he had fallen ill and his medicine chest had not helped him.

'Angus, my friend, how are you?'

He took her by the arm, ignoring me, and led her to a chair in his spacious drawing room but before they talk, he gestured for me to sit in the hall and wait for my mistress, but he left the door open. I moved to the door, and it's as if they don't mind that I can hear.

'I am well, thanks to you and your remedies. And I believe you're doing capital work on the isthmus, I hear of you all over the place.'

'Yes, it is true. But now I am going to help our boys in the Crimea. You have heard what is happening there?'

'Indeed yes, but my duties here mean I will not be able to go myself. Surely you're not intending to travel all that way.'

Mammy gave her usual hearty laugh, 'Of course I am. You know I cannot resist a challenge. I have one little problem though. I would not know who to approach in London.'

I knew Mammy had every intention of visiting a certain Florence Nightingale, but of course I was not supposed to be listening, so I curbed my tongue. Anyway, I guessed she was angling for something from her friend. I recognised the beguiling way she had when she wanted something.

He didn't hesitate. 'I'm sure I can help you. Leave it a few days and I will give you a letter of commendation and I will also find out to whom you should give that letter.'

We did not have long to wait. The next day a servant arrived with a letter for Mary. Included in that letter was the commendation she had obliquely begged for. It was in an unsealed envelope and Mammy read it out to me, proudly.

'*I became acquainted with Mrs Seacole through the instrumentality*' – listen to that, Ratia, what a long word – *of T. B. Cowan Esq., Consul of Colon on the Isthmus of Panama and have had many opportunities of witnessing her professional zeal* – and that's another lovely word – *and ability in the treatment of aggravated forms of tropical diseases.*

I am myself personally much indebted for her indefatigable – oh, what another one – *kindness and skill at a time when I am apt to believe the advice of a practitioner qualified in the North would have little availed.*

'Her peculiar fitness, in a constitutional point of view – oh how true, Ratia, for I am very healthy despite my age – *for the duties of a medical attendant, needs no comment.*

A.G.M

Late Medical Officer, West Granada Goldmining Company.

'I must say Ratia, I couldn't expect a better commendation than that, could I? I shall attend upon the highest in the land of Britain when I arrive and who can refuse me with such a letter?'

It was not long after, that we boarded the great vessel that took us to England, and Mammy decided now was the time to tell me her story. She ordered some apple juice. She insisted I drink it to settle my stomach knowing how sick I'd been in the past. As I drank, she folded her hands in her lap and started to tell me her story.

'Yes, Ratia, I was married and a very happy time it was too. You may not know that I was born Mary Grant, and my dear departed mother was a freed woman being loved of her master, as she was light skinned like me.'

I let Mammy tell her story as we sat on the deck together watching the rolling waves, even though everyone knew her mother, greatly in demand as a great doctress herself in

Kingston and running a respectable hotel. I'd been scared of her because she was stern or so I thought as a child.

'And my mother and Mr Grant loved us, their children, me, Edward and Louisa, and we were all taught business ways so we could be independent and help mother when Mr Grant was away.

'So, I watched mother pounding herbs and potions and learnt a lot from her which as you know has been of great help in our travels. Being the older girl, I was my mother's second in command, if we can use a military phrase. Edward was not very good at learning and Louisa was far too young. We always had very respectable army and navy men as guests in our establishment and we made many friends that way. I was happy being useful to my mother and her guests but one of them in particular was special to me. You must remember I was past thirty and although some locals had proposed, I could not bring myself to part from Blundells, my home, but when Edwin Horatio Hamilton Seacole proposed to me I accepted, and we were married on 10 November 1836, a day most dear to me. Even though that was eighteen years ago, I still remember it as if it was yesterday.'

She paused, and I could see that her eyes were watering and I looked away, until she took a deep breath and began again.

'Note that name, Horatio. That is why you are named, to serve as a reminder of my dear husband. I named you Horatia after him.'

Now I understood my peculiar name, but I preferred it when she called me Ratia. I listened as she continued. 'Edwin was a very special man. He believed himself to be the true son of Admiral Horatio Nelson, the great leader of the British Navy who won so many sea battles. He gave me a ring which he said was given to him by his adoptive father, a good doctor from Prittlewell, near Southend. He told me the ring was Nelson's own that he gave to Lady Hamilton. She was the mother, but Edwin did not mention her much. My dear Edwin was aware that his own health was not robust and his big disappointment in life was that he knew he could never emulate the greatness of his father. Yes, Ratia, you may well be open mouthed, but when I reach London I will prove this to you by visiting his family.

'We were so very happy and Edwin was prepared to join with me to open a shop down Black River country, which we chose carefully because of the logging business there and thought it a good place to establish ourselves. It is on the coast, and the air is fresh and the flat land around there is conducive to straight streets, and large establishments were being built, to cater for the frequent visitors. There was another reason to travel to the other side of our island home. Edwin also had cousins in the area, the Days, who I was sure would help us to become established and pass business our way. Mr Day, who we met on that second trip to Panama, was my dear Edwin's cousin and he was learning to be a merchant. I could see he was good at bartering and organising the merchandise to reach its destination at the right time. That's important in such a business.'

I never commented on her words of wisdom but stored them away and they would come in useful later, as you will see.

'You should visit the place, when we get back to Jamaica, Ratia, it has a race track and a spa, and is very up and coming.'

Mammy paused here and I could see her forehead creasing. I knew something bad was coming.

'But we did not prosper. For some reason, his relations did not welcome us as I thought they would and trade did not come easily to us. Edwin was poorly and did not visit his relatives as I urged him to do, to establish a pattern of goodwill. I spent a lot of time looking after him and my servants were not honest like you, and stole from me, and I knew it but could not catch them and so could never accuse them or stop them.'

I didn't say anything but I guess those relations of her husband were none too keen to see him married to a Creole, but even if I suggested such an idea to her, she would deny it 'cos she sees the good in all men, and wouldn't believe it of them.

She carried on, 'In the end, we returned to mother's place and I nursed dear Edwin until he died. He was dying when there was a great fire, but you would not remember that. It wiped out nearly the whole of our district in Kingston, including our hotel, and how we rebuilt our lives is another story that I may tell you some time. But it was a sad and traumatic time for all of us.

'I truly believe that Edwin died with the shock of the fire. I didn't leave the place until the flames were chasing me out. I wanted to rescue as much as I could from Blundells House.

'Oh, Ratia, that was a terrible day when he died. Eight years we were married and I never could look at another man after my dear husband, although I will confess suitors came a-visiting. He left such a blankness in my life but I devoted myself to working hard, learning more of my mother's medicinal skills, because I knew I had to be useful. But then dear mother died and I truly felt alone in the world even though Louisa was there. Again, I took up running the hotel because it was our livelihood and because my medicinal skills were needed. Hard work is the key to overcoming grief and despair, I truly believe.'

That was another wise thought she had which I learned to live by.

You must understand that Mammy did not tell me all of this in one go, but over some days as we travelled east and the weather got colder and colder and I added more petticoats under my skirt, and more shawls over my shoulders. By the time we reached England I had no spare undergarments to add and I wondered if I would ever be warm again. How would I cope if I had to put up with this cold for months?

Chapter 11: English brewed tea

'Don't you worry,' Mammy laughed, as I shivered on the harbour while we waited for our luggage to be unloaded, 'you'll get used to it. Look at the navvies working.'

I was astonished to see white men, stripped to their shirts, their sleeves rolled up, as they carried great loads down the gangplank. I could not believe I would ever get used to the bitingness of this country, nor to see white men, tall and proud of what they were doing, carrying out menial work. Even my Dadda, once he was freed, would not do such work, believing it was slave work.

Once we had left the port and were heading for London on a train, Mammy explained, 'It could become even colder in England before it warms up. There are four seasons here, that we don't have in our country back home, and spring is a glory to see.'

'Mammy, how do you know this? Did you read it in books before we came away?'

'No my dear, I told you, I've been to Britain before and stayed with distant relatives in London for some months. I will warn you though that even here in this great country there are bad people who do not see beyond your colour, and think that the darker you are, the more you should be hid away, but just remember that most of the populace are kind and welcoming.'

So I was warned and I thought to myself that I would add a rim to my bonnet because I was darker than Mammy and knew from the experience on the American ship how nasty 'bad people' as Mammy called them, could be. I sure was not going to let them see me easily.

After a silence, Mammy talked of her plans. 'I shall present myself to Miss Florence Nightingale and show her my references and I am sure she will take me.'

But it was not to be. Mammy purchased a news sheet to read on the train from Southampton to London and now she picked it up and started reading.

I don't know how she could resist looking out at the passing scenery of our mother country. My own family had instilled in me a love for England, explaining that the people were kind and we should be forever grateful for the way they had abolished slavery and made us free. I was so excited I pushed the window down, despite the cold, and leaned out, trying to catch all the scenes as we rushed past, but eventually had to stop because the smoke from the engine of the train choked me. Even so, the countryside seemed grey and dull after Jamaica. Instead of our lush trees, even in the courtyard at Blundells Hotel, sometimes dripping with free fruit, which were tendrilled around with creepers, the trees here were skeletal and I'd never seen this before. There were patches of fields, all dull brown or grey, some of them dotted with clumps of green I could not identify. Some of these were so sparse I couldn't believe anything was actually growing. I hadn't had much chance to see my own country, always working indoors and being in town, but I had seen the jungles of Panama which were always steamy and green and growing rapidly so that if you didn't cut down the trunks of trees they would sprout again within weeks, and there wasn't a bit of bare earth anywhere except where man trod.

'Mammy, what happened to the leaves on the trees?'

She laughed. 'Why, child, it's autumn and in this country most of the plants close down for winter and lose their leaves and then in spring, they bud again and as I told you before, it's a wonder to behold with the soft green of new leaves.'

I fell into a reverie, marvelling at what I saw; fields full of sheep grazing, without a shepherd in sight. Sometimes the dull squares of earth were broken up with a group of red-brick houses, with pitched roofs and windows that looked like eyes. It was so unlike my own country where there was foliage all the year round, much of it growing taller than me, and our houses were wood with verandas.

As the train chuffed through some hills and the land opened up, the fields were bare of any foliage and the ground was white. Mammy explained that this was because it was chalky. I can't say I fell in love with it; the ground here seemed to mirror the cold in the air.

Staring out of the window made my eyes droop, and after a while I had almost fallen asleep with the monotony of the train movement when Mammy made me jump, exclaiming, 'Oh no, it cannot be.'

She was holding her hand to her mouth and the news sheet had dropped into her lap. She looked at me and saw she needed to explain. 'Miss Nightingale has already departed for the Crimea. I have missed her by but a few days.'

I didn't know what to say. Was that the end of our plans? Were we to go back?

Mammy picked up the sheet again and said no more. I knew it wasn't the time to quiz her.

At the station I was totally confused by the noise and bustle, but Mammy was not put out at all and held up her hand. As I stood there open-mouthed at the crowds, a man pushed past and sent me spinning and I only stayed on my feet because I fell against our trunks. Mammy was striding along the platform, waving her umbrella, until she attracted the attention of a uniformed man with a trolley who returned with her. She ordered him to take our luggage and, as he loaded our trunks, she opened her capacious bag, and handed him some small change.

Soon we were in a hansom cab with our bags around us and it was then that Mammy said, 'I aim to go to the highest in the land and offer my services. I don't know how long this will take, but I hope to be in the Crimea within the month. There's terrible news of illnesses and injuries. We need to be there soon.'

After we had found lodgings, for somehow her late husband's family did not have room for her, although they were kind enough when she visited them, and settled in, Mammy asked me to help her get her best yellow dress ready, the one with the crimson ribbons, with matching ribbons flowing from her bonnet. She sure did look stunning, especially in this dark country where most of the people in the streets seemed to wear black or grey or violet. Although she wore a large paisley shawl this did not totally hide the brightness of her gown. The English ladies' skirts were not as wide as Mammy's either but perhaps that was because Mammy was becoming increasingly portly, although she could move as lightly as a dancer. She took her umbrella – we always carried umbrellas because it seemed to rain every day – and left, saying to me confidently, 'When I return Ratia, we will know what day we leave for the Crimea. I'm going to see the highest official – the Secretary of State for War, Mr Herbert himself.'

She was gone for most of the day and it was so dark I'd shut the curtains and lit the oil lamps in our rooms, on the dressers, side tables and in the middle of the dining-table, to dispel the gloom. I found it strange that the night came down so early in this country, creeping up on me as I sewed, not like in Jamaica where you saw the sun sinking and knew that it would be night soon, before you could wrap a shawl around your shoulders.

When she came in she said nothing. The ribbons on her bonnet and dress were bedraggled and she took off the shawl which, as I took it, I felt was wet through. She smelt of coal smoke, damp, and wet leather. Her face was dull, as if it had been caked with some of the dirty air outside. As she collapsed into an armchair, I took off her boots which had white smears where the wet had penetrated. I unlaced them and she did not resist so I could tell something was amiss. Normally she helped with her undressing, as if she didn't like me in a subservient role. That was another reason I loved her.

'Do you want a cup of tea?' I asked to break the icy atmosphere.

Mammy merely nodded. That was when I knew she was truly dispirited. Making the tea, I cut up some fruit cake into pretty star shapes, to try and cheer her, as she had shown me, and laid the tray daintily with a carefully folded coloured napkin. I made ginger tea as I knew it would calm her.

'Here we are, drink this.' I placed it before her and reached for the poker to chivvy the small fire that I'd lit into a blaze and soon the room was a-glow with the flames.

Mammy laughed, as she sipped the tea, and I knew her normal good spirits had already revived.

'Ratia, you are a true friend to me, and you've cheered me already. But this land of our fathers can be cruel.'

She stood up then, and loosened the buttons on her tight gown. Then she added, 'I have to accept that I cannot get on with all and that there will be times when an antipathy occurs.'

I said nothing and let her sip her tea and I could see the colour coming back, from that greyness I'd seen in her face. She leant forward, placing the cup and saucer on the table beside her, sighed, and told me of her day.

'I told the clerk that I needed to see the Secretary at War to offer my services as a nursing assistant in the Crimea and he smirked. I hit the table with my umbrella and spoke sternly and he ran off and returned soon and politely told me to wait.

She took up her tea and leant back, as if she was demonstrating.

'I waited in a draughty corridor and saw men scurrying and messengers coming and going, being allowed into the Secretary. At the end of the working day, when these gentlemanly young fellows were cleaning their quill pens and folding up their files, I was told to return tomorrow. So that is what I will have to do. I am sure the wrong message reached the Secretary, with my letters of introduction. Why else would

I have been kept waiting?'

She pulled herself upright, all her old energy returning. 'Ratia, this does not mean we stop here. We are going to the Crimea to help our poor sons who are fighting out there.'

The next day, I helped her get dressed and she set off again. After carrying out my small duties of tidying up breakfast platters and making beds, I spent the rest of the day studying my English grammar and reading the news sheet that Mammy had left behind from yesterday. The reports from the Crimea frightened me; there had been battles and deaths and mistakes and a journalist, a man called William Russell, was condemning the politicians in this country for not being more organised and prepared. The more I read, the more I had misgivings and, as the afternoon drew to a close and I started closing curtains and lighting lamps, I prayed that Mammy would come back and say she had had no success and we could go back home. I know that was disloyal of me, but I was becoming more and more afraid.

This time, when she came in, it was as if she had brought in the chill in a wave of anger. She was as cold as yesterday, and smelt again of the horrid London atmosphere. Even as she pulled off her shawl she explained. 'I've waited in that corridor, been chilled as people came and went, leaving the outside door open as often as not, but once again, I was ignored.'

Oh, dear, that *would* make her angry. It was not good to ignore Mammy. She continued. 'I've watched those same sundry messengers going in and coming out and even when I confronted the clerks about this they just turned away from me and scurried away. What is so frustrating is not to be told anything. I mean, is the Secretary of War too busy to see me, as they say, or is it just a rebuff? I don't know whether I can go back tomorrow, but they told me to, so I have to if I want to get to the Crimea. But I tell you this, if I don't have a meeting tomorrow I'm sure as anything going to try something else.'

When she returned on the third day, there was a different story but I was still not convinced about the effect of what she had been told.

'Someone took pity on me today and said, despite my excellent references, that the Secretary would not see me, considering that my request was not his remit. This kind gentleman, taking pity on me, suggested I transfer my attentions to the Quartermaster-general's department. So I hurried there. Ratia, it was no good. The man I saw was so insolent as to be amused by my explanation and suggested that I apply to the Medical Department, so tomorrow, I wait outside other doors in that department. But I will not give up.'

I said, 'Perhaps we are not wanted and these Britishers have their own way that we don't understand. Certainly they seem rude and insolent.'

She snapped at me even though she had said they were rude.

'How can you say such a thing? The soldiers we nursed in the camp at Jamaica treated us with respect and gratitude and I cannot believe their betters, in the home country, could do less. No, for some reason, these men have not understood what I am trying to do. It is a fault of mine. After all, they do not know of my reputation and see me as a strange woman from the colonies. I will try to explain myself better tomorrow.'

But the next day she failed as well and, that evening, sat pensively, not touching the meal I had prepared, reading the news-sheet quietly.

'Look at this, Ratia, an advertisement for more nurses to follow the first group. I will apply. My, this lady is a Mrs Herbert, I wonder if she is the wife of the Secretary of War?'

She carried on reading and then said, 'I know, I will look up my old friend who is working at Cox's, he will know to whom I should apply.'

'What is Cox's, Mammy?'

'They are the Army agents and do the general banking for

the regiments, but more importantly, they arrange the sale of commissions, so they know who is where. They will tell me where my friends are.'

You see, Mammy was never idle, she discovered everything there was to know about the military of this country and again, this would stand her in good stead, in the future.

When she came back that night, it was as a different woman.

'Oh, Ratia, I wish you could have been with me. I met with several of my old companions, one of whom had proposed to me years ago and we had a good chat over the old times. He admitted to me that he was happily married now to an English lady and even joked that that was much better for him than being married to a colony woman like me. And no, Ratia, don't look like that, I did not take offence. Because after we had taken a pint of porter together which is the English way, he gave me the private address of Mr Herbert, the Secretary at War, and tomorrow I shall present myself to his wife who is recruiting the new nurses for Miss Nightingale. I am sure we will be on our way very soon.'

That night she even allowed me to indulge in a little watered down sherry with her, which I have to say is not as tasty as our Jamaican rum, which my mother let me drink on special occasions.

The next morning Mammy let me sleep in, which I needed to do after the drink which did not agree with me – I know Mammy liked a little indulgence every now and then, but I avoided it after that – and when I awoke, she had already gone. I was hopeful that this waiting time, which was now boring me a little, would soon be over. Perhaps she would return by lunchtime and we would have time to go for a stroll as she had promised me, to see the sights of this great city.

But it was not to be. I'd shut the curtains and lit the lamps, the same as the other nights before she returned, and I could tell by the slump of her shoulders that she had not been successful. One part of me was saying, *I knew it would be like this*, but I said nothing to her, just made some tea without speaking while she disrobed and sat quietly waiting.

When she had sipped her tea, she sighed heavily and told me of her day. 'Well Ratia, I managed to get into Mr Herbert's house in Belgrave Square and very grand it is too. He has many flunkeys serving him, all in wonderful uniforms and I had plenty of time to admire the marble of his hall, and the pictures, and the furniture, for I was kept waiting for many hours. But as you will no doubt say, I am used to doing that now. Those servants were quite rude and all I can say is that they resented me sitting there.

But even worse, I saw many women coming and going obviously hoping to be nurses in the Crimea. Indeed, I heard one of them explaining her reason for being there and the servant led her to a side hall where she was asked to sit near a door. I could see that some of them were totally unsuitable, being too young. One of them even had a tiny babe with her and when I cooed over it, explained that she would leave the babe with her parents while she tried to do something respectable to retrieve her good name, poor girl.

'Another smelt of drink and another walked with a stick and I wanted to help her to rise from the chair, and wondered how she would be able to stand the hard work. But I was never called and then a servant came to tell me that her mistress now had her full complement of nurses and I was not needed. When I insisted that I had letters of introduction – well, Ratia, I had those letters from the good doctor at Up-Park Camp which was as good as a letter of introduction - and insisted on waiting, another lady, called Mary Stanley, came out and looked me up and down as if I had dirt on my clothes, and told me that I was not needed even if there had been a vacancy.

'I tried something else, and rummaged in my bag and showed her the advertisement that was in today's paper, she merely shrugged and repeated that I was not needed. *Not needed*, Ratia. That was the way she dismissed me. Oh, did she know how cruel those words were to me. If I am not needed then that is the end of me.'

For the first time in my life, I took her hand, which was icy cold, and held it and made her look at me. I know I was not yet of age, but at that moment I felt as if I was much older than Mammy.

'All I can say is they did not take to me. That is the only reason I can think of to be so cruelly rejected.'

'Mammy, do you think it's because we're not English perhaps?'

I thought that was the kindest way of putting it, that these white people did sometimes look askance at our colour but I couldn't say that to Mammy. Perhaps it was because I was closer to being a slave than she was and had the feeling in me, even though I was not a slave and never had been, that we weren't like them.

She looked astonished, but at least the listlessness was gone.

'Not English? Ratia, you may be right. But I have good Scottish blood from my father and my mother's forebears were mainly English and surely the little Negro blood that I have cannot turn them against me like that?'

Then the tears began to flow, 'Is it really possible that the American prejudices against colour have some root here? Did they really shrink from accepting me because my blood flows beneath a duskier skin than theirs? Surely not. Ratia, I cannot let myself believe that.'

I decided not to pursue the idea and patted her hands which were warming now, and stood. 'I'll make us some supper.'

'Not too much for me, just a light snack.'

But when I put a plate of her favourite pie and potatoes, with spiced vegetables, she ate with gusto and I truly believed she had not eaten all day. As we ate, I could tell she was thinking and I waited for the result, with a certain amount of trepidation. What would she come up with now? But that night, we bedded down without her saying anything. It wasn't until the morning, over her sweet tea, she told me of her new plans.

'Well, Ratia, I can try one more step, and then I don't know what we're going to do. I shall look up Amos Henriques, who I remember lived near the synagogue off Duke Street. He is in London, I believe, and is a doctor, and if he hasn't got some contacts who can be of help, I just don't know what else I can do.'

So, once again she dressed carefully, this time with an extra bright red and yellow ribbon decorating her bonnet. She took a basket of our pickles and jams, as a present, and, collecting the umbrella from the stand in the hall, set off jauntily.

I thought to make some special cakes and an apple pie for her return, as a celebration because I couldn't believe that a neighbour of Mammy's from way back in Jamaica could refuse her, and she would return with good news.

She bustled in before it was dark and took off her cloak in the hall, as she called to me, 'I'm back, Ratia, and a tale I have to tell. Let's have some tea.'

I thought this augured well and after placing the tray of tea and cakes before her I sat opposite and waited for her to tell me about her visit.

'I must say young Amos has done well. He lives in a most imposing residence and I was welcomed, and given tea. He is a kindly man and listened to my proposals with keen interest, and I was most encouraged. In fact, I could see a sparkle in his eye and believe I spoke so about the Crimea that he too is fired to go there.'

She put down her cup and stroked her hair which had been flattened by her bonnet, and added, 'But he cannot help me. He has expenses with his practice, and knows nothing of the war. He is not a military man, and knows of no-one who could help. He even told me how much it costs to travel to the war, which made me believe that he, too had thought about going. I truly felt sorry for troubling him. So, Ratia, I cannot think how we can get to the Crimea, and he did worry me with the cost of getting there.'

I returned to the kitchen and put the apple pie in the larder because I knew that even though Mammy had a good appetite, this disappointing result would dampen even her enthusiasm for food.

The next morning she did not go out and I was pleased because there was such a deep brown fog outside that I could not see the houses on the other side of the road.

Mammy explained, 'It's called a London particular, as I read in one of Dickens' books, and wonderfully describes its brownish yellow colour. Apparently it only manifests itself in this city.'

I made us some thick porridge, the way she'd taught me, from her Scottish forebears, which looked like the fog when I dished it up with brown molasses, swirling on top. As we spooned it up, she read the Times, the only broadsheet she took. Suddenly she slapped the paper down beside her porridge.

'There's one more place I can try, Ratia, look at this.' Every now and then she gave me articles to read, to see how my learning was progressing. I always found the print very small but could just about manage to read it.

The article was written by W. H. Russell and it described how a special Crimean Fund had been set up with donations from the public after the awful battles of Balaklava and Inkerman which had shocked the nation. The fund was to help those poor soldiers.

'I'll apply to the fund to see if it can sponsor me. Surely they cannot refuse because what they describe the fund for is exactly what I want to do. Get my bonnet, Ratia, I have to go out.'

'But Mammy, can't you wait until tomorrow? This fog will give you a bad chest.'

'No, I'll wrap my shawl across my face to stop the bad airs

from getting to me, but I cannot wait, Ratia, we must be going soon.'

I knew that she would find her way in that thick air, hadn't she travelled the world? But I *was* concerned about the reception she would get.

Need I describe the homecoming? The same dark evening – but even earlier this time, when even the midday had been without proper light, just a yellow glow outside which I shut out as soon as it turned greyish. I swear it wasn't three o'clock in the afternoon that I lit the lamps even though I was beginning to think about the cost of the oil with the enforced inactivity in this cold dark country. She returned. It was with the same sad entrance, enveloped in that cold stinking London smell, and with the same despair on her face.

I said nothing, but my stance must have said it all. 'Yes, you have guessed. Turned down again. What can we do?'

I did nothing except what I usually did which was to carry out the common sense tasks of getting her warm and feeding her. I hoped this was the final straw and we would be heading back to the warmth and welcome of Jamaica very soon.

I had not been treated well when I went out to buy food, even though I kept my head down. Some of the shopkeepers had pretended not to see me and, when they did, they couldn't understand me at first, until I spoke slowly. As I walked home, I thought I was being stared at but would not look at passers-by to confirm my feeling. It made me distinctly uncomfortable and I thought sadly that the *mother country* was not what it had been made out to be by people back home. I also felt as if I would never be able to trace Robert in this strange land.

I was beginning to believe that it would be better to be on my own island, and wait for my Robert to come to me there, rather than trying to find him. So, in a way, I was happy that Mammy had not been successful and began secretly packing, ready to depart.

Chapter 12: Sour sorrel

How wrong I was. The next day came a visitor – Mr Day. I opened the door and when I saw his dark face, with the thick eyebrows which made him look as if he was frowning all the time, I nearly shut the door and was willing to tell my mistress a lie, that it was just a tinker. He put his foot in the door, so he must have guessed, with a rictus smile on his face.

'Who is it, Ratia?'

'Why, Mammy I do believe it's that merchant man from Navy Bay, Thomas Day.'

Mammy had come out into the hall and when she heard this she hurried forward to greet him. 'Come in, come in out of the cold.'

'I've tracked you down, at last,' he said, as he came in rubbing his hands and giving me his damp scarf and hat, without even looking at me. 'Mrs Mary Seacole, I have a proposition to make to you.'

I didn't like the way he said that, without any introduction or giving Mammy a chance to be hospitable and offer him tea. I made some anyway and listened as he spouted forth, in the abrupt manner I would learn was his habit.

'I had to go to Cox's to find out where you were and they were very interested in a proposition I made to them, supplying me with goods to take to the Crimea. I need a partner. And you could well be that person, Mrs Seacole. Your reputation as a doctress and a fine hotelkeeper has spread far and wide.'

I didn't like the way he flattered her, knowing she would preen at such words, and allow good judgement of character to be suspended.

She bowed her head in acknowledgement, with a little smile, but said nothing. Encouraged, Mr Day continued.

'I can trust you as being a close relative to work with me, can I not?'

As I brought in the tea things, hoping to stop her making any rash decisions, which of course was a vain hope, she was all smiles and I must say that when Mammy smiled, it seemed the whole world lit up.

He continued. 'If I can obtain the funds to purchase supplies, I'm bound for Balaklava and, with you as my partner, such funds are assured.'

'Of course, that's it. I knew it would be possible somehow. You may not know, but all my offers to go as a nurse have been refused.'

And I knew well why Mr Day wanted my mistress as his partner. He would capitalise on her acquaintance with the doctors and officers in the army and their willingness to vouch for her skills as a doctress. Clever, this man, I thought.

'Yes, I heard,'

So he knew how desperate she was getting. Oh dear, I would have to watch this one. Yes, Mammy was skilled and knowledgeable about her herbs and she could cook a mean meal out of virtually nothing, but she had a wonderful way of trusting people. I had already learned that she was not good at charging for her services, although we picked up enough to live from day to day by providing herbal remedies to visitors, sent by the Amos's and other of Mammy's relatives.

Mammy's philosophy, was that, if people were good, she would get the best out of them, but rarely commented on those who had a mean streak, and took advantage of her. She would *put it down to experience*. Yes, she would fight for what she thought was right, but she did not look out for herself, that was the trouble. I realised that now, if I hadn't seen it before.

I couldn't say anything while he was there, but once he had gone, and she was walking around our small lodgings, enthusiastically picking up items and putting them down again as if her brain couldn't work unless she was a-doing,

I tried to warn her. 'Mammy, does this Mr Day have the money to pay for those supplies?'

'Ratia, he assures me that Cox's will give us credit and we can repay them as soon as our first customers come through the door of the hostelry. It will be built quickly like the one we created in Cruces, and with good supplies, it will be a great success with all those British officers, I know. I will call it the British Hotel, and it will be almost next door to the army quarters, near the front.'

She approached me and put her hands on my shoulders, even though I was nearly as tall as her now, and her eyes were shining. 'We will soon repay any debt and then we will make a tidy sum, to allow me to set up my own hostelry either here or back home in Jamaica, you wait and see.'

How could I dampen that enthusiasm? How could I refuse to go with her? She needed me to keep a tally and watch out for the thieves, as I had done with the American and his extra eggs. In any case, now that we were definitely going my hopes of meeting up with Robert grew. He was always in the back of my mind.

Chapter 13: Crates of sherry and champagne

The next weeks were frantic with preparations. We hardly noticed the Christmas festivities as Mammy made lists even on the day itself, as it was not possible to visit suppliers. Mammy obtained the loan from Cox's and organised some cartes des visite and sent them to her contacts, such as Sir John Campbell, in the Crimea to announce her forthcoming arrival while Mr Day organised the shipping of supplies.

When I saw the lists of items I was a bit bemused and questioned this. Crates of sherry and champagne? On a battlefield?

'Oh, Ratia, we must trust Mr Day to know what he's doing. Remember we will be running a high class hotel and will attract the officers who will pay us handsomely to entertain them with good food and drink – and then we will have sufficient funds to nurse the men in the ranks. We will not provide accommodation because the army will do that, I trust.'

It was true that medical supplies were also ordered and Mammy's precious box of herbs and potions was carefully packaged, together with bandages and splints. She would refuse to let this box, the size of a small crate, or sailor's box, out of her sight.

So *Seacole and Day* was formed as a partnership and I had to go along with it.

Mammy spent the rest of the days in London visiting those officers she knew. She discovered they met at the United Services Club so visited the place, and when she returned she was full of enthusiasm.

'If only you could see them, so smart in their uniforms, and so eager to get to the front and prove themselves. And how welcoming to me. Our mission cannot fail, they are all so encouraging and tuck my carte de visite into their pockets with a promise to visit our hostelry when it is built.'

I pretended to be enthusiastic for her sake but I wondered how many of those little cards, so carefully designed and paid for by my mistress, would be discarded before the men embarked for their duties. I hoped I was wrong but I was trying to be practical. The cards announced that *'she has taken her passage in the screw-steamer 'Hollander', to start from London on the 25th January, intending on her arrival at Balaklava to establish a mess-table and comfortable quarters for sick and convalescent officers.'*

She couldn't have made her intentions clearer, so could I doubt her now?

The weather was taking a turn for the worse and I saw snow for the first time that January, and what a wondrous thing to see, as it floated down like so many angels. I watched, fascinated at the window until Mammy chided me for being lazy. But it wasn't so good when I went shopping the next day and the pavements were iced over with trodden-down snow that had gone slushy and then hard overnight. I had to learn to walk carefully and marvelled at the other pedestrians who strode out, confident in their hob-nailed boots.

When I got home, the hem of my skirt was like a board, with snow and ice stuck to it so I had to shake it off in the hall, if I wasn't to carry a load of it into the rooms, where, no doubt, it would ruin the carpets and we would have to compensate the landlord.

It stayed like that for some days and I never got used to it, finding it frightening as the pavements became more hazardous the more people trod the snow into impacted ice, so when Mammy said she had the tickets, and we were sailing on the 27 January, I was mighty pleased. She explained how all their preparations were complete; 'I have handed out so many cards, and written so many letters, that the whole of the Crimea will be waiting on the dockside of the harbour for us to arrive, I am that sure,' she laughed, and I smiled and made her some tea.

We boarded the *Hollander* and here we had a pleasant surprise.

We were greeted with, 'Well, I don't believe it. Mrs Seacole, a name that my mother insisted I remember, and if I was ever in the Caribbean to be sure to look you up. And instead, you come to my waters. Let me introduce myself, James Macworth Smith, younger son of Dr Henry Macworth Smith.'

Mammy shook the man's hand and her forehead creased up in that thinking way she had. 'Why of course, I can see the resemblance. Your mother was mighty kind to reply when I wrote to say your brother Charles had died in my arms. Such a gentle, kind soul, and he was a good doctor in the making.'

James had taken Mammy's trunk and was leading us to our cabin, and he kept his face down, and I truly wondered if he didn't have tears in his eyes.

'I'm in charge of the ship's cargo, Ma-am, so whatever you need you just let me know. And I'll make sure that anything marked with your name is above the water line and kept dry.'

'That's mighty kind of you.'

I could see he was bursting with curiosity and sure enough, as he opened the door into our cabin, he asked, 'And why are you on your way to the Crimea, Ma-am?'

'Why I'm going to supply the Army with victuals and ensure they have the advantage of my nursing skills, just like I did your brother, although I was sorry to lose him.'

He leaned against the door of the cabin as I pushed past him to follow Mammy into the cabin, and took one of the bags from him, not looking at him, for again I was sure Mammy's words affected him.

He paused before answering. 'Well, I am convinced you'll succeed. From what I've seen, supplies are sadly lacking and there's many a man out there that would welcome a bit of home cooking and some kindness. You'll do well, I'm sure.'

With that he departed and we were left to fend in the tiny cabin that we had been allotted, even though Mammy had paid for a superior cabin.

Maybe I was wrong. Perhaps Mammy's fame had spread as far as this distant war.

This was not the only acquaintance she would meet as we travelled. In Gibraltar she decided to disembark, and wander the high roads of this strange rock on her own, but I insisted on going with her. I knew she did not like it but I called after her, 'You promised to show me the sights of London and I missed out on that, please let me come now. There's nothing to do in the cabin.'

She turned then and smiled at me, gesturing for me to join her. She hired one of the local guides, after surveying the group that surrounded us. She pointed at one of them who I could see was more tidily dressed than the others, and he didn't have the dark unshaven chin that most of the rabble had, which I'm sure Mammy spotted as well. 'Take us to the English fort, please.' He looked surprised.

'You don't want to climb the rock and see monkeys?' Mammy had chosen right though; he said it in a cynical way as if to suggest that was the boring place that all tourists wanted to go to.

Mammy laughed and he gestured for us to follow, setting off at a good pace, probably thinking he would leave us behind. What he didn't know was that, despite her bulk, my mistress could move quite smartly when she wanted. He pointed out the garrison and the church and the view, but the uphill walk had made us both warm and after an hour Mammy dismissed him. 'We'll sit here in this square and relax. You can go, as we can find our own way back.' He did not argue with that after she gave him an English florin for his trouble.

I gratefully collapsed onto a side wall and Mammy joined me but, just as I was drifting off into a comfortable day dream, our peace was shattered by a shout. 'Good old Mother Seacole, can it really be you?'

I looked up as did Mammy and, strolling across the square, were two English officers.

'Mother Seacole, what are you doing here?'

'Oh, my dear boys, is it really you? Captain Brown and Major Strudden, what a pleasure.'

After hand-shakes all round, Captain Brown said, 'You must come and have a drink for old time's sake and tell us how you have left Blundells Hall, which we remember well, don't we Captain?'

'Indeed, I do, that's where I was sent, to recover from that bout of cholera, and you worked your miracles on me. I'll never know how to thank you. I swear you saved my life.'

Mammy looked down, embarrassed. 'No, sir, you saved your own life by fighting it, even though I gave you the herbal weapons to do so.'

They were standing either side of us now, and I realised that it was not etiquette for Mammy to introduce me as, in my dark plain clothes and white blouse, her acquaintances would know I was her servant, so I kept quiet.

'Now, you must come with us for old time's sake, and your maid here can have some ginger beer, what say you?'

Mammy stood in between them, taking an arm of each and I followed them as they led her to a small bar at the corner of the square, where there were tables and chairs set outside in the sun. It reminded me of home, where drinkers would loll outside small shacks serving rum. The men ordered some drinks and I waited outside, where my ginger beer was soon brought to me. The warmth of the sun made me dozy and I thought Mammy would spend hours reminiscing but she did not stay long and bade farewell to her friends, with a 'see you in the Crimea.'

As we walked downhill to the ship, she staggered a little and took my arm, in a most unfamiliar gesture.

'I do declare, young Ratia that the local Spanish wine is very nasty and I may have to retire to my bed when we board the *Hollander*. I must say though it is very encouraging to meet old acquaintances, for they have made some very good suggestions as to who I should contact when we get to Balaklava and no doubt, when they arrive they will seek us out. Yes, I am truly positive that our venture will succeed.'

Our next stop was Malta but neither Mammy nor I can say a good word about the place and we agreed that it was good to be gone. For one thing, there were many poor English women, trudging around with bairns holding on to their skirts, begging for work. One of them approached us, and explained that she was trying to get to the Crimea to find her husband and could we help. Mammy was sympathetic and gave her a coin but could do no more.

I discovered from James, who became quite friendly with me, that many of them turned to whoring to find the funds for a loaf of bread to feed their children and I was so glad that I had Mammy as a mistress who paid me well as feeding me and making sure I had good clothes, so I could save as well. She would give me the dresses she no longer wanted, because she did like to keep up to her idea of fashion. I was handy with a needle and could always cut them up to fit my slender frame, and have material over to add pretty collars and cuffs to other items. I usually dispensed with the bows and ribbons Mammy loved, and might even turn her brightly coloured materials inside out, to achieve a plainer look.

Compared to the poor soldier's wives, the officers' wives were even more offensive to us. They patronised the large hotels and when Mammy entered they pointedly ignored her and some of them even left the restaurant where we took tea, putting on their gloves in a way that I could decipher as *we don't want to get our hands dirty fraternising with these black women.* Needless to say Mammy ignored the exodus, but I knew she noticed it.

While we were there, we learned of one desperate wife who had made her way to Malta dressed as a soldier and nearly got away with boarding the ship to the Crimea, except for a heavy period that she had not expected. Mammy said it was probably caused by the stress and the unfamiliarity of being on board a storm-driven ship. The poor woman was ejected, her man clothes ripped and her bag thrown after her, where it burst on the ground, revealing her womanly undergarments.

The only highlight of our visit to Malta was that Mammy met Doctor Henderson in Valletta, whom she had known in Kingston. He was the doctor who had asked us to help in the yellow fever outbreak. She told me about her meeting with him, as I refused to disembark after our first few walks in Malta, and he came to visit us on board.

'He has just come back from Scutari, Ratia, where Miss Nightingale has set up her hospital. Scutari is in Constantinople, and he is most encouraging about me paying her a visit, before I go on to the Crimea.'

I could see how she set to work on him, explaining her plans as she plied him with his favourite Caribbean ginger syrup cake that she had taught me to bake and it was a fresh one that I had made that morning. That was how Mammy persuaded people; through their favourite foods or by comforting them with her good humour and good conversation. As you may realise by now, from her explanation of her exploits with her husband, she was a great story teller, not that she told lies, but through her enthusiasm, she coloured the telling with exotic additions. People seemed to like to listen to her and she would bewitch them with her story-telling and then, when she had them all good-humoured, she would ask them for help or favours or introductions.

As the good doctor left, burping discreetly into his handkerchief, Mammy leant against the door that had closed upon him and said exultantly, 'He did not reject the idea of my approaching Miss Nightingale in her hospital. How could she refuse me when I am present at the very place where I am most needed?

'I'm sure he will send letters before me which will stand us in good stead, accentuating my medical skills. I know I cannot call myself a doctor, but doctress will do just as well. He explained that he had been working with Miss Nightingale herself – imagine - and he has given me a letter of introduction to her. We are ready to face anything now.'

So when the *Hollander* left Malta we were both content, for I was always happy when my mistress was happy. It was also because the weather became warmer, although not as warm as our home country. After England, though, it felt as if we had been blessed. The sea was calm for one thing. Mammy enthused about all the little islands we passed, with their white, domed, buildings and sandy shores but I found them quite boring and arid compared to the lush growth on Jamaica. I never really shared Mammy's enthusiasm for these foreign climes.

Soon we reached Constantinople. We had travelled past little villages clutching the sea shore, all of which had their own small domed building which James, who stood beside us as we sailed along the coast, explained were mosques, and I became familiar with the shape of their domes with two or more minarets at the corners. It was evening when we finally docked and the sun shone on the golden towers and minarets of the large mosques which dominated the skyline, and glinted luminously. Here they seemed huge, with many domes and minarets, the city boasting about its greatness by the glory of its buildings.

As we watched the activity of the ship edging its way to its berth, amongst many other ships of all shapes sizes and designs, the sun hid behind the cityscape, so that the buildings became black silhouettes, and the horizon looked as if it was made of soft hills pierced by so many lances of cavalrymen. The sky became a cavalcade of reds and oranges and yellows, pierced by the gold of minarets. I soon learned the purpose of these minarets and within a few days I had become used to the chanting call to prayer that emanated from them and haunted us across the water.

James approached us in the evening before we were due to disembark, and whispered, 'See those men loafing around? They will offer to be your guides. Be careful, Ma-am, and choose wisely, remember those who wear turbans will stop to pray five times a day, and you'll be left waiting. Sometimes they abandon their charges,'

Mammy looked towards the group. Some were smoking, some were crouched on their heels, and others were looking expectantly at the ship. Mammy thanked James for his advice.

Next morning we disembarked and we were soon surrounded by a chattering crowd of porters and guides and opportunists. I recognised the type by now, being the same as those in Cruces and other harbours we had landed at. I stood aloof as Mammy looked around and pointed to a tall clean shaven man who did not wear the turban of the Mohammedan.

'Here man, come here.'

He approached us and bowed low and very respectfully.

'What is your English like? Tell me.'

'I spik very good English. I work for diplomat at English Embassy. I show him and his guests our city. My family are merchants and disappointed that I don't take part, but I like to meet people like you.'

It was a long speech, made in very broken English, and others were elbowing him and speaking in their own tongue or saying the odd word that I understood. I guessed they were trying to persuade Mammy to take them on as well. Mammy ignored them and asked loudly, 'What is your name?'

'Johnny Ebraugaglou, Ma-am.'

His name sounded like so much tumbling water to me and Mammy also screwed up her face at the sound of it.

As we were having this conversation James, the cargo chief, strolled down the gangplank and joined us.

'They're all called Johnny here,' he laughed. 'It's the common name they use because they know you cannot pronounce their individual names. What did you say your name was, sir?'

Johnny bowed to him and gave his name again and James explained to Mammy, 'He is one of the Jewish faith. He will be a good servant if you treat him right, and he probably has very good contacts with suppliers.'

Mammy thanked him and turned to our chosen man and confirmed the appointment. 'Very well, sir, you will be our guide and our agent in this city, but I will call you Jew Johnny to differentiate you.'

I detected a slight frown from the man but Mammy did not notice it and as I stepped forward he looked closely at me and I smiled. He smiled too and I put out my hand to shake his, 'I am Mrs Seacole's personal servant and hope we can get on together.'

He looked at me sharply and I could tell he understood me; we would be friends and compatriots if he treated my mistress right, but if I ever found him cheating he would be the subject of my wrath. That was how I had matured on that journey; I could intimidate people as much as Mammy, but I never let her know that.

'Come Jew Johnny, you must show us the wonders of your city.' She turned to James, 'We can return to the ship to sleep or do we have to find lodgings for the few days we are here?'

James assured us we would be welcome to stay on board at night for the six days his ship was in harbour, and he would take care of our cargo.

'Mother Seacole, you deserve to be looked after and I'll ensure that all your supplies will be delivered to the next ship that takes you across the Black Sea.'

Johnny called a carriage and ushered us into it, but Mammy

asked him to stop when we reached a lozenge shape square. Johnny explained this was the Hippodrome and walked us round it, telling us that it had been a Roman racing track but when Mammy asked to enter the great mosque on one side, Johnny refused.

'You're not Muslim so not allowed. But also, women, they are only allowed in the balcony,' and he turned tail and took us down a side road and we came to a great gate and through the gaps we could see landscaped park so we followed him. We spent the day in this pleasant garden which was the outer section of the Topkapi Palace, but were not allowed into the inner sanctum. Johnny informed us that the Sultan's harem was beyond the high walls, together with many chambers where the Sultan kept his jewels and collections of artefacts. As the afternoon became warm, Johnny cold see we were in need of somewhere cool and he led us out of the great gates, and into a bazaar which was huge and I rather feared that we would get lost. Johnny marched confidently through the narrow alleys, greeting stallholders from time to time who shouted at him but he shrugged and moved on.

We were looking for a place which sold pots and pans, after Mammy explained she needed a selection for her cooking when she arrived at her destination. As he guided us through the crowds, Johnny spoke quietly in his broken English. 'It is not a good idea to pay the price asked. You refuse the first price and suggest one that is one third of the man's asking price, and then he comes down, you have to go up and it is good to settle at half the price originally mentioned. Understand?'

Mammy let him talk and said nothing. As if she didn't know what to do. I'd seen her haggling in the Panama with rogues and thieves, and she'd always beaten them down to what she considered satisfactory. This would be no different. Johnny carried on telling us the tricks of the locals. He became silent as he ushered us into a shop full of cooking utensils. I looked around, to see ladles, sieves and large knives hanging from the ceiling and upon rows of shelves were piled copper pans, pewter pans and gaily coloured pottery. Oil lamps were cleverly interspersed between the goods to make them shine so that it looked like an Aladdin's cave.

We were greeted with bows and clasped hands and led to an elegant sofa which edged the walls of the shop, below the shelves, and handed what we were told was apple tea. I sipped it gingerly but Mammy quaffed it as if she had been drinking it all her life, so I followed her lead. It was hot but delicious, with only a hint of apple in it.

Mammy explained what we needed and the proprietor gestured to an assistant, who spread a coloured cloth on the ground, and proceeded to collect different varieties of pots and pans. The proprietor waited until there was a good collection and then explained, in a censorious voice, about the qualities of each of the designs. Needless to say, they were all excellent, but some of them were more excellent than others, according to him.

Johnny whispered something to Mammy and pointed to the more expensive copper pots but Mammy picked up others and started to bargain. I drank my tea and, as the bargaining went on and on, with Mammy beating the owner down, I drifted off into a doze. I was awoken by a metallic cacophony as the pots that Mammy had eventually chosen were collected together and placed on the counter. After some more negotiating, Johnny persuaded the owner to deliver the parcels, which were quite large, to the ship and we left. It was nearly dark when we got back but the city was lit with great flares which reflected on the goods being sold on street stalls and, as the sun set behind the mosques and minarets, the call to prayer began and I felt a great sense of peace and happiness, knowing that Mammy was happy with her purchases and we would soon be on our way to the Crimea. The insistent rhythmic sound of the chant always appealed to me.

We spent six days in Constantinople and Mammy was not impressed with the way the locals treated her, staring at her as if she was an oddity. I pointed out when she complained, that she *was* an oddity in this country, where we did not see many local women out on their own. Indeed, even the European females had chaperons and guides – it was only Mammy that strode ahead, looking to right and left, absorbing all, instead of keeping inside a carriage, and being modest. It might have been because they saw her as a coloured woman dressed in European clothes that made them stare, for it was true that this was a great metropolis with people of all colours and nations mixing together, and there were plenty of people of my colour in the city, but they seemed to be workers of all types, so Mammy stood out with her commanding ways.

The only people who seemed to tolerate her pushiness – for that is what I realised it was – were the French, who had a peculiar way of shrugging their shoulders and looking up in the air, as if to say, *she is a one.* I kept quite close behind Mammy and learnt to keep my eyes down, for many of the passers-by would try to waylay us, with offers to take us to their uncle's carpet shop, where the carpets were the best in Constantinople. It was no good Mammy explaining that she did not need carpets, they still bothered us, even though Jew Johnny would return quickly to us from the errand he'd been sent on, and shush them away, like so many bothersome midges, similar to the ones that plagued us in Jamaica.

On one of those days, something momentous happened. Mammy decided to take a caique across the Bosporus and visit Miss Florence Nightingale in Scutari, on the Asian side of the Bosporus.

I sat her down for her breakfast and I sat opposite her. She looked surprised but did not comment but ate her porridge steadily. I had never before confronted her about her intentions but this time I really wanted to save her from certain humiliation.

'Mammy, can I say something?'

She did not look up but nodded, and I knew the way I acted had non-plussed her, for once.

'Let me recall, you tried to become a nurse in London with Miss Nightingale's group?' I didn't wait for an answer. 'You were rejected. You tried everything in London and I saw how it affected you. I've brushed your hair and can see the grey hairs that accumulated in those weeks. Your eyes looked sad, you were frozen and dispirited.'

'But not for long, girl, and it gave me time to think of this much better idea, didn't it?'

You see, incorrigible, nothing could get her down, but I persisted. 'You were rejected. What makes you think she will welcome you now? She could well not accept your letters of introduction and what will that look like? An outright snub will do no good for your reputation.'

She looked up then. 'An outright snub?' This person is a lady, an English lady, and brought up to know the highest in the land, as I have been in my own country. It is not ladylike to *snub people* as you call it, and I have every confidence she would not do that from one lady to another. I am going.'

With that, she stood and made her preparations, but before she went, she came to me, and put her arm around my shoulder, which was difficult for her because I was now the taller.

'I know you have my best interests at heart and I will not take it amiss that you have spoken to me like that, and I will think on what you have said.'

She turned away then and looked in the tiny mirror in the cabin and eyed me through there. 'I am glad you have learned wisdom through being with me.' Her eyes had that old twinkle in them and I couldn't help but laugh with her, and wish her well in her venture.

I had to wait many anxious hours for her return. When she did not come back at night, I sought out James, but he assured me he would have known if anything had happened to her.

'News like that spreads like wildfire amongst the crews here, even from locals to foreigners. I assure you she is safe. I'll wager she left it too late to return. If she doesn't turn up tomorrow by mid-morning, I will start making enquiries.'

He was right of course, Mammy came in late the next morning, calm as a Jamaican lizard sleeping in the sun, when I was mad with worry. I could not detect from her demeanour what had happened, which was unusual, so I said nothing but ordered a fresh pot of tea from the orderly at the end of the corridor, and told him to find James and make sure he knew of Mammy's return. While we waited for the tea, I helped her take off her outdoor clothes in our cramped quarters. It was warm but she had still gone out with several shawls and her favourite bonnet, and now I could tell she was hot and, despite her calmness, something bothered her.

'Do you want to wash before our tea arrives?'

'Indeed, yes, I must, Ratia, and ask the steward for some carbolic soap, the strongest he can find.'

I did as she asked and discreetly left for a late morning walk while she carried out her ablutions at the tiny sink in our cabin. I returned with the tea when I guessed she would be dressed.

I found her in fresh clothes but I was disturbed to note that she was unusually quiet, and put it down to tiredness. I could always tell when she had overdone herself because the bags under her eyes turned to grey and they were very grey now.

Once she had sipped some of the tea she sighed and looked at me.

'Ratia, you have grown very wise, and I should listen to your counsel.'

I blushed but said nothing.

'I have witnessed some terrible scenes but also met some of my old friends from the 97th but it is wicked to see how they are wounded and how they are being treated. What a terrible place that Scutari hospital is.'

'Oh, tell me all, Mammy, you know how it eases your mind to talk about it.'

She nodded and began, but as she spoke, she started to scratch and I was surprised at this as she was very particular about her hygiene. 'It was not until late afternoon that I stepped off the caique and made my way up the hill. The first place I saw was the British cemetery, a sad place showing the tragic deaths of many already. The hospital is a dull looking, square block of a building, dominating the skyline but inside there are corridors of beds, filled with the wounded. They say those corridors are a mile long, and I truly believe that is so. The windows are high up and at mid-day the sun sends rays of warmth down on the beds but this does not last long because of the height of the windows. It had a strangely quiet air, as if the men were resigned to their fate.'

I said nothing as she sipped her tea and sighed. She took a deep breath and continued in a measured voice, which I knew demonstrated she was too shocked by what she had seen to embellish and use her usual dramatic way of story-telling.

'The nurses smiled at me but did not confront me, and they seemed subdued and willing enough in their work, but they do not talk to the soldiers, or hold their hands, or be at one with those dying. It is all so much dressing this one, or taking the bedpan from that one, or holding a cup to a thirsty one, all done in a very clinical way.

'I was beginning to despair of finding my way to the nurse who oversaw this, when I recognised Joshua, a Sergeant in the 97th who indeed spotted me at the same time. Ratia that was endearing, as a cry went up, "Well, bless my soul, if it isn't Mother Seacole from Jamaica. Boys, it's our Mother Seacole, bless her." Somehow, the ward seemed warmer.

'I noticed many of the men I had known when they were stationed at Up-Park Camp and it was a sight that made my heart sink as I saw how ill they all were. I could do no more than start to nurse them, adjusting a dressing here, and helping another with water, gently holding his head and speaking quietly but encouraging him in the drinking. A group sat together as one of their number read from a newspaper but when they spotted me being welcomed they turned and the whisper went around the ward as to who I was. Some of the more able-bodied came and shook my hand. Ratia, I know where our men are and I know I am needed. I asked Sergeant Joshua to show me to Miss Nightingale and he willingly did so. But it took a long time because, as we travelled to her quarters, I stopped and ministered to the men, giving one a drink here, and there holding the hand of another who was obviously dying.

'Oh Ratia, it would break your heart. One man was obviously blind and as I held the cup to his lips he held my hand and gasped. "Surely that is the hand of a woman. Bless you, dear, bless you." And he wouldn't let go, until I explained gently that there were others who needed my services.

'As I stood, a doctor was passing and he nodded approvingly and thanked me. I knew then that I was in the right place and my man, who was waiting patiently, led me away from the sick, to Miss Nightingale's quarters. I realised that it was now getting quite dark and my friend said, "How are you getting back? It is too late to go on the Bosporus on one of those caiques, it could be dangerous."

'I will throw myself on Miss Nightingale's mercy and see if she can find just one spare bed for me to stay the night or else I will stay up all night and nurse the men.'

'He smiled at me and I knew he approved of my answer.

'We reached her office which was in a corner tower. My man knocked and a sharp voice ordered us to enter. The room was quite small but very neat, with her papers stacked on her desk, a chaise longue in one corner where I imagine she sleeps when she can, and a circular staircase leading to other quarters upstairs. I had time to look around as my man introduced me with an air of respect. There were one or two comfortable armchairs as well as a window seat. When I gazed on Miss Nightingale she was inspecting me sharply. I could well see from that look that she was most particular about who she would take on to work for her, as I had heard. Eventually she broke the silence.

'Yes I have heard of you, how can I help you?'

'I have here some letters of introduction,' I explained and handed her the letters I had gathered as we came out.

'She read them carefully and put them on the desk still saying nothing. I watched her. Ratia, I am sure you are interested in what she looks like?'

I nodded, although I had seen a drawing of her in *Punch.*

'She is a slight figure with a tiny waist – it looks to me as if she is living on will power and not stamina as she has no reserves, unlike me! She was dressed in a type of nurses' uniform with a high collar and belt at the waist, which accentuated her tiny face which seemed pale and pinched. She has so much nervous energy and as she stood facing me her foot tapped as if she was impatient to be away, doing.

After a pause, she asked, "What do you want from me?"

"I do not now want to work in your hospital, Miss Nightingale," I said but with the utmost respect of course. "I am now bound for the front where I know I can be of more use. But my immediate need is for a bed for the night, or to be given permission to help your nurses care for the men. I dread the journey across the Bosporus and may not be able to find my ship, the *Hollander* in the dark. I had not realised how time slipped by as I came through the wards."

'She eyed me sternly before answering. "You realise that we do not have spare beds here? Indeed some of the soldiers who are not so ill sleep in chairs all night. It is not ideal but we have to make do with what we have. I will see what I can do, however, as I realise you cannot return, a lone woman, across the water, at this late hour."'

'Ratia, I made no comment but it did cross my mind how we

made do in Cruces, sleeping under that table.'

I grinned, yes, we had been most inventive.

'I did not suggest that to this eminent lady though, as I realise that such people would be shocked at what we have done.'

I could see the mischievous look in her eye. Miss Nightingale may have tried to show she was superior to my mistress, but it would have rolled off Mammy's back like water – although she would have been aware of it. Mammy knew her own worth.

'So, what happened? Where did you sleep or did you keep awake all night? You look as if you have, with those bags under your eyes.'

Mammy did not rebuke me for talking so personally; I think by now she realised I was more of a friend than a servant.

'No, eventually they found me a bed with a washerwoman in the basement and I found her most congenial. Her name was Beatrice and we spent a long time chatting before we decided to sleep.'

Again Mammy started to scratch and added, 'and I was visited in the night by some unwelcome visitors, as I slept. *Fleas,* Ratia, jumping on me like a cloud. It was truly unpleasant. You will need to clean my clothes in boiling water to get rid of any eggs. The bites will go and the carbolic soap has helped.'

She scratched as she explained and I too started scratching, in sympathy.

'I had some breakfast before I left and said goodbye to Beatrice, who was already up to her shoulders in soapsuds; I found her a truly congenial and kind woman.'

I noticed that Mammy had not made that claim about Miss Nightingale who was said to be an angel in the night to the men, but I wasn't going to point it out.

'So that was quite an adventure and I'll always remember meeting Miss Nightingale, who I will predict will be known as one of the most important women of our time. Now, we need to go to the post office to collect our letters and start planning for the next stage of our journey.'

Chapter 14: Lavender bags

At the post office there were letters from Mr Day and from home, and from Cox's giving details of items that had been sent at Mr Day's instructions.

We walked through the staring crowds back to the ship, being familiar now with the way the Turkish ladies, heavily veiled, fluttered around us, asking questions in their own tongue, which we didn't understand, so couldn't answer. Mammy had opened the letters quickly and scanned them but put them into her large bag saying, 'I'll read these properly when we're back in our own quarters, and then I can digest them and make such arrangements as are necessary.'

I agreed with her as it was getting warm and after leaving the post office we had to walk through a fish market, and the odours from the produce was most unpleasant. We were constantly bombarded by what Mammy called Greeks, trying to sell us goods, by shoving them close to our faces, and I had to grimace and pull away as large slices of pink fish were displayed so the smell almost suffocated me. I felt like telling them that my eyesight was perfectly good and I didn't need the fish to be put right under my nose. Mammy didn't seem to mind and waved them away with good humour and a smile. I realised the reason they were accosting us was because they recognised Mammy as the weird lady from afar who never spoke sharply to them.

When we reached our cabin, and we had taken off our outdoor clothes, Mammy laid out the letters in date order on the tiny table between our beds. She then took a small notebook and proceeded to make notes. I said nothing but read from my grammar book and also a little book showing how the French language was different from ours, because I wanted to surprise Mammy with my learning.

Soon she was finished and leant back on her chair. 'Well Ratia, it looks as if the venture is going to be a success, although Mr Day is obviously not enamoured of the area. Listen to this.' She held up one of the letters and read, "It is very muddy here and there are no proper roads so the mules behave appallingly, refusing to budge unless whipped, and become more impossible to deal with every day, and there is much thieving from the locals so we have to be constantly on our guard."' She looked up and added, 'So, Ratia, don't we know all about that? I should imagine it's the same wherever you go, that poor people see others with items they want and don't understand that we work hard for them.'

'Well, Mammy I sure had experience in the Panama and I reckon that, if we have the right people with us, like Johnny, we should be able to keep our eyes peeled and the thieving at bay.' I hoped I had given her a hint because I was sure we needed Johnny's services where we were going, and I had grown fond of him. He reminded me of Mac who we had left behind in Panama.

She nodded and went back to reading, '"The harbourmaster is not our friend and makes all sorts of excuses for not being able to deliver our goods when they arrive, pointing to the bedraggled army and explaining that they do not even get their supplies, so why should we expect him to help us? I have asked the local Tatars to help and they will, but of course the expense of the delivery is going to be much higher than I thought. Can you organise more horses, as they are in very short supply here as well as making sure the champagne and other luxury goods arrive? I have made friends with some officers who cannot wait to have a slap-up meal, as they have heard of you, Mary, and know that you will cater for them very well."'

Mammy turned the page, and paused, reading silently, but I could see that little smile playing at the corner of her lips. Then she stopped smiling.

'Listen to this, Ratia, would you believe it. "In the meantime, there is a lot of drunkenness, and the soldiers are most dispirited. There are many men dying in huts, or even on the harbour side, without any shelter, waiting to be shipped to the hospital at Scutari. Even worse, the sea is littered with the corpses of animals and men. It is most unpleasant and I would suggest that we abandon the venture."'

'What is he talking about, Ratia? Abandon our plans now? At the same time as ordering me to find horses. The man is confused. The sooner we get there the better.'

Mammy put the letter down and looked at herself in the small mirror. 'All these problems can be overcome, can't they? It doesn't seem as bad as some of the places we've been to but it certainly sounds as if we're needed, and that's what's important. If we have friends out there, as we obviously do, we shall do a good trade and make some money, and I can spend time nursing the men who need it. Now I will reply to Mr Day.'

'Mammy, I will go and check on that washing with James, and leave you to it.'

She agreed and I left her to find our good cargo man because I wanted him to accompany me back into the city. The truth of it was that I had hoped to get letters as well from the post office, from Robert, but I had not liked to ask when I was with Mammy and hoped that James or one of his men could accompany me, because I was not like Mammy, I felt threatened by the crowds and noise.

James found me a sailor who had completed his *at berth* duties and we set off.

His name was Tom and he was taciturn so I did not bother to engage him in conversation as we pushed our way through the crowds. We *were* stared at; a very black woman dressed in European clothes, even though my bonnet since London had an extra rim to it and ribbons fell down around my face, and a young white sailor accompanying her. I could understand that, even in this cosmopolitan city, there were always going to be gawpers and sights for them to gawp at. I stared off into the middle distance to avoid any acknowledgement of the stares or comments.

But my little trip was to no avail; there were no letters for me. My family back in Jamaica were not likely to write, even though I wrote to them, which letters were read out to them by the local know-all, for my parents had never had the luck I had, and never learned to read and write.

My disappointment was soon forgotten when we returned, for other matters occupied me. It had started to rain, the torrential rain I had become used to in Panama and I rushed on board. In the cabin, Mammy was her old active self, packing and checking her supplies, with letters on the side ready to be sent on their way.

'We leave today, Ratia, I have secured our places on board the *Albatross*. James is to help us transport the supplies there by boat. And other goods will go in another ship called the *Nonpareil*. Both ships should arrive at the same time, God willing.'

'Mammy, it's raining very heavily outside, can we not wait until it stops?'

She turned and looked at me and put her arms on her hips. 'No, we are not important. The transport ship that is about to leave for the Crimea *is* important and we cannot hold it up because we are afraid of a little rain. While you've been out, I've made all the arrangements and we must go, rain or not.'

You might think she was criticising me for 'gallivanting' while she did all the work, but I knew it was not meant so, it was just a statement of how busy she had been.

So for the next hour or two it was hard work, even with James' cargo men who were used to hauling such bales and parcels from harbour to boat and from boat to ship. Johnny helped and begged to stay with us and Mammy pretended to think about it but I knew she would agree because she'd already told me how useful he was, and I had confirmed it by my subtle hinting.

Soon we were berthed in the *Albatross* and, as it left that great port and sailed through narrow strips of land, so narrow that I thought we could touch either side from the ship, Mammy made the acquaintance of the other passengers. Through the mooing of many cattle, stored in the hold, she laughed and joked with the commissariat officers, making sure they knew what she was planning to do, knowing they would be useful if she wanted supplies that were hard to come by. I couldn't help admire the way she dropped it into the conversation as if it was the most natural thing in the world to tell them, and made sure they knew her name, and the name of *Seacole and Day*.

It didn't take long to sail across the Black Sea. A friendly sailor told me that, due to the 'sea' being landlocked, there are of currents caused by the sea crashing against different beaches, fighting with itself. Our ship, despite being a modern steamship, was rocked like a cradle being manhandled by an angry slave-nanny. We made one stop at a town called Varna to take on fresh vegetables from the locals and then we steamed across still waters. I was lulled into a kind of dream world, as I leaned over the side of the ship, watching the waves lap and splash over the lower portholes, and the slapping sounds become rhythmic. The sea was dark and I could see my reflection in it and it was constantly moving as if I was a sea-maiden looking up at me and trying to tell me something. I don't often reflect on the life I have but I did then, wondering if I'd ever meet my Robert again; if he'll still want me and if we will ever marry. I have a strange yearning and I remember Sarah and her baby and what she said about a light coming into her life.

I was in the same strange mood when I saw before me a dark coast and some thin wisps of smoke that were almost welcoming, signalling a warm house with a hearth. We had to wait for permission to enter Balaklava and, after what seemed hours, the pilot came to lead us in.

As we slipped into it, I was soon shocked out of my reverie by the noise, the smells and the palaver that was going on and what I at first thought strange; the mooing of many cows, echoing as if in a great barn, not just from the hold of our ship but from the land. The entrance into the harbour was a surprise in itself as it was so narrow that I swear I could hear the ship scraping the sides and there were so many masts and funnels that I couldn't see the end. It was as if all these ships stretched onto the rising hills either side. The water in this harbour was littered with planks of wood and other floating debris, including the corpses of animals, as Mr Day had described. The stench suddenly hit me and I retched. It was the sick-sweet odour of decaying bodies, filthy men, manure. On either side the land rose like walls and on the right hand side of the entrance, high up, was the ruins of a castle, standing sentinel over the whole scene. The hills were dotted with low houses, looking so much like carbuncles on the side of a ship. One building had the skeleton of what looked like an onion on a tower and I later learned that this was the locals' design for their church. The sky was a bright blue and so was the sea but it was churned up by the many small caiques sailing amongst the great ships and had dirty brown foam floating on the top. The smell came to me again and this time reminded me of rotten vegetables and rancid meat and I gagged again before I left my place and sought Mammy.

She was calm and gathering together her bags as normal. 'Ratia, you're here at last. I was beginning to worry although I thought you needed some free time.'

See, again, she knew instinctively when to leave people alone as well as minister to them. That was a healing thing in itself, I learned. In the bustle of all this activity, people needed sometimes to be alone.

But then practicality took over. 'Come, we have much to do

here. Take this lavender bag and hang it round your neck, like this, as it will mask the smell.'

She too wore such a bag and as I tied it on, the soft sweetness of lavender perfume wafted up my nose and although I wasn't sure whether it would cut out the awful odours outside, it was certainly a great relief. As we went on deck, she pointed out those thin strips of smoke and disabused me of my belief that they were welcoming hearths full of warmth. 'Look; that is the fighting around Sevastopol. They have big guns which are shelling the town. We will definitely be of use here, after all. The battle is being fought even now.'

We watched as the little boats guided our great ship to its mooring which was a slow affair, trying to find a way through the multitude of ships.

Mammy was watching all the activity, and even she was silenced. I too watched and realised that there was some order, men in charge instructing others, and labourers following those orders, unloading ships. There were crates that were moved further along the landlocked basin and navvies working in a chain gang and I believed they were building what looked like a railway. By the side of where they worked, there were crudely built low buildings which I learned were the warehouses and everywhere I looked there were piles of metal and wood.

'Ratia, I'll write a note to Mr Day and ask one of the sailors to deliver it. I don't think we'll disembark this evening, but will wait for Mr Day to come to us and he will apprise us of the situation with our enterprise. I shall also send word of my arrival to Codrington of the 97th, and solicit the aid of Captain Peel and all those medical men we know. Oh, and I mustn't forget Sir John Campbell, one of my patrons, who I know has high command out here.'

She started naming all these names and I'd never taken much notice before but remembered some of them, who she'd written to before leaving England. I realised that her time in

England had not been wasted; she already knew many of the officers who she could summon to her aid.

'You know you can't stay on board much after tomorrow, Madam, don't you?' pointed out the captain of the *Albatross*. 'We leave as soon as we are able. We don't have to wait for the tide to turn here.'

'Of course, I quite understand. I will find other quarters.'

I looked around at the harbour. The small houses I'd seen appeared unoccupied but looked miserable and were, anyway, too far up the steep hills either side. The ground was muddy, churned up by all the activity, and I could see it would be too slippery to climb to them anyway, and there didn't seem to be any pathway up the hills. All traffic was moving along the flat shore to the end where the hills met, the way split by the rails. The only building nearby, I discovered, was the cattle shed, full of milking cows; that was where the echoing noise had come from.

'Mammy, where are we going to sleep?'

'Now, don't fret Ratia, we'll find somewhere tomorrow. Remember, we have managed it before.'

I didn't answer but I *did* remember; sleeping under Mammy's hammock on that uncomfortable boat on the way to Cruces, beneath her brother's dining table and behind a thin curtain elsewhere. I was older now and probably wouldn't fit into the nooks and crannies of the past and, now that I was a woman, I felt I needed the privacy of four sturdy walls around me. But I had to trust to Mammy, knowing she was ever resourceful.

Chapter 15: Wormwood

Our first journey off the ship confirmed my fears; the ground was muddy and slippery with untold filth, with the rotting bodies of starved horses and, something I'd never seen before, dead camels, which made me laugh with their funny long necks, even though they were dead. Sick men lay on rude stretchers along the quayside, as others were being loaded on ships and it was as much as I could do to stop Mammy starting to nurse these men. It was only that the orderlies shoved her to one side and, I think because she was tired, she allowed them to do so. When we returned our skirts were caked with mud and worse, and the odour tainted our cabin all night.

The next day I set to and scrubbed the caked-on muck off our skirts and into the sea, and tried to freshen our skirts as best I could while Mr Day and Mammy bent their heads together. When I'd finished I spent the time reading an old timesheet that someone had left behind as Mr Day and Mammy made plans. I had some sewing to do but I let this drop as I watched them at the other end of the deck, with a makeshift table set between them, writing and nodding and watching as our supplies were unloaded. What were they planning? I truly hoped it was that the venture was a hopeless one, seeing all the disarray around us and they were working out how we could make our way home to Jamaica. My dreams of finding Robert were impossible anyway in this muddle.

My attention was caught by the wheedling way some of the idlers on shore were moving around our supplies that were being unloaded. I spotted what they at immediately.

I called to Mammy and Mr Day, 'I think I'd better organise Jew Johnny and myself to watch the packages. Look, Mammy, how they circle, waiting for a quiet moment.'

She saw at once what I meant and agreed with me, and I

saw her jump up and shout at the loafers, as I ran to find Johnny who was sitting below deck, out of the sun, with a bored look on his face.

'Quick, we need to guard Mammy's goods. They're being eyed up by the locals and I'm sure they'll filch some of it if we don't watch out.'

He eagerly jumped up, and followed. I took my broadsheet and an old umbrella, for it was beginning to get hot, and we disembarked and I sat on the best packing case, my back to the water, and Johnny leant against the wall of the cattle shed nearby. I saw that the thieves soon disappeared, knowing there would be no pickings today.

From where I sat, the conversation between my mistress and Mr Day drifted down to me, but it bored me with its exchange of figures, and *bills of lading* and *letters of credit* and *payments* so that I almost dozed. Johnny kicked me awake and I grinned at him, to thank him, for I would not want to be seen wanting in my duties.

Mammy was insisting. 'We must negotiate with the captain, to get our supplies off before this ship leaves and make sure all the goods on the *Nonpareil* are moved as well. You must go to visit the captain of that ship to make sure he knows what we need and check the goods as they're landed.'

I watched Mr Day and I swear I saw him *squirm*. 'I don't like to talk to that captain, he's a mean man.'

'And so I have to do it? Is that right?'

'With your womanly charms, you might be able to persuade him to stay awhile so we can organise a collection of men to get the packages off, you know you're better at the talking than I am.'

I sighed and knew what our first trip would be. Eventually, as the sun rose to its zenith, Mammy and Mr Day shook hands and they disappeared and soon approached me as they disembarked. She said something to Mr Day, he nodded and then departed, without looking at me. I think our feelings for one another were mutual. Mammy turned to me, 'Come, girl, we have some organising to do. And Johnny, keep a close eye on our supplies, and you will be well rewarded.'

'Where are we going, Mammy?' I asked as I kept pace with her, which was easy to do as she carried some bulk and I was slender. She was not heading to the *Nonpareil* which was docked a few ships away from the *Albatross* but walking towards the smartest building on the dockside, which I discovered was the harbourmaster's quarters.

'We have to approach the Port-Admiral first and I'm not at all happy to do so alone. I'm happier with Army men. Now, let me see.' As she spoke she looked around her and spotted someone she knew.

'Look, there's the captain of the *Diamond*, William Peel, he'll do.'

I saw a young, handsome sailor and didn't know how Mammy knew him but when she called to him, he greeted her with pleasure and immediately nodded, and led the way to the Port-Admiral's office, to see if he could organise dock labourers for us. I kept close to her as I didn't like the way the railway navvies stopped working and leaned on their shovels and stared at us.

Mammy pushed her way in and did not wait for the occupant to stand up before she addressed him. 'Admiral Boxer, I would ask that you let the *Albatross* and the *Nonpareil* stay for a few days until I can discharge my cargo. And I would enlist your help with some men to do it,' I could see the man was about to explode, but Mammy carried on. She spoke quietly but deliberately and I knew she was determined to get her own way. 'And if you have any dry storage to spare, I would welcome it.'

I could see the Captain who had accompanied her backing out of the room, but I stood in the door, and he couldn't move round me without being too obvious, so he stopped.

'Christ's bells, and damn your eyes, Madam, this is a

military port and you expect me to help you? How the hell do you think I can ignore my instructions and help a civilian?'

I was shocked and waited for Mammy's reaction. I knew she did not allow swearing in her establishments, but this was not her home territory. I waited for that look of Mammy's to darken her brow, but instead, she pulled out the chair on this side of the man's desk and slowly sat down, gesturing for the Captain to join her. I pushed him forward.

Mammy then answered the harbour master, in her gentle voice. 'Port-Admiral Boxer, yes, I remember that name. Your son told me how uncouth you could be, when riled. I had the pleasure of nursing him, when he was with his regiment in Jamaica, but he also told me that once you had had your say, you would be kind and helpful.'

Port-Admiral Boxer hesitated. Mammy continued. 'All I am asking is for you to allow the *Nonpareil* to dock for a few more days so I can unload my merchandise – it will be to your advantage as I am sure we can find a case of wine or another beverage that you like?'

He hesitated, but you could see that all his swearing intentions had evaporated. He turned his gaze to the Captain who said nothing, but shrugged. The harbour master picked up the quill he had been using and turned it over in his hand, as if considering, but I could tell he'd been won over.

'Very well, but I really don't see what *you ladies* are doing in a place like this. It is not fitting and how can I do my job properly when I have to contend with female nagging?'

Mammy did not seem to notice the derisory way he called us 'ladies', neither and did she rise to the bait of being accused of 'nagging'. She merely bowed her head and thanked him very gracefully for seeing her.

We swept out of the room, Mammy for all the world looking like a merchant ship with all its sails unfurled, the Captain following her. Outside, she thanked him and he said he'd been glad to help, not that I thought he had done anything.

Before we could set to work, I asked Mammy where we were going to sleep, knowing that the *Albatross* was due to leave soon.

Mammy answered jauntily. 'Mr Day tells me there is nowhere to stay on land, which if you think about it is good for us. Once we have set up our hotel, we will have a monopoly.' She was smiling but it was the sort of smile I'd seen on her before when she was out to be determined about something.

'But don't worry, Ratia. He tells me that the captain of the *Medora* which is moored here to keep supplies safe, is willing to help us and give us a berth for the time being. So we are heading there next.'

I followed her up the gangplank of the *Medora* and stayed with her when she ordered a member of the crew to take her to the captain. When she asked politely for a cabin, for a few days, he looked surprised.

'Madam, this is no place for a woman, what are you doing here?'

'That is no business of yours,' – I realised that she thought he might believe us to be in competition with him – 'all I ask is for the common decency of a little help. I will not be in your way at all after a few days, I sincerely hope.'

He smiled and it wasn't a pleasant smile. He came round from behind the desk where he'd been sitting and leant against his own desk so that he was almost touching Mammy's knee. He said, grimly, 'You do realise this is an ammunition ship? If the Russians reach within firing range, we will be blown to bits. That is my position and I am here willingly to do my duty, but I do not like the idea of placing a *lady* in such a dangerous situation.'

I could tell my eyes widened in horror.

'Yes, your servant understands, so what do you say now?'

Mammy pulled herself up to her full height, and answered, 'If you can accommodate me, as I request, I will not mind that danger. If God wills it, then it will happen, but I believe I have been sent, like you, to fulfil my destiny, and I am not afraid.'

His shoulders sagged. I thought he gave in too easily and I wanted to protest, but I couldn't show Mammy that I was afraid.

'Very well, I will let you have a cabin here but only for the few days you claim until your business is done here.'

As we returned to the *Albatross* to collect our personal belongings I tried to remonstrate with Mammy but she did not listen. I resigned myself to my new temporary lodgings. Instead of listening to me, she was looking around her as we returned to the *Medora* and this time, as she noticed the contingent of sick and wounded being delivered from the landward side, she did no more but start to care for them, using an old tea can that had been left with them by the orderlies, to aid their thirst. This time nobody stopped her and I guessed that word had travelled that Mother Seacole had arrived. I followed her example and we worked for some time before I noticed that it was darkening, as the sun set behind the high hills.

The next few weeks were a blur of activity, with Mammy being visited by many of her old acquaintances including Mr Vicars who I remember visiting her in Jamaica. We were constantly looking after the sick and injured not only of soldiers but the engineers and navvies of the railway who also got sick. These navvies were made to work all day, under the heat of the sun and would suffer from sunstroke and burnt skin, and Mammy showed them how to make hats out of old paper and insisted they wear them to keep the sun off.

On one occasion, the chief engineer, approached her.

He was polite, as he stood before her and stopped us, 'Madam, I've heard that you can nurse sick men?'

Mammy merely inclined her head. He continued. 'I'm William Doyne, in charge of building the railway. Some of my men are sick, with a fever. Can you come and help?'

'But of course, tell me all the symptoms,'

As we stepped over the railings and followed him, Mr Doyne led us up a steep incline to some rough built sheds, and he described the symptoms. 'They are hot and tossing and muttering, and although their companions try to make them drink, they refuse. I've quarantined the worst in this furthest shed.'

Mammy nodded, and I could see she was not smiling. Of course we had a bag of medicinal herbs with us, the usual ginger, cloves, and many other dried plants. I was carrying an urn of black tea which I'd been using to quench the thirst of the men we worked on at the quay.

When we reached the first shed, the door was opened and the usual terrible smell of sick men all close together cloyed my nose and mouth. The shutters were firmly closed. Without asking, I opened them not only to let in some light but fresh air as well. Then I could see some of the men who had leered at me when I had first walked by the side of the railway they were building, now laid low, and moaning. They hardly acknowledged our existence, so bent over were they with stomach pains. We set to, giving potions of ginger and other stomach-calming herbs and spices. Mammy whispered to me, 'It's only a bad case of diarrhoea I believe, not cholera, thank God.' Within a few days Mr Doyne had his full contingent of workmen back digging and laying the rails and, after that, he allowed us many small favours.

A few days later, she returned from one of her visits to Port-Admiral Boxer bursting with news.

'He has kindly found me a corner of his warehouse, and we can now arrange for our packages to be brought to land.'

I was pleased about this as I was growing tired of making tea for Mammy's visitors on board the cramped quarters we had, quite apart from being afraid of it being blown up at any minute. Mammy had several visitors during the early evenings, all being welcomed aboard.

Stephen Lushington was one of the people who visited her.

He'd been at Blundells when I was very young, recovering from a long illness, and I remember he'd been sent back once he was fit enough, to his family. Now he did not recognise me until Mammy called me by name to make the tea and then he looked at me keenly. 'This cannot be the young nipper with the tight braids and sulky look about her?'

Mammy laughed, 'Indeed, it is, and she has grown to be a fine young woman and I consider her more of a friend now than a servant, do I not, Ratia?'

I couldn't help smiling, and my heart swelled with such words. Oh, Mammy, you made me so happy saying that. I forgot how dangerous our quarters were afterwards, and slept soundly at night. Probably because I was exhausted with all the work we had to do.

He was later to be one of my favourites and he was always generous with his small coin, but more of that later.

Mammy decided that the port of Balaklava was not a healthy place to set up her hotel, and we went exploring. The only way out of the harbour on the land side was between the two hills at the furthest end of the narrow strip of sea. We walked it first and found that the land opened up into a narrow canyon and then became relatively flat, although there was a small incline as we travelled further inland. Mammy decided to follow the path of the railway which was being built, to take supplies to the front. She managed to acquire a pony and one for me, but I refused to ride it. I had never gone on the back of an animal before and I wasn't going to start now. I could walk fast, and Mammy was kind enough not to force her steed to go too fast, so off we set towards Sevastopol.

'Look out for a likely place, Ratia, a dip in the land which will provide shelter with water nearby, and that is where I will set up my hotel. If we build it alongside the railway, I'm sure we'll be able to use that to ferry our supplies to the hotel.'

As we went further inland, the wisps of smoke I'd seen before became more numerous and there was a booming sound that frightened me, but I wasn't going to let Mammy know. We passed rows and rows of tents, with some men lounging about and rough fences constructed to keep in the horses now at rest and grazing. Some of the men called out to us, and it was obvious that Mammy's advance letters had reached their destination. At one point, a horse rider came galloping towards us.

'Captain Peel, I do declare, how are you?'

Mammy stopped, and the officer, who stayed mounted, bent down to her and they shook hands. He answered, 'I thought it was you. I'd recognise your figure from miles away.' They laughed at his little joke but before Mammy could say anything he continued. 'I thought you would stay in Balaklava, so what are you doing around here?'

'Well, young man, we're scouting for a place to build our British Hotel, and when its built you'll be both welcome.'

Mammy almost curtseyed and Captain Peel, laughing, answered, 'Im so glad to see you, Mother Seacole, and I hope you get settled soon as we have need of some good cheer.' He then reached in his pocket and produced one of Mammy's cartes des visites that she had sent on ahead.

'Look, I have one of your cards and have spread the word amongst my men and we are all eager to visit your premises. Are you going all the way to the front? I hope not, as it is too dangerous. The Russians' shells reach a long way into our defences.'

As he spoke, he nodded to me in acknowledgement but Mammy was too busy looking around and answering him to notice.

'I would like to find a place half way so that all the regiments can visit me. And it's not too far to pick up fresh supplies from the port.' she explained. 'And we are looking for such a place now.'

He rode around us, trying to calm his horse and gestured the way we were heading. 'I know just the place, it is on a slight incline just above Kadikoi, near enough for us to ride to you but you will be protected by the hill behind. There is also water close by, which is important, of course. I know that the railway is planning a station stop near there so you will have the privilege of feeding their men as well. I'll ride with you and show you.'

Soon he pointed out the place, just after we had passed a tiny collection of rough huts which he said was the halfway point for the Army's supplies.

'The railway should reach this spot in a few days and then they have to negotiate a way around this hill to continue on to Sevastopol. So there should be some navvies and engineers stationed nearby.' Mammy nodded, and dismounted. I could not see anything that commended the place except that it was near the railway.

Captain Peel pointed to the left and added, 'The French are stationed over there, not more than two miles away and,' he pointed over his shoulder. 'There is a Turkish contingent over there. You'll be bang in the middle.'

Mammy smiled at him but I could see she was still considering the place. While I stood and watched, holding the reins of her pony, Mammy marched off and I saw her bending and picking something from the ground. She smelt it and rubbed it between her fingertips. I realised then that the meadow was full of tiny pink and white flowers, and the grass between was quite green. Of course, it was spring, and I wondered what this place would look like in summer. Would it have more flowers, the whole place covered in a cacophony of colours? Even if it was, I still felt it would not look as succulent as Jamaica, with its climbing flower-covered vines.

Mammy returned, and held up her hand to my nose. I could smell a bitter-sweet scent, unlike any I had encountered before.

'Wormwood,' explained Mammy, 'a good herb for the digestive system, I've been told.'

I looked at what she was holding, some grey-green stems

that looked like crushed up grass, and I was surprised that such a boring looking plant could smell so strong.

'Yes, this is the place.' She turned to Captain Peel. 'Do you know if we can solicit aid from any of your men or of another regiment who can help build my new hotel here?'

'I'll make enquiries.'

He was as good as his word, for soon he'd found some sailors who were carpenters, and some Turkish soldiers with their officer, who took orders from Jew Johnny who could speak their language. I discovered that, although there was fighting beyond our valley, there were still times when the men were at ease and their officers were pleased to put them to work, to relieve their boredom, to assist us.

Mammy would sometimes ride out to supervise but used to come back dispirited. 'It is just not going up quickly enough, that's the trouble. We need more men but there's none to be had, as they keep on being sent to the battlefield. Ratia, I have an idea, and you need to come with me tomorrow, as I am making a visit and need to impress.'

She made me wear my best cloak and I helped her into her colourful blue and yellow dress that had stood her in such good stead in the past. We had learnt from our various forages to walk within the rail lines, so long as a train was not coming, because here the earth had been impacted and at least we could keep the mud off our skirts.

'And bring a basket of our bottled beer,' was her last command.

I knew better than to ask her where we were going, and, once we were ready, we set off. We passed the building site of her hotel and I could see it was a sorry sight, with hardly any walls and certainly no roof. She guided her pony around the hill, which we called Spring Hill, for the simple reason that there was a small spring near our chosen spot, and I realised where she was going.

'Mammy, you can't just walk into the Turkish encampment.

What will they think? At least ask Johnny to come with us.'

Mammy stopped and looked at me. 'Yes, you are right, run back and ask him to accompany us but make sure he looks smart, and puts his jacket on at least.'

We must have looked a peculiar sight to the men in the Turkish encampment, a rotund lady on a pony, a negro servant and a Turkish assistant. Mammy did not flinch and asked Johnny to tell the soldiers who stopped us that she wanted to meet their commanding officer. Johnny explained he was called a 'pasha' which meant 'leader' and Mary took to that immediately.

'So take me to your Pasha,' she said. We were led to a large tent and after whispered conversations with those inside, the flap was opened and we were invited to enter. Inside it was comfortable with low tables dotted about and beautiful patterned rugs on the floor. On a large armchair, sat an imposing gentleman, heavily bearded and wearing a fez, with a tassel falling down one side of his head. He stood and came towards us and as he did so, his coat flared out from his waist. I found this strange because it looked like an army uniform jacket but it had skirts, and he also wore loose pantaloons. I stifled a giggle as a cough and immediately he said something in his native tongue, but when Mammy turned to Johnny, he explained. 'He is welcoming you and says that he can see that the journey has made your companion – he means Ratia - thirsty. He is offering us some coffee. I assure you, Mother Seacole, they make it differently to us but it is a most refreshing drink.'

Although we had passed through Turkey, at Constantinople, we had not partaken of the local coffee and I was to discover that this was brewed in a very different way to the way we made it in Jamaica.

Mammy told Johnny to say that she was glad she was welcomed and accepted the hospitality. The pasha clapped his hands and one of the men left, and he then gestured for her to sit in his large chair and he brought forward some stools for himself and me and Johnny. Mammy demurred and insisted he sit on his own chair and there was a miming of both of them bowing and edging around one another, until Mammy gave in, laughing and saying, 'well, Johnny, tell him I accept as his guest. And, Ratia, offer him the drinks we have bought with us.'

I leant forward with my basket and gave the Pasha a bottle of the beer which was quite warm by now.

The Pasha was delighted at this and smiled warmly, taking it as I showed him how to open it. He had dark eyes and although he was not as black as me, he was swarthy with a curled up moustache, and his face was gentle. When we were all seated, the pasha, taking a sip of the beer and smiling broadly in appreciation, turned to Johnny and addressed him. I guessed from the tone that he was asking a question. Johnny replied in the same language, and all I could discern was, 'Mother Seacole' and 'doctress' from which I guessed they did not have such a word in their own language.

The drinks that he had ordered arrived and there was a pause as these were handed around, together with some mixed nuts. I sipped my coffee, which was thick and sweet, and tried to follow the exchange between my mistress and the pasha, with Johnny turning to one and then the other, interpreting for them. It was a halted conversation, but as Mammy explained what she was about and Johnny repeated her words, the Pasha became more and more animated. When she put her plea for help in building her hotel, with a further offer of more beer, which the Pasha took eagerly, he stood up and approached her and took both her hands in his and pulled her upright and spoke very positively.

Johnny was grinning when he interpreted. 'He is saying you must call him Omar, which is his real name. And he is quite taken with you. Of course he will help you as he thinks it is very enterprising of you to come to this out of the way place with such an ambition.' He stopped as the Pasha was still talking, and listened to him. Then he nodded, and added, 'But he asks a favour of you, as he thinks you are a very good gentlewoman.'

I didn't like the way Johnny said this, as he had a glint in his eye. I knew Mammy might lose her temper if the favour was an improper suggestion. 'He wants you to visit him often and speak English with him as he would like to learn the language.'

Mammy roared with laughter then and I knew it was a laugh of relief. I could tell what was going around in her head, as we had all heard of the harems in these countries and indeed had seen the outside of the harem in the Topkapi palace.

'Of course I will, it will be my pleasure.'

I rather suspected the Pasha had developed a taste for the beer that we had brought but I wasn't going to say anything. If it meant Mammy had help with her building then of course I was pleased. The sooner we moved out of the stinking hell hole of Balaklava the better.

Chapter 16: Warmth, nourishment and fresh air

I don't know why the Admiral had queried our presence in Balaklava, because all sorts of people arrived while we were there, one of them being the wife of an officer, and she was known as Fanny Duberly. We often saw her riding out on a wonderful horse. But she was a snooty one and never deigned to glance at us and, after a while, Mammy ignored her too.

'She's no use, not at nursing or anything else, just here to gawp, I wager, and note, Ratia, how she stays on board her ship, and doesn't even attempt to be with her husband,' was her summing up of this lady.

One of the wonderful sights we saw before we moved out of Balaklava was the delivery of a fantastical carriage that looked like a large container with dark curtains hiding the interior. We discovered that this was a photographic box belonging to a man called Roger Fenton and we were lucky to catch the spectacle of it being delivered from the ship it had arrived in on to land.

We'd heard rumours about his arrival but it was six days later that we were told that he'd got permission to get the carriage onto land. I was friendly with some of the railwaymen by this time and they told me that it was not going to be easy for the item to be unloaded and they were taking wagers as to whether it would land in the drink.

The problem was that there were so many ships in the dock that there was no room for a large barge to go alongside the ship so it had to be hoisted off and swung across to the smaller vessel that would bring it to land.

I explained this to Mammy and, because we didn't have much to do while the hotel was being built and it was in between the sick being brought down from the battlefield, we decided to join the crowd on the wharf that had gathered to watch the spectacle.

Everyone who was there seemed to have their hands to their mouths, confident that a disaster would occur. And Mr Fenton was there, looking very anxious.

It is a wonder that all the world, whether they be officers, ordinary servicemen, sailors or masters, all love to watch when there may be a potential disaster. And we were no exception, of course, Mammy and I, waiting for it to happen. I realised we were no better than the other spectators.

Mammy nudged me as Mr Fenton ran from side to side of the dock as his precious vehicle was hoisted into the air and then delivered onto a barge so small that it looked as if the contraption hung over the sides of it. It fell with a great pounding noise. But, when the barge did not sink, nor the contraption fall off, there was a huge sigh from the crowd.

'Let's wait though,' said Mammy, 'I can see that thing being much too heavy for that barge and it could still sink before it lands.'

I was astonished at Mammy, you would have thought that she would not wish such a problem on anyone, so we stayed. All was well as it moved slowly through all the ships to the dockside. Again, we watched as the ropes were tied around the contraption and it was slowly hoisted up, across the narrow slip of water that separated the barge from the dock and then was lowered carefully onto the muddy road beside the rail track. Everyone who was watching clapped approvingly as it trembled and stood upright. All this took hours and Mammy found some shade in the shadow of the cattle shed and we sat on makeshift benches, drinking tea and enjoying the spectacle. I suspect there was a little disappointment when the episode did not result in any disaster.

Mammy whispered to me when it was safely on land, 'Go and ask Mr Fenton if he would like to meet the famous Mrs Seacole.'

I hesitated because the man looked imperious but as I approached, he turned to me and said, 'I suppose you and your mistress have enjoyed the afternoon's entertainment?'

I blushed – but he wouldn't notice that, of course. 'Sir, my mistress is Mrs Seacole, the well-known doctress and she wondered if you would care to take tea with her?'

'I don't have time, I have to get to the front to start work.'

I then thought to be bolder. 'Why, if you want to take photographs, you could take one of my mistress. I know she would welcome it.'

He turned away to check some strapping on the carriage which was now being fitted onto its wheels. 'I have not come all this way to take photographs of ladies. I am interested only in the military and the campaign.' He did not even look at me.

I shrugged and returned to Mammy and told her what he had said and she stood up and made as if to approach him herself.

'Mammy, I don't think you should, you'll only be rebuffed. Look, he's shaking his head at the navvies and they've been bothering him all the time, as soon as they knew he was a photographer.'

She turned to me and followed my gaze and she could see by the way that Mr Fenton was forcing his way into his carriage and ignoring the pleas of the navvies that I was right and we made our way through the throng back to the ship where we were still sleeping. Even this rebuff did not prevent Mammy inviting him to visit us once the British Hotel was open because when we were in our quarters she hastily wrote a note and ordered Johnny to take it to *that photographer man* as she described him.

'Even if he doesn't want to photograph us, he can still pay for good hospitality, can he not, Ratia?'

That was the way she was, never bearing a grudge. I would have snubbed him from then on, but Mammy, she never snubbed anyone.

Of course, while all this was happening, we were still seeing many men coming from the front badly wounded and I became immured to it although all the time, at the back of my mind, was the fear that one of these men would be Robert.

For all I knew he could be dead but because I held out hope that I would one day be reunited with him, I treated all the men as if they were, indeed, Robert, and tended them gently and kindly, as Mammy had taught me. Mammy kept muttering, 'What they need is warmth, nourishment and fresh air, not this rancid place, lying in the open. We have to do what we can for them, Ratia.'

She was treating me as if I was one with her, and remarked on it one day when we had had a particularly harrowing time, with men unconscious and ready to die all around us.

'Ratia, you are almost like me, now, and I can trust you to do the nursing without watching. You are a good, kind girl.'

'Thank you Mammy, if I can be half as good as you, I'll be content.'

We carried on working without saying anything but when we had finished and were walking along the quay to our quarters, she took my arm, and I knew I was her equal. But it troubled me that she leaned heavily on me and I realised she was tired. Her face often looked grey and, in repose, serious, except that, it only took one man to say, *thank you Ma-am*, and she would be all smiles and her eyes would be as bright as ever.

Chapter 17: Lemonade and cake

Our lives became regular, nursing the men, and visiting the building works. I watched Mammy cajoling the motley workers she had there. I was excited seeing the structure emerging even though it was made up of odds and ends.

Mammy still enjoyed her visits to the Omar Pasha and it was true that his Turkish soldiers worked very well at the construction of her hotel and she was constantly praising the Turks and her *dear Omar,* and her face would crease into smiling when she spoke about him. But I was hearing gossip among the English navvies who were building the railway as I was doing my chores and travelling from the port to Spring Hill. As I described, we walked between the rails and when I approached the workmen, banging down the earth, to flatten it for others to place the rails, there were always some of them standing around and gossiping, waiting for their skills to be used in the next stage. Some of them sat on the bank beside the work, eating their rations, and, as I approached, they deliberately talked loudly, rudely and raucously.

'An English mother throws herself at the Pasha, doesn't she?'

Another would remonstrate, 'But she ain't English, is she? She's only doing what they do in the colonies. Can't expect anything else.'

The group all laugh, looking at me, making sure I can hear, and I hear these jibes on several occasions.

'The pasha is *throwing his pocket handkerchief* at Mother Seacole! She'll soon be Mrs Pasha and give up on her nursing ways. What'll we do then, boys?'

Raucous laughter followed that comment.

I felt embarrassed, annoyed, and frustrated at what I heard. I was too scared to say anything to them because they were always fighting amongst themselves and I wouldn't put it past them to beat me up for any angry response I gave in reproaching them for their rude comments. After a while I realised they were talking so loudly to see if I responded, but I would never do that. I would find out first from Mammy how the land lay in that direction, although in my heart, I knew the visits were innocent. But I had to think of Mammy's reputation.

I decided to broach the subject to Mammy when we were alone that night, although we were both so tired after tending the wounded on the dockside. I thought it best to just come out and say it. 'Mammy I think you should be careful. Perhaps you shouldn't visit that Pasha so often. People are talking.'

She roared; the same laugh as she gave when she first met the Pasha.

'Oh, Ratia, you know me better than that. Johnny is close by and nothing untoward can happen in a camp full of men. But, to put your mind at rest, Omar has freely admitted to me that he has three wives already and the discord in his home is bad enough that he would have no wish for another. There, I am quite safe.'

She turned serious. 'You must also understand that if I was not the widow of Mr Seacole and hold his memory most dear, I would be married to the British army; that is where my love lies.'

I felt ashamed and blushed but she assured me. 'Ratia, it is good that you tell me these things. We should not keep secrets from one another. should we? We are friends now, I've already told you that.'

Again I swelled with pride but also felt a little discomfort for I could not tell her of my love for Robert and my hopes for the future; that was my secret. I could not bear it, if I told her and then she tried to help me and such help failed. I would pray that God would find a way for Robert and me to be together one day.

We continued to help the sick who were brought down by mule train and lay waiting on the shore to be put aboard the ships. It was a sorry job but Mammy carried on in her smiling ways and even found time to make cakes and her own special lemonade, which she gave to the men who were fit enough to eat and drink. We even helped some of the navvies and railwaymen, with Mammy teasing them, about having strange ideas. They had the good sense to look abashed, and, after that I noticed that the talk about her changed and soon even they were calling her the *good mother Seacole* and all gossip about her stopped.

On one occasion the stern Port-Admiral came and watched us as we tended to the wounded, his face not flinching at all. I thought him a cold fish but when a loud groan came from a soldier as he was being carried onto the ship, he called out to the carriers, 'Careful, men, treat them tenderly.'

It was shortly after that, that he approached Mammy and I steeled myself because I thought he might be going to reproach her for interfering. Instead, I was astonished to see he tapped her on the shoulder and whispered something to her. She later told me that he had a tear in his eye as he thanked her for her kind ministrations. After that, I had no fear of him.

In the meantime, the hotel grew steadily, despite the Turks breaking off for their prayers five times a day, and then to smoke and sleep if it was warm. It was the biggest mish-mash I had ever seen and I had seen some messy buildings going up in the Panama. Our new hotel would be created from old packing cases, the flotsam of timber from the broken up ships sunk in the storm the previous November, iron sheeting and other metal that the men salvaged. Somehow the workers were fashioning what I could see would be a welcoming place and I was becoming quite excited about starting to serve the soldiers, and officers.

Indeed, when we had enough supplies, Mammy and me set to and made some lemonade – good for scurvy as she explained to me – and some simple cakes and took them to Spring Hill. We set up a makeshift counter that was shaded by a tarpaulin and served the soldiers and officers who frequently travelled between the front and Balaklava, taking messages and obtaining essentials for their regiments. The railway helped them to get there quicker but that had not gone much further than us so they still had to walk or ride past us and they thought it a good place for a stop and some refreshments.

All the time there was the rumbling from the front and we heard there had been assaults on the Redan and other places, all of which had been repulsed by the Russians. We heard from men coming from the front that there was not much progress being made in the war, and that the Russians defended their city well and some of our men were becoming depressed because it seemed a hopeless war. Some even suggested that we could lose because we did not have the good supply lines that the Russians obviously had, because it was their country.

I tried not to think about it, but in the nights, sometimes, I would shudder and wonder if the enemy was creeping up on us. But in the days I kept busy and happy, seeing Mammy's establishment taking place. It was at one of these skirmishes that Mammy's dear friend Sir John Campbell was killed and our friend William Peel was wounded. He came to Mammy and she nursed him as best she could. But she didn't stay sad too long, her natural optimism conquering. She also concentrated on making William Peel, one of her favourites, better.

'Knowing he will recover, and be able to take his place in the fray, cheers me, Ratia,' she explained.

Men came and went and she soon found another Campbell to make her friend, this time a Colin, who was much more important, because he was commander of the Highland Brigade of the 1st Division. He was quite old, and a stern officer, but he did us a good turn eventually by enjoying a glass of wine in the corner of our restaurant, and keeping a beady eye on his men, as you will see.

But Mammy's luck was beginning to run thin. Just as our building was nearly finished, a disaster occurred. It had been raining steadily for some days and I was getting mightily fed up with scraping mud off our skirts and trying to keep them decent, let alone trying to keep ourselves dry. We were attempting to keep the place rain-free with tarpaulins covering the dry goods when I heard a great roar and ran outside.

A group of soldiers who we knew, were running towards us shouting but I couldn't hear them for the roaring. They were waving their arms and I could tell they were warning us of something.

'Mammy I think something terrible has happened,'

Even as I said it, I noticed what the soldiers had already seen. We had chosen this spot because of the little stream that ran alongside the nearly complete building, but it was no longer a harmless flow of gentle water. Suddenly a torrent, as wide as our main building, was racing towards us, passing the men as they came, and I just had time to pull Mammy to one side before it hit the back of the construction and broke through it as if it was so much tinder wood and rushed over our makeshift floor, tearing up the timbers as it went, and taking much of our supplies which seemed to be picked up by giant hands and thrown and tossed in the water.

I watched horrified but Mammy screamed as her best herb chest passed us and she stretched headlong out for it. She toppled over and I could do nothing as she was swept away with the torrent. The men had arrived by this time and we all ran alongside watching her bobbing up and down and reaching out for her cabinet. She grasped it and was swept under, then came up again, as we watched, helpless.

'A dam further up the spring has burst with all this rain, and we couldn't stop it,' shouted one of the soldiers, with true despair in his voice.

I could only scream loudly as she was swept along and we

followed the bank of muddy, churning water trying to see something to throw to her or for some other sort of help. Mammy was rolling over and over but her bulk meant she was strong. I saw with relief she was slowly pulling herself to the side and then, miracle of miracles, there was a tree hanging over the water and I yelled, 'Grab the tree, grab it.' She turned and saw her chance and moved quickly and wedged herself into the tree and then there were others around me and we managed to pull her out. She sat on the bank, clutching the retrieved herb chest, panting so heavily I thought she'd never get her breath back.

She was soaked through and I knew I had to get her into warmth quickly and somehow get the chill out of her, so I asked the men to help me get her to the railway and they kindly gave us a ride back to Balaklava where we were helped by the Port-Admiral. He allowed us a room and I ran to the *Medora* and found shawls and extra clothes and towels.

When I got back Mammy was chatting amiably to the Port-Admiral and waiting for a pot to boil. She turned to me, as calm as if she had just been taking afternoon tea with her friend.

'There you are. I'm making myself a hot drink of ginger and other spices to warm me and get rid of the nasty taste in my mouth. I'm sure I must have swallowed some filth as well that will ruin my stomach.'

'Mammy, come, you must be exhausted and I think you should wrap up and rest.'

'I know how to care for myself – if I cannot take responsibility for my own health, how can I help others? Now Ratia, I'll sit here for a while and drink my concoction and you go back and see what can be retrieved. Go on now, I'm perfectly safe.'

I watched her for a while as she busied herself drying her bonnet and trying to put it back to shape, rubbing her crinkly hair which had lost all its style and was as tightly curled as mine. She turned and shushed me away and it was done with such good humour that I felt satisfied that she had not suffered any ill effects and, with a heavy heart, returned to Spring Hill to see what could be salvaged.

When I got there I could see Johnny working away collecting boxes from all over the place and putting them back in order behind what was left of the walls of our building, while at the same time serving soldiers and their officers arrived with various goods such as beer and cake that Mammy had baked and brought up that morning, offering them back to customers for free. I could see they were rather moist and the men had to almost suck them from their hands, but still seemed to enjoy them.

Johnny smiled as I joined him and explained, 'The news of Mother Seacole's dipping has spread like wildfire throughout the camps and the men have come to buy what we have left before the supplies are totally ruined. Giving them the damaged cakes is encouraging them to buy drinks to go with them so I am doing a roaring trade but it is hard to tidy up as I serve as well.'

I took over the serving as he stacked up the goods behind me. I was amazed that these men took most of our muddy stock and insisted on helping us as well. Many of them offered to pay even though the goods were damaged. Even Sir Colin Campbell, who I was a little in awe of, because he was in charge of many men, came down and supervised, making sure the men did not cheat us. We had not lost too much and I was pleased to take enough from that day's sales to make sure Mammy could re-order more than she had lost with a bit of profit was well. It felt to me for the first time that Mammy's enterprise would succeed, despite the flooding.

But the building had to start again which was a setback. It was late spring now and the news was that the combined forces of the English, French and Turkish were moving forward, and there were rumours that they would force

Sevastopol to surrender by the autumn. I wondered whether the war would last long enough for us to be in business.

Mammy was soon back running up and down and I visited the site often. She hired more staff, and a cook who became special to us, whom we called Black Francis, because he always wore black.

When the roof was on again, we started moving the remainder of our supplies to the spot. Mammy had arranged with Mr Day for more to be ordered from home, but they would take some weeks to arrive. She ordered shelving to be put up and a counter in front of the shelves and tables and chairs were acquired from somewhere. She insisted on a strong store room, with double walls, to try and prevent thieving. Again, the fittings were all odds, and rickety but the carpenters were put to it to reinforce the chairs and tables somehow. When there were three walls and the roof was finally completed, Mammy decided that we would decamp there and greet all those who passed by, telling them of the fine food she would cook – when the stove arrived. This was a difficulty that Mammy solved with her usual alacrity.

'There's a rumour that the army have commissioned a famous chef to come out and organise the army's kitchens and I am determined to meet him as soon as he arrives. His name is Alexis Soyer, and my liberal friends who are in the army swear by his cooking as he was the chef at their Reform Club in England. So, dear Ratia, if you hear any news of this man arriving you must let me know at once.'

Mammy had recognised by this time that I had a good source of information from the navvies and the sailors who I spoke to on my forays to organise deliveries and buy basic foods for us. I soon heard of the great man's arrival. Surprisingly, he was travelling with another who I was not at all keen to see. Florence Nightingale was coming to see the front, accompanying Monsieur Soyer who was to oversee the food for the army.

Surely even Mammy couldn't organise a meeting with Miss Nightingale and the Monsieur. But luck was on our side. We soon heard that Miss Nightingale would not be passing our way because she was ill and had been prevented from leaving her quarters, so Monsieur Soyer would be in our neighbourhood alone.

I discovered that everyone thought he would bring with him nourishing foods and warmth. From the rumours I gathered he was a bit like a male version of my mistress, except he did not minister to the sick.

He turned up in early summer and Mammy soon engineered a meeting with him. My trusty friends working on the railway warned me of the day he was travelling to the Army headquarters near Sevastopol and so, on that day, we made ready. There was a makeshift road between us and the railway, which was still used by the officers who rode by on their horses, the railway only being used to transport supplies to the front, and the wounded to Balaklava.

'Ratia, we must get some of our most supportive officers, and organise a little tea party in the yard, where we can be seen from the road. I understand some of them know Soyer from his time as chef at the Reform Club so they can bring him over to us.'

She was kneading bread dough as she spoke and added, 'And we'll find a French flag and put it up with the English one, to show he's truly welcome.'

Sir Colin agreed to the ruse, when I asked him. 'Indeed, yes, it would be capital to see how they get on. I suspect there may be a ladle fight between the two of them and that would provide great entertainment.'

So the charade was set up and, as a little group of riders from Balaklava reached that part of the road near us, our group started laughing and calling to them. They stopped and stared at our makeshift camp, Sir Colin and his friends calling to them.

'Soyer, here, come here.' The man recognised some of the group, from their time at the Reform Club, and there was a general astonishment all round as he came over and they all sat down on the rickety chairs. Luckily the sun was shining and our place always looked more attractive when it was bathed in sunshine and there was a light breeze so both flags fluttered in the wind and showed their full glory. I greeted him with a 'bonjour' but he stopped me and explained, 'I've been in England for many years, young woman, and I am happier speaking your language than my native French.'

He still had a heavy accent though, although he dressed like an Englishman – well he certainly didn't look like the French soldiers called Zouaves who I'd seen riding past. He had a neat beard that made his chin look determined and I wondered if Mammy had met her match. I had time to observe him like this as I waited for my mistress to emerge, choosing her time, when the men were relaxed and happy in each other's company.

As she arrived, she asked in her pleasant voice, 'Who is this? Who is my new son?'

Sir Colin stood and introduced them, 'Why this is Monsieur Alexis Soyer, Ma-am, have you not heard of him?' and Soyer, this is the famous Madam Seacole, restauranteur and doctress.'

'God bless me, my son, are you the Monsieur Soyer, of whom I have sold many of your relishes in my home country of Jamaica. Indeed, your fame spreads.'

She called him 'my son' but I guessed he must have been about the same age as her. But he did not seem to mind. He stood and took Mammy's hand and answered her. 'Indeed, of course I have heard of you. You are as famous as I am.'

He had a jovial smile on his face as he said it.

'You must partake of a glass of champagne with Sir John and his companions, I insist.'

'Champagne? In this place of war?'

'Yes, sir, courtesy of this great lady. Champagne all round, Mother Seacole, capital idea. And put it on my bill.'

Sir Colin insisted, despite Mammy saying it was on the house and eventually they all settled down and I found some cake and other refreshments to make sure they did not get drunk on the champagne.

I heard Monsieur Soyer say, 'Madam Seacole, I have heard of your nourishing foods and I must see your kitchen when it is set up and how you concoct such dishes. I hear you are famous for rice pudding without milk and that your spiced meat patties are very popular.'

'Really? A great chef like you could never learn from such as I, surely? Of course I have heard of your reputation and that you have been commissioned by the Army to improve the rations out here. What can you learn from old Mother Seacole?'

'Madam, I cannot agree with the description of 'old' – you do not look old to me, but in the prime of your life.'

Mammy sat up straighter and waited as I served more champagne. I was happy to raid our supplies for I could see he did not flatter Mammy so much as speak what he thought the truth; it was the way he said it.

As I watched the party, I realised that these two were equals. Mammy didn't have that quiet air of defiance that she often used to get her own way with the officers, nor did she have the compassionate air of the doctress, and certainly not the roaring humour she exhibited with men like the Pasha. She folded her hands neatly in her plaid skirt and looked down as, after the pleasantries, he said gently, 'I may have officialdom behind me, but we are both in a place where provisions are hard to come by and I need to find out how you manage to supply such good food.'

'Monsieur, I would like to find out more about your recipes, especially your soups and stocks, so I truly believe we can help each other.'

'Can I visit your kitchen now?'

She laughed, and agreed, and she led him into the side building where the kitchens had been set up and I left them to it while I kept an eye on the regimental party that was now in full swing, encouraged by the champagn, no doubt. I was going to make sure that Sir Colin kept to his word to pay for the drink, as I often found that the best of men might forget about payment once the drink had disappeared down their throats.

Shortly after that little party, we acquired a large military style stove and I discovered it was very much like those that Alexis had introduced in the Army billets, but nobody said anything.

Mammy might have been good at persuading people to do her favours, but I too had my ways of getting hard cash out of them, making sure they paid handsomely for their *comforts,* so we made a good team.

After that, Alexis, as we learnt to call him, often came by and he and Mammy would discuss the best way of preparing the skinny animals that we had. Mammy discovered his secret of using the blood and offal from the animals, which most cooks discarded, chopped up fine, and boiled hard, with seasoning to add flavour to his stocks.

'It is more nourishing for the men to have such ingredients in their soups. In England I saw many butchers throwing these really useful pieces of the animal away, but they make such excellent ingredients. I know the English are fastidious and only like the joints of their meat. Such a waste. Here, I also cook the horses that have died, and with judicious basting and soaking in wine and other stocks, it can be made more tender than beef.'

Mammy challenged him to a cooking match but he was too good-natured to take part. Despite that, he listened when she showed him how to spice up the chicken for our Jamaican dish, and he took away with him her recipe for rice pudding without milk. This was a speciality which we used a lot as the men liked it but also because our tinned milk was kept for other special recipes. Mammy knew how to spice up the rice pudding with nutmeg and ginger so that the lack of milk didn't notice.

'Perhaps, when all this is over, we will open the best restaurant in England – what say you, Mother Seacole?'

Mammy laughed and they spent many happy hours working on the idea and I would have been happy to agree to that as well, and hoped that it would come true very soon. I liked Monsieur Soyer and he was truly Mammy's equal.

Chapter 18: Lignum vitae

I suppose I ought to mention Sarah Seacole, who turned up when most of the work was done. She'd been sent out by a relative of Thomas Day's but she was also a relative of my mistress, as her name shows. I at first thought she was a spy for Mr Day and did not take to her immediately.

There were always rumours abounding amongst the soldiers and navvies and at first some said Sarah was Mary's illegitimate child she'd kept hidden. She was younger than me, by some years, and I'd never heard mention of her.

I should explain that in Jamaica, we have large families with cousins and second cousins and as we don't much care for keeping records so that, if someone turns up with the same name as you, and says they're a cousin, you accept it. That's how Sarah came to us and as she'd been vouched for by Mr Day, Mammy welcomed her, as another pair of hands. Some of the men wickedly said she looked so much like Mammy she must have been her daughter, but I soon scotched that idea. After a while, she became known as Sally, which suited her much better than Sarah.

I at first felt side-lined because she was always at Mammy's side and was learning her ways as a doctress, and I felt as if I was no longer Mammy's confidante. But in another way, this meant I had more time for my own private occupations.

Now, this is my story about Mammy and not about me, so I won't say much about it, except that sneaky Sally discovered my secret and that was how we became close friends.

She was hardly out of puberty, and quite inexperienced, or so it seemed because she had just travelled from the home country. I felt middle-aged by comparison, although I had only just passed into my twenties myself. Like her cousin, my mistress, she was inquisitive and adventurous but in different ways to Mammy. She was curious about men and what they did to you – in the baby making way you understand. When the men came in to the British Hotel, where she helped out, she would twirl a stray hair behind her ear and look at them through half-closed eyes and I could see exactly what she was doing because it was a trick I had used to attract a soldier that I thought had some ready money to release to me in exchange for my special favours.

You must understand that although I wanted to find Robert, and, in my heart, stayed loyal to his memory, I still had feelings that had to be assuaged, and when the men eyed me, I felt it was only right that we should *take advantage of the situation* and enjoy ourselves. And if it meant that I had a chance to save a little nest-egg, and they felt it was only right to pay me, then why not?

It was when I was entertaining one of these soldiers in the hay in one of the outhouses, where I had made a sort of nest for myself, that she discovered me. As the soldier gasped his last orgasmic groan, I felt as if we were being watched and covered up quickly although usually I liked the aftermath of my exertions, and allowed the soldier to rest awhile. When we returned to the dining room, separately you understand, with me carrying a tray full of pies from the kitchen, to justify my absence, I saw a smirk on Sally's face. It was not possible to say anything then and I hoped that she would never confront me, if it was her that was peeking.

As I say, she was inquisitive and I should have known. When we were baking a few days after that and Mammy had gone visiting the Pasha there was a silence, which was unusual because she usually prattled on about the men she'd served the night before and describing one as handsome, and another with strong shoulders and some such nonsense.

'What's it like then, going with a man?'

'Why should I know?' I countered, feeling lucky that blushes did not show too much with my dark skin.

'Of course you know. I saw you.'

I couldn't help it, I snapped, 'You shouldn't have been looking. It's private.' I rolled the pastry angrily so that the flour on the table whipped up into a fog either side of the base I was rolling.

'I won't tell, I promise, if you tell me what it's like – and how you don't have babies. I guess you must know something that stops them, and I've heard rumours back home about black magic that can prevent babies. I got all excited and hot watching you and I really want to try it but I'll be sent home if I grow a baby, in disgrace.'

'Try it? Have you anyone in mind?'

She looked at me and, with one pastry covered hand, twirled that piece of loose hair around her ear so that a piece of damp pastry stuck to it. I felt jealous because she had fine dark hair, streaked with blonde, and blue eyes, which came from an English forebear I suppose. They stood out more because she had a dusky skin. Now I was also curious about her. I waited, raising an eyebrow in question.

'Well, yes, that cook, Black Francis, he's been making suggestions to me and I think I love him.'

I scoffed. 'Love? You're too young to love.'

Even as I said it I remembered another Sarah, with her child, when she was fourteen.

'No, I'm not. Anyway you don't worry about love. You go with half a dozen of them.'

'But I do like them, and I choose who I go with because they're the ones I like a lot. I wouldn't go with anyone, and anyway I do it for a purpose.'

'Oh yes, what is that?'

I stopped my rolling and held up the rolling pin as if I would hit her but then I dropped it and stared at her. I suppose it did look bad. I looked at her and she was grinning at me, and suddenly all my anger disappeared and I could see how it looked to her.

'Let me explain, Sally, and if I do, you must never breathe a word of this to your Auntie. If you do, I will kill you, because I value her good opinion of me and if I lose it, I'll die too. Understand?'

She really changed her tune then and backed away from me and I realised I'd learned from Mammy how to be fierce. She nodded.

I looked around because at any time one of the cooks or Jew Johnny could return, but it seemed to be that part of the day when water had to be fetched, or the horses tended to, or the chickens needed their necks rung and the carcasses plucked.

'I do it to make money for Mammy. You've not been with her long but you'll see, what money comes into this hand' – and I held out my right hand – 'goes out from this hand' – and I held out my left hand. In good causes, you understand.

'I love Mammy for it because she is giving love and care and good food to these poor soldiers, who may die. But I can see that unless someone does something we'll be left destitute in this strange country where we can't even say 'help' in the local language, if we're starving.'

I carried on, talking quietly but earnestly, even though I was worried that someone might come, but I felt I had to make her understand that I was not really a bad person.

'And another point is that she doesn't understand what these men *really* need. They're away from their wives and their loves, and you can feel the urge yourself, but it's even worse for a man, he builds up into a crescendo and has to release his longings somehow, so that's how I help – two ways; I give them true comfort and they give me coin, real coin.

'I won't tell you where my stash is but I know that one day I can use that stash to help us all, God willing.'

She had sat down on a stool behind her as I made this long speech, probably the longest I've ever made and probably ever will make in the future, and at first she said nothing but I could see she was impressed. What she said next made me love her and it was the start of our great friendship.

'I know I said Black Francis wants me, and I want him, but if you help me – and can stop babies from coming – I can help you with your work, we can both work it together.'

Minx that she was, I agreed, because I knew that if I didn't she would fall one night into a seduction and would probably get pregnant, because that's the way of the world.

Chapter 19: Fig-tree sap

It was July before the British Hotel was truly finished. We hung the banners of cloth we had bought and put curtains at the window and Mammy used flour paste to stick posters and pictures from the *Illustrated London News* and *Punch* to cover the cracks and joins in the walls. After the main hut was completed, she took advantage of the Pasha's good nature and asked him if she could use his men to provide outhouses including two little houses where we would sleep – and one for Mr Day *when he was there.*

I have to say now that Mr Day was an elusive creature as far as I was concerned and seemed to spend all his time *doing* away from us so I never really worked out what his contribution was. He certainly didn't hump supplies from Balaklava to Spring Hill; that was for us, with the help of Johnny and the muleteers we managed to hire from time to time. Mammy did the negotiating for that, and she seemed to be working on Port-Admiral Boxer a lot to persuade him to help us move our goods. She stayed friendly with the Pasha which I know stood us in good stead, as he provided us with guards once we had the stores in place.

I discovered from the navvies that Mr Day was known for his horses and quite often we had horses in a fenced-off area which would disappear one day, and Mammy never really questioned it. Perhaps she knew that Mr Day was dealing in horses and looked on it as his own business and nothing to do with us, although hay that we purchased disappeared into the horses' mouths.

Makeshift outhouses were ordered to be built and somehow she acquired a pig and some chickens. I wasn't with her when she found these and all she would say was that the Pasha had influence with the local community. I had not realised that the locals still remained but they kept well away from the camps themselves.

It was growing now, Mammy's little empire, and she maintained it was over an acre in size but as I have no idea what an acre looks like, I couldn't dispute her. It certainly was impressive, with its outhouses, and the main long room where we would entertain. I found plenty of hidden places that I could use for my own purposes and hoped that Mammy would never discover my way of making money – which stood us in good stead later as you will discover.

On one glorious summer day Mammy, me and Johnny, who had become as familiar to me as Mammy was, all stood outside the construction and we watched as one of the carpenters nailed up the sign over the entrance – *The British Hotel*. The Union Jack was then hung again and we were open for business.

Yes, it was hard work, trying to keep our supplies dry and fresh and safe from the thieves. It was not easy for us to concoct Mammy's soups and patties from the limited raw materials but we managed somehow and then what laughter and good cheer was had by those who visited.

Mammy greeted the old companions she'd known in Jamaica and I was surprised at the number of soldiers that had visited our island in years gone by. They introduced others and soon we were working every day except Sunday.

On one occasion, when we were all overworked because there was a lull in the fighting and it seemed as if every officer was visiting us, Mammy let out a little scream so I thought she'd hurt herself. When I looked, she was rushing towards a couple of plain-clothed gentlemen who were coming towards us from the Turkish camp.

'Amos, Amos, is it really you?'

She enveloped one of the men in a great hug and he returned it and they seemed to sway together for some minutes, before they broke away from each other and Mammy took his hand and let him to our camp. I stood there, open-mouthed, and Mammy, with her great laugh, explained. 'Ratia, this is Amos Henriques, who, you remember, I visited in London, a great neighbour of mine.'

She sat him down and as I poured him a soft drink, at his request, she asked, 'Now how are you coming here, and where are you based? Ratia, he is a doctor, and shouldn't be here; he should either be at the front, or with Miss Nightingale in Scutari.'

'No, Mother Seacole, you are quite wrong. You remember I told you I had no influence with the Army when you visited me in England? You fired me with enthusiasm, and I decided to help with my medical skills, but the only way I could do it was to join the Turkish medical corps, so that is where I am based. When I heard you were just over the hill, and you visited our leader, I couldn't but come to see you, could I?'

Mammy then asked him questions about what he did, how he found the war, and what injuries he treated and how, but I was called away by other officers so did not hear his answers, but I was pleased Mammy had discovered another old acquaintance.

Mammy usually worked as hard as me and the others who now helped; two black cooks, the one we nicknamed Black Francis, and I will tell more about him later, and some Turkish servants to kill the chickens and other animals and prepare them for the cooking.

If the soldiers and the navvies and the ordinance men had their way we could be working a twenty-four hour seven-day week, but Mammy insisted that apart from Sunday which was our day of rest, we closed at eight each night.

'They can go down to Kadikoi if they want anything important after this hour,' Mammy said, 'we need to eat and rest as well, Ratia.'

The truth was that Mammy's hair was getting flecked with more and more grey and her face more drawn but it was only me that saw how exhausted she became, although I was surprised that she never became ill.

I have to say that I had bouts of dysentery and bad colds that would lay me low and Mammy always ministered to me, giving me concoctions of thistle seeds and fig tree juice, as she did to her 'sons' and even on one occasion encouraged me to get better by telling me I was like a daughter to her. I turned my face to the wall and cried when she'd left, frustrated that I was so useless as to get ill when there was so much to be done but also because I was so touched by her feelings for me. It was at times like this that, even if I'd met my Robert again, I wasn't sure that I would leave Mammy to go with him.

Each day would have a pattern to it. In the early morning we brewed good fresh coffee for the first travellers on the road who had not eaten and gave them good Turkish fresh bread that we bought in Balaklava, or, later in the day, made ourselves. Then the rest of the morning we cooked and baked and roasted, ready for the lunchtime rush. Once we had finished, and before lunch, we would head to the harbour and for a few hours we would minister to the sick and wounded, before rushing back to the British Hotel to welcome the first of our guests who would arrive in the middle of the day and then there would be a constant coming in and going out all afternoon and early evening. Mammy didn't mind the guests drinking – even champagne – but she couldn't abide drunkenness and refused to serve any man who became overbearing and rude. She would do it with good humour and the other guests would help by cajoling the drunken man outside and helping him on his way back to his tent. Poor men, some of them suffered so, it was a relief for them to collapse into a drunken stupor. Mammy understood that but she also insisted on keeping a decent house, as she described it. We were helped by some of the senior officers who made sure that if there was a build up of aggression, the protagonists would be moved off, by force sometimes. Sir Colin Campbell was one of those who sat in the corner, talking quietly, smoking a cigar and slowly quaffing wine, but you could see his gimlet eyes were roaming the room, making sure there was peace and his soldiers knew he was there and behaved themselves.

Chapter 20: Plantain juice and mercury rubs

We were so busy we didn't notice that the booming noises from the shelling of the city of Sevastopol were increasing. But one day it seemed to penetrate our consciousness, because we noticed that we didn't get so many visitors and there were more men returning on stretchers, and the train was going backwards and forwards more often, with its hell-fire of smoke belching out behind it like a little London fog. We knew it was carrying shells and ammunition to the front and wounded men back to the hospitals.

'Of course, it's carrying a greater number of weapons, Mother,' explained one of the ordinance men who was waiting for the train to return. 'I've been in the wagon yard trying to get more wagons in good order. The bombardment is increasing and we need to transport as much weaponry as we can get to the front.'

Omar Pasha had ridden up and greeted the few diners in the hotel at the time. 'Mother Seacole, beer and champagne all round. We have been mobilised at last.'

I ran to get the drinks and Mammy was sitting down with him and the others when I returned. I heard the Pasha say, 'Of course you can come with us dear lady, but I wouldn't want you to be hurt.' You understand this was said in very broken English and one of the other soldiers was interpreting as well, so it was a very staccato conversation, but that is what I heard, I know it. I became alarmed. Was Mammy going to run off with him, after all?

I said nothing, waiting for an explanation but none was forthcoming. As Mammy made to depart the next day I set about my tasks with thin lips and decided to be taciturn; I could only remonstrate with her if she confirmed that she was leaving us to go with the Pasha. Could she really abandon all this? And her workers? I knew she was fond of the Pasha and the earlier comments came back to me. I just didn't how to express my sorrow and anger at what I thought she intended to do and wouldn't know what to say that would stop her losing her reputation.

I know on occasions she said she felt like my mother and at other times that I was her great friend, but she had not revealed to me what she was going to do and it hurt. Quite often, she would leave me to work the hotel and restaurant while she went out on missions of her own, and never told me where she was going and why should she? Although she said I was more a friend than a servant, I never lost the feeling that I *was* her servant, even when I sometimes spoke bluntly to her.

I suppose she could tell by the way my shoulders were hunched over the patties I was making that she eventually came round and looked me in the face. 'What's the matter, dear girl? You haven't spoken all morning.'

I looked at her and tears came into my eyes. She immediately led me to a stool in the kitchen that we used when dressing the chickens, and sat me down and pulled another stool so she was sitting close.

'Now, what is it, tell me.'

'Oh, Mammy if it makes you happy you must go, but I fear for you.'

'Now, you mustn't be worried. The Pasha has promised to look after me.'

'But he has three wives already, you said, and how will I fit into that? You weren't thinking of abandoning me here?'

Mammy looked puzzled for a minute and I thought, *yes she was going to leave me.*

Suddenly a great guffaw came from her, the laugh she used when she was enjoying the Pasha's company which made me even more worried. Before I could stop her she gave me a great bear hug and was kissing my face.

'Ratia, oh, my dear Ratia, how could I ever leave you? You're such a wonder.'

Then she released me, and explained, 'I am following the Pasha to the Russian outposts near Baidar, to see the fighting that is going to take place. His regiment is following the British and the French to support their outer ranks and he has kindly allowed me to go with him. And I will return before nightfall.'

I slumped back on the stool in relief.

'Why didn't you tell me? I heard the conversation yesterday and he certainly said he would look after you if you went with him.'

'Ratia, I know you like to listen secretly but let this be a lesson to you; that if you hear half a conversation you could be sorely misled. How could you think that I would become Omar Pasha's consort?'

She was laughing again and I was mightily ashamed. I got up and found the biggest pie I could and packed it in one of the bags we used when preparing food for the soldiers on the move, and gave it to her, as a peace offering.

'Very well, if you're going to be out all day, take this with you and at least have a good meal with the Pasha. But I will still worry about you being near the fighting. Please come back.'

'Of course I will, Ratia and I'll tell you all about it.'

Which she did. Later on, as we sat in the candlelight in our little sitting room, after the British Hotel was shut for the night, and she tucked into what was left of the Irish stew, and sipped at some porter, she narrated the events of the day, and she was so vivid, I felt as if I was there.

I can only let her tell her tale.

'As you know I followed on horseback and it was a grand sight to see our English with the bright colours of their red uniforms, and French cavalry riding in formation, with the Turkish regiments flanking them, when suddenly the Turkish detachment made a flurry of advancement up the hills to the right of the River Tchernaya where there were Russian outposts and they were so brave, that the Russians just seemed to give way and disappear. It was very pretty to see them advance, with little clouds of white smoke coming from our men and then from the distant hills, which of course was where the Russians were. It was very exciting and I can understand how our sons go into battle without thinking of themselves and their lives; they are just part of a great army fighting the enemy.'

Somehow I couldn't see it, the word 'pretty' seemed to me wrong for men going out to kill each other. Even though Mammy had witnessed the sick and injured from such skirmishes, I believe she didn't see it as so much waste of men as I did. I just kept thinking of my Robert being at the receiving end of one of those 'pretty little clouds of smoke' and falling, smitten, and suffering pain but not dying. Mammy was a good doctress and kindly but, in her eagerness to be involved, and *useful*, perhaps she had become immune to the reality of it all.

Luckily, after this excursion the rumbling noises seemed to desist and we had a jolly time with many visitors. One of these I have to mention, as it shows just how gullible Mammy was despite her age. I should tell you that she was past childbearing by this time, as I could tell from the private things I had been washing for years. I hadn't washed bloody rags for her for some months, so you can tell she was aging and you would have thought she would have grown wise with all what she had seen. But when Captain St Clair arrived, I could see she was, well, the only word that describes it, smitten.

But I could tell at once that he was the sort of man who relied on his good looks to get away with, perhaps, murder. He smiled at me as I approached him to ask what he would like, and the smile was confident and I read it as saying, 'hello, you can see I'm handsome and you will like me and give me just what I want.'

In fact, he said, quite charmingly, 'Good afternoon, pretty

maid, can I have a glass of your best red wine please.'

It was the *pretty maid* sentence that confirmed my suspicions. I know I'm not ugly, but no-one would call me pretty and I'm sure not bothered about it. I knew I had a pleasant face with a welcoming smile, but pretty I wasn't.

I served him and hoped that Mammy wouldn't spot him, but she did of course and greeted him with her usual 'And is this another of Mother Seacole's boys?'

He ingratiated himself with her by flattering her good cooking, the taste of her best wine and her genuine good nature, and she allowed him to stay although we did not have guest rooms. Mr Day's room was, of course, frequently available, because he was often travelling between Constantinople and Balaklava now, no doubt in the comfort of a guest cabin in a cargo ship. So his room was vacant and that is where Captain St. Clair made himself comfortable.

I tried to warn Mammy, as always. 'Has he paid yet for the services he has had so far?'

'Ratia, you're heartless. He is due for the front and may die in the service of his country and you're thinking of money. How could you doubt a man with such a name, indicating sainthood and clearness?'

'Mammy, it's just a name, and in fact, how do we know it's not made-up? Nobody else has vouched for him, although the others like him. No doubt because he is always standing drinks – which have not yet been paid for.'

Mammy said nothing but that night she was more than hearty with Captain St Clair and I have to admit that I heard her mentioning the fact that her *partners* were looking to her accounts and did he think he could pay his bill to date.

That night, again when all was quiet and we were together eating, she triumphantly produced a bill upon his agents, which I looked at most carefully. It did indeed confirm that, upon production of this bill, his expenses would be paid for by Cox's.

'You see, Ratia, you really must learn to trust people.'

I shrugged, but a few days later I heard that Mammy had received another bill from him and she had kindly given him cash to see him on his way home – not to the front – because he pleaded the lingering death of his father and had to get back to England.

We would not be able to cash in the promises until we too returned to England and we didn't know when that would be.

There were so many people coming and going that I couldn't keep track of them but Mammy was able to sit down and reminisce and talk about those she had known in Jamaica and it seemed that the men liked it when she mentioned their comrades who had fallen and they had a good laugh about the foibles of some of their commanding officers. I discovered by listening that most of the younger officers considered that those leading them in this war didn't know what they were doing and they despised them.

'When did they fight? Fifty years ago, Ma-am, with muskets and old fashioned ships. They rest on the laurels of Nelson and Wellington and most of the men here have starved because they haven't thought about how to supply simple things like boots and overcoats. If only we were in charge…'

This was an age-old mantra, as I had learned, the young always thinking they knew better than their elders, but Mammy and me, when we had our quiet evenings together, tended to agree with them, although supplies were now getting through.

Mr Russell, whose articles we had read in *The Times* when we were in England, was one of Mammy's favourites, although he was not of the military and I couldn't make him out. Being a journalist, he listened to what the men said and then wrote and wrote and wrote – more than me, even, and sent the packets back as soon as he could. We knew where these missives ended up because we had read his stories before we came out, and many people were influenced by what he said.

He even mentioned Mammy on one occasion as a kindly doctress who ministered to the men at the front. For that, I would always like him despite his peculiar job. I was with Mammy on that, both of us always felt that a man who did not fight for their country were lily livered.

As I say, many people came and treated the place like a holiday hotel, but didn't stay long. Even that photographer man, Fenton, returned home in the late summer, taking with him many plates for his photographs, and I heard he made a lot of money out of the trip. But I forgave him for snubbing Mammy because the navvies told me that he did in the end, take photographs of them, and they felt as if they would have a little immortality for all their hard work. Not that he would ever know that I'd forgiven him or that he would care what a black servant would think, but I know it made me feel better to forgive him. Despite my misgivings about the people around Mammy, I stay with her because I agree with her philosophy of always seeing the best in people and not holding a grudge against those who do you bad – it only festers inside you and makes you a bitter person, all that rankling. Even so, I would try to protect Mammy from the out and out bounders, like Mr St Clair.

At about this time, the booming started to increase again and Mammy became stern and sad. I listened to her breathing at night and knew she wasn't asleep and she knew I knew, but she would toss and turn and mutter and worry and not say anything to me in the morning. I know what upset her more than anything. She loved all the *boys* who came to the hotel, and learned about their lives, and their families. She knew those who were married and who had little ones back home. She had her favourites as well and generally I could understand why.

There was one young man, I'll call Sam, who was in the artillery, and he was an especial favourite and it wasn't because he was blond with large blue eyes, which looked soulfully at you, as if he didn't know how he had gotten here and *why* he was here. It was his courtesy and deference to his Mother Seacole that endeared him to her and to me. I could tell by the way Mammy gently stroked his hair out his eyes, and gave him a little extra meat, that she adored him, in a maternal way of course. It was true that Mammy always had a special fondness for blue-eyed blond men and I wondered sometimes whether her husband had had that colouring although she never said.

Sam came to us firstly because he had the cholera and Mammy nursed him, holding his head in her lap and muttering endearments to him, while he looked into her face and smiled as if the very look of her would get him better. And it seemed to work, because he was soon back at his post but no sooner had he got there then a Russian sniper caught him mid chest and Mammy closed his eyes and helped bury him. This was about the time that burials took a deal of our time, because there were so many.

One strange thing that kept occurring was that both officers and men would come and dine with us the night before they had been ordered into the trenches and this is what many of them said to Mammy, 'I can't say goodbye to my family at home Mother, but I'll say farewell to you so that if the Russians get me, you see to it that my family at home know I was thinking of them to the last.'

Mammy answered, as light-hearted as they, for they did speak quite light heartedly despite the serious words. 'I will do all I can for you. For now, rely on God's providence, he thinks of all.'

Not that Mammy was particularly religious at that time, but she knew how to comfort and use such platitudes. Even as these little scenes were being played out, I wondered how Mammy was going to travel the breadth of England – or indeed Ireland, for many of the ordinary soldiers were Irish – to meet with their families. I know she would do it if she could.

My mistress was often called away to the front where an officer was so badly wounded he could not be moved and she told me when she returned how dreadful it was to see them, and try to comfort them, and close their eyes at the last.

Even though the battle was intensifying you wouldn't believe how some of the men behaved – but it was all to the good for us. They organised race meetings and cricket matches and when they were in full swing, we were at double time, providing picnic baskets and drinks for all.

I said one day to Mammy, as we were both rushing backwards and forwards, 'It feels as if there's a desperation in the air, that it's all going to blow up in one big event and all the men know it and want to enjoy themselves before they go down into the trenches one last time.'

Mammy puffed as she lifted a joint of beef onto the table, and started carving it before she answered me. 'You may well be right. I heard that there is to be a great push in a few weeks' time and Sevastopol will fall. I mean to be there, and help the wounded, you understand that?'

I took some of the slices of beef and laid them carefully in a box with some bread rolls. As I reached for the jar of pickle I answered her, 'And I mean to be with you. I don't think I could bear to wait here on my own for you to return,'

'Bless you my dear, I was hoping you would say that. You are an immeasurable help in these things. You have learnt well. Prepare some mercury rubs to disinfect wounds and plantain juice to ease bleeding from the wounds, as well as bandages, splints, and we'll take some laudanum to dull their pain.'

I wouldn't say I had cause to regret that conversation but what we saw as Sevastopol fell was not something I ever wish to see again. Yes, I'd seen men and children sick with cholera and yellow fever; I'd tended those with dysentery and I'd also seen my fill of those wounded as they came through from the front to Balaklava but to see these sights multiplied on a battlefield, with bodies strewn all over the place, on top of each other, some moaning, others trying to crawl away, not knowing that as they did so, they left a severed arm or leg where it had been blown off; guts hanging out, and brains splattered all over other bodies. Some were fully conscious but holding their hands vainly to a hole in their leg, which had been punctured by a huge cannonball, and shattered bone showed through the engorged blood. There were craters with bones and guts that could not be identified as men.

Before this, I'd imagined a flat field, like the pictures of Waterloo I'd seen in London, but when we approached the slopes before Sevastopol, I found it was split with deep trenches which we had to negotiate. Inside these trenches, the ground we walked on was thick slime with mud, blood and dangerous from discarded bullet cases. Bodies blocked the way and it was difficult to scramble out of these trenches to move further up the hill. When I first arrived at these hellish battle scenes the smell of body odours and sour blood, faeces and sick, made me retch but as I moved among the wreckage of humanity, I think I lost my sense of smell, or I became used to it and didn't notice it.

The crest of the hill was covered with a basket-shaped structure which was the Malakoff from where the Russians had fired their huge cannon. These had caused great destruction and had left the shattered remains of our boys on the lower slopes, beyond our help. This is where Mammy headed as she knew it had been the centre of the battle, where the French had broken through the structure. When we reached it, we found there were injured men piled on top of the rough pile of sandbags and woven fence-like structures which were the main defences. It surprised me that it had stood out so well, but it was thick and the Russians had abandoned the huge cannon, still facing out towards our trenches. Here, many of the French and English had lost their lives, but there were also dead Russians, some still gripping cannon balls, or leaning over their deadly weapons. The stench of ordure was so strong that I nearly turned back, but the groans of some of the men showed that some were still alive, and I followed Mammy's lead, by comforting the men who could be comforted.

The bombardment still continued though. Our men would look out for us and shout to warn us when they thought a Russian shell would fall close to us and we would dive down either in a trench or behind a small rock-fall on the hill, although I thought this was silly. If the shell hit us what did it matter whether we were standing or lying, except that by lying we would not fall.

On one of these occasions, Mammy fell sharply on her hand, twisting her thumb and although we treated it immediately, and one of the doctors put a splint on it, it never really recovered. I think the reason was that Mammy would not rest and carried on using that hand, to minister to the injured, so that her poor thumb never got a chance to heal. But that was typical of her, she would never think of herself, especially with all that needed to be done for *her men.*

We moved among them, me holding a great container of water, tinged with lemon, and Mammy quenched the thirst of those she thought would survive. We called those stretcher bearers who were not laden already, to the wounded who we thought would benefit from being taken from the battlefield and closed the eyes of others who died in front of us. There were Russians, English, French and many other soldiers from places I did not even recognise from what was left of their uniforms and we treated them all. The moans and cries were horrendous and my head began to swim, not knowing which way to turn to help, but I followed Mammy and carried out her instructions, just to keep sane. The smell of congealed blood and guts, cannon fire, and faeces where the men had let go, made me retch each time we went back to that battle scene, but then something took over – compassion? Concentration on the job in hand? I did not know what it was, but we got used to the smell and didn't notice it until afterwards.

We were not the only comforters, we came across a Russian lady, with a rough scarf tied over her head, who was also moving among the wreckage and she, too, was ministering to anyone, not just her compatriots.

Mammy suddenly screamed and I could see her finger in a man's mouth, who I recognised as Russian from the torn remnants of his uniform. I called to others and some doctors came and forced the dying man's teeth ajar and she pulled her finger out, but I could see the bone in the middle of the teeth marks.

'Whatever were you doing, Mammy, putting your finger in a man's mouth?' I asked later as I bathed it with hot water tinged with lemon to try to clean it.

She looked at me ruefully, 'I wanted to find out where the musket ball was lodged in the back of his mouth, I could see it and thought that, if I could get it out, he might have a chance.'

Then she started laughing. And I joined in, because sometimes both of us realised the stupidity of what we were doing and laughter released the tension of the awful day.

We were not the only nurses there. Apart from the lone Russian woman, the French had their vivandieres, and both Mammy and I were impressed by their neat uniforms although they rapidly became filthy, as ours did, and their efficiency and hard work. We also saw more Russian women, with gaily coloured scarves around their heads and huge crosses hanging from their necks, ministering. We all worked in the mayhem, not caring whether the men were from the British Army, the Russian, Turkish or French, because they were all mixed together in a ghastly mess of ghoulish heaps.

Mammy was given a ring by a grateful Russian, for helping him to find a stretcher and be taken back to his own people to be nursed, but we're sure he would not have survived. 'Otherwise, I would not have taken the ring, Ratia, as he might have needed it later.'

We returned to Spring Hill when the nights came and we

could see no more. Then I set to, scrubbing our discarded clothes with carbolic to get rid of the gore that clung to the hems and the odours which had seeped onto them unnoticed as we stumbled our way through the carnage.

And we went back the next day and the next. Mammy was moving slowly towards the burning city and I watched as she climbed the ramparts of a redan and disappeared over the ruins of the fort, into the ruins of the now abandoned city. I knew that the Russians had built a bridge of boats and the population, after fighting so fiercely, had left.

She was gone a long while and in panic I returned to Spring Hill at dusk, not wanting to be with the sick and injured at night, when the thieves came out to rob the dead of what little they still had on them. When she returned, almost at midnight when I was beginning to despair, she sat down and because I knew the only way she could recover from ghastly experiences was to talk about them, as if by doing so, she was releasing the horrors from her memory, I made her some tea, and said gently, 'Tell me about it.'

Instead of launching into a description, she put her hand in her pocket and at first kept her fist clenched, but slowly she opened it to reveal a beautiful jewel-encrusted cross, a little bigger than her hand.

'May God forgive me, Ratia, I've seen dreadful scenes today, babies wrapped in cloth and left to die, old people dying because they couldn't move, and dead soldiers at their post in the ramparts still clutching their weapons as if, even in death, they would defend their city. I had to step over them, there were so many but they were all dead. Unburied, it is starting to be rank and soon, I suspect, there will be disease.'

She still held the jewel in her open hand so I asked, 'And where did you get that?'

'Ratia, I took it from one of those soldiers, may God forgive me, the only thing I will ever take, because it was as if his God was talking to me and thanking me for my kindnesses to them all. I held his head as he died and he looked at me and I am sure in his own language he said *thank you, Mother*. I am sure of it.'

I saw tears in her eyes and I realised she was at the end of her resources. I stood up, and took the jewel from her and said, 'Come you must rest, I insist, and you must not get up early. I will make sure everything is ready in the British Hotel tomorrow.'

When she was in bed, and I watched until she fell asleep, I took the cross and found some ribbons in her favourite yellow, blue and red, and plaited them and threaded them through a hole at the top of the cross and hung it on a nail in her room so she could see it as soon as she woke. I cried myself to sleep partly for her but also for my own sadnesses.

It was about this time that she began to read her Bible and I noticed her praying more. That battlefield had affected her in terrible ways, so much so that I forgot my own fears and hopes. All the time I followed her it was with horrible trepidation that I would recognise Robert as a corpse, but truth to tell, some of them were so mangled, with faces blown off, and I hadn't seen him for so long, I doubt if I would recognise him even if he had been one of the many hundreds of bodies.

Chapter 21: Sauces and stews for sustenance

Despite the carnage, we had jollities at the British Hotel and I maintained a smiling face, as did Mammy and Sally Seacole, for all those who came.

'They need to have a little normality and we'll give it to them,' explained Mammy as we slaved over the hot stove and listened to the laughter from the dining hall, which began to sound manic with fear, to my ear.

Little did Mammy know how real her words were, when she said, *we give it them,* but Sally and I did not smile behind her back; we truly believed we were doing our best for her and for the men. As the men went to war, and told Mammy to say goodbye to their loved ones, they were saying goodbye to me and Sally in their own desperate way.

It was that summer that we were plagued with the biggest flies I'd ever seen, as if they were one of the ten plagues of Egypt, and Mammy helped the Duke of Cambridge, the cousin of the Queen, by rigging up for him a muslin tent to keep the flies off him at night. For that, he was always grateful and became one of Mammy's greatest friends and supporters later on.

Then there was a lull and winter came but the booming went on and we learnt that the British were trying to destroy the harbour of Sevastopol because it was large and very deep and could take any ship that tried to moor there. They thought that by destroying the structures, they would stop the terrible Tsar from trying to use the harbour ever again. I kept thinking about the poor Russian people whose homes were being destroyed. Every night there was a red glow in the sky and I dreamt of people wailing, and pulling their hair out in despair.

It was a strange time, the jollities continuing against the

background of destruction and mortality. On one occasion the men decided to put on a play and a makeshift stage was erected and they pleaded with Mammy to provide ladies' clothes. They didn't ask Sally and me, knowing that our clothes would not fit the men who were to play the female roles. Mammy raided her trunks to provide the costumes and I blushed as she pulled out her petticoats and underwear, even though I knew that most of the men who were taking part had seen mine.

On another occasion we worked throughout the night, nearly, with Sally whispering to me that she *had to go outside* and would I cover for her as we made pie after pie, because there was to be a race meeting the next day and the orders for picnic baskets kept on coming.

And so we lived through the bitter winter and although we still served our customers, the numbers were dwindling as we lost the men we knew and loved. Sir Colin Campbell, who would keep order in our establishment, was killed and he was sorely missed.

There was a particular Irishman, Paddy, who typified many of his countrymen, in that, when he got drunk was particularly aggressive. All of us heard the stories of these Irish who had often joined up through desperation, and they told us of families starving to death in a potato famine, so we often felt sorry for them but their melancholy would make them drink more, perhaps to reach oblivion, but liquor often turned them violent. Mammy watched what she gave him to drink, but sometimes it seemed as if he swaggered in, already the worse for wear, and pitching for a fight. He would stagger against another customer whose drink would spill, just as he was about to take a swig.

'Hey, watch it,' the aggrieved man would call, as he turned to see who had pushed him, and Paddy would already have his fist clenched, and raised, ready to punch the man in the face. It was at this point that Sir Colin would stand, gesturing to several of his soldiers. It might take four to 'persuade' Paddy to leave for fear that the fighting would escalate, and that he and the other men, who were all willing to join in, would wreck the place by throwing tables and chairs at each other as the initial contretemps became a fracas that affected the whole of the bar. Just a word from Sir Colin Campbell, and the soldiers would take Paddy home, as he swore dreadfully and flailed about, but he soon weakened, as they dragged him to his bed. As the war escalated, more men found a way to get drunk, without our help, to stop the terrible experiences from overwhelming them.

'It's the French and the Turks who give them the drink, that awful raki, and when they get to us, they're so tanked up that one slug of our good whiskey will send them over the edge,' Mammy explained to me, as I moaned about Paddy and others who we frequently had to eject.

'I keep a decent hotel,' she maintained, 'No drunkenness and no gambling.'

She tried so hard to keep to this mantra but, as she knew, there were others in Kadikoi who were willing to pander to a man's taste, and provide them with the cheap raki. I have to admit that Sally and I chose carefully as we had a similar mantra to Mammy; we didn't allow drunken men to come to the hay with us, nor those we thought were using the other women who, by that time, were becoming numerous. It was probably out of desperation, poor women, as their men died at the front and they had no means of supporting themselves.

The winter seemed to fly by with all the hard work, and the news from the front, and we still ran a good hotel with many customers.

Then, one day, I noticed the greenery increasing and that strange warmth that heralds summer. We'd had a new delivery of port wine and champagne and although Mammy watched with annoyance the large boxes being delivered by the mule trains sent by Mr Day, she did not refuse them. Several large deliveries came about this time, as if, with the fall of Sevastopol and its destruction, a joyous stream of cargo was getting through.

'I hope Mr Day knows what he's doing, arranging for all these supplies to come now. We could well have done with it six months ago but I've heard from some of my sons that their commanders consider the war is now over and they're going to dismantle everything and go home. So give our boys a jolly good time, Ratia.'

I was happy to do so as I knew that Mammy had very little money in her coffers as she trusted me to keep the books. I managed to squeeze out the last coin, whether it was a Levant, French, or an English one, from the soldiers who were kind enough to use my services to the end. It was all very well for us to give credit but the locals didn't work that way and if Mammy wanted to supply good chicken patties, or a beef pie, then I had to give coin when I purchased the ingredients. You have to understand that these soldiers were not paid while they were out in the battlefield, because their superiors thought that it would be a bad idea if they were captured, or even left on the battlefield, with ready money on them, and we had many bills of honour to encash when we got back to England, which Mammy took willingly. I was much happier with real money, the odd penny or shilling that the men managed to keep on them or even, as I say, if it was Levant coin. I preferred these to bits of paper, knowing we could use such currency in the Ottoman Empire. I rather feared that the proffered paper would prove to be just that – useless bits of paper.

I never openly voiced my concerns to Mammy though, because she seemed to have recovered her good spirits and I could see that this was good for her and good for our visitors. In fact, the jollity seemed to be louder and more desperate than before, with men who came, telling of lost friends and colleagues and toasting many who had fallen in that last desperate battle.

Mr Day had sent horses and mules to her, but they were either stolen or they didn't produce foals, but Mammy ordered more because they were in demand and she thought she could sell these easily. Then the supply dried up and none had been forthcoming for months. Suddenly, with the warm weather, several horses arrived, when there were few men who needed them now. *He* was safely ensconced in Constantinople and my guess was that he wouldn't be making the trip to the Crimea again.

All of these thoughts I kept to myself, as I say, but they played on my mind. There was another problem that was niggling at me. Mammy was, I am sure, becoming forgetful and would stare into space sometimes, and then say, 'My, what was I thinking?' At those times I kept a close eye on her and reminded her, 'Mammy, you were serving the captain his red wine,' and she would laugh that raucous laugh of hers and carry on with the task. I put it down to exhaustion.

Within a few weeks the railwaymen started to leave and we soon saw regiments, in the best gear that they could muster, march past us, some of them giving us a little salute without their commanding officers noticing. Others, ignoring their officers, gave three cheers as they marched past.

It was true; the army was going home.

'What am I going to do with all these supplies? Ratia, we'll have a sale. Come, let's get the table outside and fill it with some of the goods. Look we have a large box of handkerchiefs here, they were always popular and we've sold out of them before so we should be able to dispose of these.'

So as the men marched past, Mammy would call out in her loud voice, 'Come, my sons, one last purchase before you disband. Buy a handkerchief for the little woman at home. We have beer and porter and champagne for the journey home.'

But to our horror the men did not stop and carried on marching. I remembered something Robert had told me. If his superiors told him that he had to go, he went, and he had to obey their every word. Had the officers told their men not to stop? To keep marching past us? After all the hospitality we had given them?

What did happen though was that her loud voice attracted locals, both Russian and Tartar who came flocking round, offering her pennies for what was worth pounds. She complained that a box of wine that had cost her £4 had to be sold at 4d a bottle – the empty bottle was worth more than that.

Her friend the Pasha had long since gone, whether to his maker, or back home, we never discovered, and suddenly I was frightened. We had no friends here now, and were at the mercy of thieves and beggars themselves. Jew Johnny helped as much as he could and tried to barter with the crowd to pay more but these people were canny. They suddenly realised that we were stuck, stuck in this strange country, with a shed full of supplies that no one wanted – well, not at its proper price.

The crowd were laughing and jeering at us as we offered our goods at the going rate. Suddenly, Mammy strode off to the sheds where Johnny's tools were kept and returned with a hammer. Her face was thunder and I felt afraid of her and for her at the same time. She attacked the largest barrel of best port so that it spurted out on all sides and she continued to hack until it was spouting like a dead soldier who'd had his throat cut. The crowd surged forward and held their hands out, or any makeshift container they had, to catch the spillage. Both Johnny and I tried to stop her as she approached the next barrel.

'Mammy, Mammy, please stop it,' I cried but she was powerful in her anger and Johnny could not hold her. She broke away and faced us, arms on her hips. Sally came up with Black Francis by her side and remonstrated with her, 'Auntie, Mammy, please don't. We could try to get some of the good stuff back home.'

'If we can't get a good price here then no-one will have my goods. This will show them. I have worked so hard, so hard, and now it comes to this that we have nothing but food and drink that nobody will buy.'

She collapsed onto the ground, in one heap and put her head to her hands, and started moaning. The crowd just gaped and I turned to them and by waving my hands and screaming, made them to understand that they should leave us.

Jew Johnny and the other servants stood helplessly, watching me as I rocked Mammy in my arms as she sobbed away her heartache at the loss of her business. Through it all, I noticed that Black Francis took Sally in his arms and held her tight as she, too, sobbed.

All crying has to peter out in the end, no matter how long it takes and eventually Mammy's stopped with a great gasp of air as if her innate optimism took over. She rubbed her fingers through her thick hair like she was wiping away the pain and looked at me. Her face was swollen with the crying and my heart went out to her.

'We will dismantle all of this and take it with us, Ratia. I can't leave anything behind. And when we get back we will start again and build a shop in Aldershot where all my boys have told me they will be stationed when they get back home. We'll make a living there.'

She pulled herself up, stiffly, and I could see how she'd aged. Sally, Black Francis and Jew Johnny, stood around and we listened and said nothing. What could we say?

Chapter 22: Peruvian bark mixed in brandy and water

To add salt to the wound the Army organised a special farewell ceremony for all the troops on the wharf in Balaklava with a grand band and speeches from the remaining officers. It seemed to me that they were arrogant and unthinking, leaving us civilians to fend for ourselves.

'I don't think you should go, Mammy,' I advised, 'The officers have treated you appallingly, not letting their men stop for a second even if it might be to purchase a wad of tobacco or a handkerchief. They could have supported you a little more, knowing that you would be left bereft.'

She was about to say something but I had to have my say and continued, 'They're not even helping us to dismantle the building or take it down to the harbour and whether we will even get a passage, we don't know. They sure have time to organise a *ceremony* but can't help those in need, who have helped them.'

I believe I had every right to feel bitter but Mammy, even from where she sat could see thieves making off with our chickens, shook her head.

'You have to understand the Army. They are fighting units and cannot let discipline be broken. I'm just a poor sutler, doing my job supplying the Army, and if, as well as that, I can help my poor boys to recover from their wounds nobly obtained, then that is my purpose in life. I thought you had matured, Ratia, but you will still have to learn that I am happy to serve and expect nothing back. I have had a moment of weakness, but now I must show my support for my boys and forget my own troubles. All will be well in the end, you'll see.'

I couldn't argue with her. I just marvelled at her eternal optimism and misguided belief in the British Army. I watched silently as she stood up and moved slowly to the door and shouted at the local thieves who were running all over the place trying to catch the squawking fowl. They retreated but I knew that, as soon as our backs were turned, they would be back. Sally and the rest of them were working in the main building trying to pack up the best of the remaining tins and taking down the sheets of iron that formed the walls. One of the important items they were packing was a fine window frame that had been delivered to us from the ruins of Sevastopol.

'Look at those poor fellows,' Mammy said, still watching the thieves who knew she was there but were ignoring her. 'They're as hungry and desperate as us – that's the way of war. We can't take the animals with us and they won't sell so they might as well go to those who need them.'

I made no comment to that because I could see the sense in it. She turned to me and said, 'But I will go to this ceremony and I'll wear something that will be talked about and I will smile and be at the front. That's the way Mother Seacole faces her defeat – with courage and aplomb. Come, let's get that roll of plaid we ordered for that poor Scotsman who died before he could order a new kilt, I'm going down to Balaklava in style.'

She showed me what she had in mind and while she made the full skirts from the tartan, I rooted around in our trunks and found some white lace from an old table cloth and cut and stitched it into an elegant fichu. Mammy went out and came back with a variety of large feathers and, producing a bowler hat she tucked the largest, brightest feather into the band. When we had completed the costume, she went into her room, like a giggling girl, to put it on. A short while after, she came out, hand on hip, and grabbed an umbrella which was lying nearby and, using it as a walking stick, pranced up and down and twirled before me.

I called to Sally, 'Come and look at your Aunt, she looks splendid.'

Sally came running, with Black Francis and Jew Johnny following and they all exclaimed. It was true, Mammy did look wonderful. The outfit suited her girth and she took on her usual air of authority with a swagger of jauntiness. All the sadness of the last few weeks was hidden for now, and she looked years younger.

'Come, Sally and Ratia, I think you both deserve to accompany me to this event.'

I wanted to say I had nothing so grand to wear but thought it didn't matter. I'd always hidden in Mammy's shadow so I would wear my usual dark clothes. Sally though, argued 'I don't have anything for such an event'

Mammy dismissed her fears. 'You just wear that sweet dress you wear in the bar, and we'll find a shawl that you can wrap around your shoulders and you'll be fine.'

I concurred, 'Yes, if there's any of our boys down there, they'll be grateful of another sight of you in that dress.'

I hoped Mammy didn't know what I meant but Sally smirked at me and ran off to change, into *that dress.* This was a frock in the latest purple colour, striped with silver, with a bodice pulled tight at her waist and then billowing out into an openness that I knew suited Sally's activities in the hay stack. It was low cut at the neck, and if I had worn it, I would have tucked in a collar of lace to hide my body. The tight waist accentuated Sally's ample bosom, and she only just hid her décolletage with a flimsy fichu when she was serving the men. I had watched her as she leant over them to put their porter on the table before them and saw the looks of appreciation in their faces. Sally truly had learned how to flirt with the men; my way was a lot more subtle than that, I always thought.

We all arrived at the harbour early and Mammy ensured she was near the front, with Monsieur Soyer, who wore a stunning white suit that I thought would soon be soiled but he doffed his hat at us and complimented us all, calling Sally, his own sweet girl and allowing Mammy and her to take each of his arms. As we moved through the crowd, Mammy called out to those she knew, 'Hello, my sons, what a great affair, hey? See you back in England, and can you spread the word that your Mother Seacole is going to set up shop near you all at Aldershot. We'll have the same comforts and good food ready for you, my boys.'

You see, she never gave up. I thought it was a mere idea that had suddenly come into her head, when she was in despair, but it seems that it had become fully formed now. All the civilians we knew were there – and the remaining officers. The band played and boring speeches, which I lost track of, were made. To see the regiments, in their columns, with their red jackets, was indeed a sight to remember. It was a grand affair and I was so proud of Mammy but when we returned to our half dismantled British Hotel, a quietness came over all of us, as none of us knew how we would get back to England.

Chapter 23: Opium

My greatest fears were realised. When Mammy went down to Balaklava to get a berth for the five of us – the other cooks and servants had disappeared into the crowd and I think that Black Francis only stayed because of Sally – nothing was to be had.

'We have to get the troops out, Mother Seacole, and you'll have to pay for your passage.'

'I have these bills of exchange, written on Cox's and others, from noble officers, and even if they're dead, I know they will come good when I get back to England.'

'Sorry, we need more than that. We need cash.'

They named a figure of which I knew that Mammy could not produce a quarter, from the books I kept. We had gone with her, a sorry band, not caring whether the locals raided our British Hotel; both Sally and I knew that even though we had money, it would not be enough to transport the tinned goods, flour, chickens and goats and pigs that were still there. Sally had whispered to me as we walked the way. 'Let us hope that some of it is taken and perhaps we can negotiate for what is left and it will be better.'

I agreed with her and hoped that Sally would stay with us forever because she had what I can only describe as common sense.

While Mammy was trying all her remaining contacts, Sally and I waited and walked away from the men who accompanied us.

'Let's reckon up and work out what we can do,' suggested Sally, and I agreed. I told her how much I'd acquired one way and another and she told me how much she had. We were jubilant. We knew we had enough to pay for all our passages and take some of the building materials with us.

'But how are we going to tell Mammy, without her knowing

how we acquired this?' asked Sally.

I thought about it. 'I'll go and see the master of the ship and explain that we can pay but he must not tell Mammy.'

Sally approved of this so, when Mammy returned to say she had not been successful, we feigned disappointment and fear and helped her back to Spring Hill. Here, I have to say, we carried out something I am a little ashamed of but in my time with Mammy I'd learnt how to give someone a sleeping draught that would give them a refreshing sleep and that is what I gave Mammy in the drink I offered her. She sure needed it but it would also help us to help her.

Once she was well asleep, Sally and I, accompanied by Jew Johnny and Black Francis, in whom Sally insisted in confiding, although I'm not sure she ever told him the way in which she had acquired the money, returned to the harbour and spent some time bargaining with an English captain – no less – to ensure our passage out of the Crimea and at least to Constantinople. When we had completed our negotiations, and returned to the hotel, Mammy was still groggy from the opium that we'd given her but, when she came to, we convinced her that she had slept so long because she was plain exhausted. We didn't have enough funds to pay for all the supplies but felt pleased that at least we could all escape from this place.

Mammy always glossed over this part of her story but I don't mind about that; all of us loved her and would do anything for her so it was just an extension of what had always been; us secretly caring for her.

When we got to Constantinople I had the biggest shock of my life and this is true. Jew Johnny wanted to return to his family and that was natural and of course that wasn't the shock.

It was the night we landed, and I was lulled into a false sense of happiness listening to the call of the imams and seeing the pigeons, catching the last of the sun, circling the minarets in the dusk in a rhythm that mirrored the chant, as if it had become solid. I really felt they were dancing to the sound of the call to prayer. I was interrupted in this reverie by Sally coming and plonking herself down beside me – she had developed the heavy hips like her aunt, andwas not graceful when she wasn't being deliberately provocative. I resented being interrupted as well, sure that anyone who saw me could see I was in a reverie. Instead, she started talking.

'Me and Black Francis, we want to stay here, and how can we tell Mammy? He says there's lots of opportunities for a cook and now he's learnt so much from Mammy he will easily get a good job.' She stopped and said shyly, 'I told him what I done and he don't mind, he thinks I'm noble and that you're noble, but he wants me for himself and I'm old enough now, but Mammy might take it bad, that I want to leave her. What should I tell her?'

Without me saying a word, she went on, 'Perhaps if I tell her I'm budding with child, she'll be so ashamed and annoyed that she'll abandon me.'

I was shocked at her thinking this, as I was sure that Mammy would never abandon anyone and would not be ashamed that someone was having a baby, even if she might help if that woman didn't want it. Sally didn't understand about Mammy even though she'd been with her a couple of years.

She carried on, 'Me and Black Francis, we could just disappear without saying goodbye, but we didn't want to do that. What do you think?'

Well, that one was easy to answer. I took her hands in mine and was surprised they were so cold, and realised that Sally was a good girl at heart, and she'd worked herself into a worry about the situation. She didn't want to hurt anyone really, it was just that she loved her Black Francis and didn't want Mammy to say it was wrong to love him.

'I'll come with you and you tell her, simple like, what you told me, that you and Black Francis love each other and want to be together and she'll accept that, I'm sure.'

So, in the early evening we told Mammy and she gave that raucous laugh of hers and says, 'As if I didn't know. You think you can hide from me when a man's making sheep's eyes at you, and you a-twirling your hair at him. Black Francis is one of the best cooks I have ever had, and he will provide well for you girl, and if you want to stay in this city, then do so, but I'd like to see you married and what'll you do for money, hey, until he gets a job?'

I interfered then, and maybe I shouldn't, 'Don't worry, about that Mammy, I have a little saved and I will make sure Sally and Francis have enough to keep them going for some time until he get himself established.'

Mammy looked at me in that sharp way and sure, I know, as sure as eggs make omelettes, that she knew what Sally and I got up to in the hay, but I also know she won't say anything and she would never mention it.

So we had a grand farewell slap-up dinner in a restaurant behind the Blue Mosque, where we sat upstairs in the cool of the evening, and watched whirling dervishes, which was a weird and wonderful thing to me.

Then it's time to leave, but my money is halved by Sally remaining behind, and I offer to negotiate us passages back with the little that remains.

'How would you like it, Mammy if we visited some of the Greek Islands, and Italy and southern France?'

I had studied my atlas and the ships' routes and knew that trading ships would take us for a quarter of the price that had been paid to get us out to Constantinople all those months ago.

And she agrees because both of us know that, if we take these local trading ships, that hop from port to port, it's a lot cheaper, and we might make it back to England with a little money to spare to provide a lodging before we work out how to make contact with Mr Day and start the business at Aldershot.

Chapter 24: Blistering the patient

When we finally reached Southampton there was no greeting from Mr Day as Mammy expected. Instead, there was a letter in which he told us that he was in London trying to trace those men who had left us letters of credit.

'There you are, already anticipating what we need to do. He's a good man, Ratia.'

I'd never said he wasn't to her but once again she'd used her instinct to work out what I really thought. I didn't say anything, just shrugged.

We made our way to Aldershot third class and I found cheap lodgings. As soon as we were settled I could tell Mammy was itching to be out there, to find suitable premises for her next enterprise, but I wanted her to rest, just for a day or two because I could see how grey she was getting.

'Mammy, do you think it a good idea to take stock? We should go to the warehouse where the materials from the British Hotel are kept, and check what we have, before we commit ourselves to anything, surely. We need to discover how much it will cost to hire suitable premises and how much we have left.'

'Oh, you worry too much, girl, I'm sure that Mr Day will come up with the money. But you're right, we ought to seek him out or at least try to collect what we're owed. I'll contact Cox's and at least we can cash in that Captain St Clair's letters of credit.'

My heart sank, but then I thought, *why not? The sooner she discovers whether they're good or not, the better.*

It didn't take long for her to be told the awful truth – both from Cox's and from Mr Day. Most of the money owed to us was irrecoverable; either the bankers would not accept the letters of dead army officers, or they claimed they were fraudulent. I was of course vindicated – Nobody knew a Captain St Clair, and if they did, they weren't saying. I always knew he was a fraudster, but I merely comforted Mammy. It would do no good for her to be reminded how gullible she'd been, and I hoped she'd learn from the experience.

Mammy was not to be put off that easily. She propositioned Cox's and suggested they provide her with further credit to set up the Aldershot business, in order to build up her business and then pay her debts, but they refused.

'Never mind, we'll inspect what's in the store – I know we brought back pickles and tins of milk and other non-perishable items. I'm sure we'll have enough to bake some good sponges, and it's August – there's plenty of soft fruit and vegetables in the markets. We can start pickling and conserving, like we did at home, and sell what we make.'

Aldershot was a peculiar place. Surrounded by heathland, it did not have the lush vegetation I was used to, and very few trees as we approached it. I knew Mammy liked foraging for wild berries and other delicacies to mix into her conserves, which was what gave them that extra flavour and goodness. I doubted whether we would find anything of value in this dried up scrubland. I found out later that it was because this was *heathland* with poor soil, and the local labourers, who had very little work on the land, were pleased when the army started building and giving them work. It had a small village at its heart with the quaintest timber houses and shops you ever saw, surrounding an old church, called St Michael's. It was just like the pictures I'd seen in books at Blundells Hotel as a child that illustrated 'olde England', but it was swallowed up by the building works all around it, of the low huts that had been so familiar in the Crimea; the quickly-built quarters for soldiers. It was flat and you could hear the hammering of the building all day long. But more disturbing than that, Mammy had been beaten to it by many army sutlers who had set up shop in and around the town, and prices for premises were expensive.

'We'll take a stall; that will do for us for a time.'

Mammy's answer to everything – always find a solution, no matter how impractical.

Our stall was visited by those soldiers who remembered her, but we did not fare well. After our first concoctions were sold, we had little money for more ingredients, and I was right when I guessed it was not good land for foraging. I was beginning to panic because my savings were dwindling as well. I wondered if I should go back to my old game to raise some much needed capital, but it wasn't so easy here. I couldn't just slip out *for a crate of beer* and take a little detour. Besides, the army men I had known were at home now, with their wives and girlfriends and some I recognised didn't even acknowledge me in the street, which suited me, as I would much prefer my extra duties not to be mentioned. Ever.

Despite our hardship, Mammy announced one day in late August that she must go up to London, and I didn't know how to stop her.

'It will be a great time for me to meet up with some of my friends and soldier-boys, my 'sons', and see what they can do for me. Look, there's a celebration to honour the non-commissioned officers and privates of the Guards battalions who were in the Crimea. I know most of them. I'm sure if I tell them how hard done by their Mother Seacole is, they will help.'

Mammy waved the *Illustrated London News* under my face so that I could not really see the details but I took her word for it. I wanted to stop her, thinking of the expense, but I could see she was determined to go. I was seething inside, partly because I thought she would be rebuffed, as in the old days in London. There was also the shortage of cash. This was the nearest I ever came to having a real argument with my mistress.

'How can you think of going, when we have no money even for more supplies? Some of these men have let us down already, and you know which ones, and you are going to mix in their company. Surely they will laugh at you or turn away if they have any shame.'

'Listen, girl, I know what I'm doing. You've always trusted me in the past, haven't you? And it'll come good, because my sons would never let their Mother Seacole starve, I'm sure of it. All I have to do is show myself, in my best blue, red and yellow and they'll come flocking. I also need to see Mr Day and go with him to seek out those who owe us money.'

'Let Mr Day see to that, if he can. If you stay here, we might be able to find some work as cooks or in the other sutlers' shops.'

She looked horrified at this suggestion. 'You know I've never worked for anyone else, except my mother, who taught me all I know. How can you think I would ever lower myself to work as an employee?'

She was truly angry, and I could feel myself growing hot, just because I could not make her understand. I said, as sarcastically as I could, 'I've heard there is an English phrase, beggars can't be choosers, and that is how I feel, Mammy, for how else are we going to get food on the table, if we have no money?'

'Beggars! You go too far, my girl, although I love you dearly, I just will not hear any more of this despairing talk. I'm sure my credit will be good with the likes of Cox's if I go and explain my dilemma, just wait and see.'

She flounced out of the room, if a large woman like her can be described as flouncing. She left me standing, anyway, speechless and annoyed. I could do no more. Her dignity was such that I knew she had made up her mind and nothing, absolutely nothing, I said would dissuade her from her unassailable confidence in her own abilities. Perhaps it was for the best, and I ignored her as I heard her dressing and preparing to leave for the great London ceremony. I picked up the *Illustrated London News* that she had dropped before me, and read the details. It was to be held in Surrey Gardens, in

Kennington and over two thousand troops were to attend. Perhaps she was right, and some of them would help her.

I set about trying to find ingredients in our depleted stores to make a nourishing pie for her return when I thought she would be dejected and might need cheering up. One thing I'd learned from Mammy was that it was no good sulking and it was better to get on with things and accept that the argument had finished. Like I said, she never took offence and I'd been learning from her for some years, so I would not be angry with her and I was sure she would not be angry with me, especially if she had met with some of her friends and shared a glass of porter or two. So I placed the finished pie in the middle of the table, with a setting of knife and fork and plate and waited for her.

When she did get back, very late, she said nothing, and suggested I go to bed. It was the way she said it that I knew I could ask no questions. She was not in the mood for talking. What had happened? I could not believe she was still angry with me. I tossed and turned most of the night, in a fever of worry that we would be turned out of our temporary lodgings, as poor as they were, in Aldershot and then where would we go?

The next morning, as I tried to make some coffee out of the meagre supply left to us, Mammy sneaked out and returned after only a short while. She said nothing but deposited a folded-up copy of *The News of the World* newspaper on the table where I was sitting, clutching my cup of coffee. I glanced at the headline which was at the forefront of the folded part.

I read the headline:

A GREAT CELEBRATION FOR OUR SOLDIERS.

Underneath, it gave details of the decorations in the hall where the celebration was held, and particularly mentioned a 'handsome trophy of flags and laurel wreaths, with Redan and Malakoff on each side and Miss Nightingale's name in the centre.'

My heart felt heavy. This must have been like a physical blow to my mistress, she knowing that Miss Nightingale was not part of these battles, whereas she was. When we both were. I read on, while she watched me. And then I knew why she had made me read it. Three-quarters of the way into the article, it mentioned my mistress, in the upper side of a gallery, as 'Mrs Seacole, whose dark features were quite radiant with delight and good humour as she gazed on the pleasant scene below.'

I said nothing, but when I looked up my mammy was smiling.

'That was not all, my girl. When the men saw I was there, they gave great cheers for me and then suddenly some of them headed my way and placed me on a chair, and carried me around the hall, throwing their hats in the air, and calling out "Mother Seacole, it's Mother Seacole." For a while I was balanced most precariously until two burly sergeants took charge and pushed the crowd away and carried me steadily amongst my boys. It was a wonderful day and I also managed to mention to one or two of them that we were in Aldershot and they should visit us, and they promised to do so. You'll see, we won't be forgotten.'

'But did you get to see Mr Day?'

She hesitated. 'Indeed, yes, but he has explained that he has a great deal of trouble tracing the men who gave us the letters of credit and claims that he has lost a lot in the venture himself because his horse trading did not go well. You know that is true, when we had turned our backs, that man he had hired disappeared with his best steeds, and that wasn't Thomas's fault. He is doing his best, Ratia, I'm sure.'

Again, how could I tell my mistress what I knew about this event? Yes, the man had disappeared with the horses, but I heard from some of *my men*, if you know what I mean, that he'd been seen trying to sell them to a group of cavalrymen who'd had their rides shot from beneath them and, lucky to be alive, were keen to get back into the saddle for the rest of the battle. I tried to trace the horses with the help of my friends, but in the mayhem of fighting it was impossible. I guessed that the proceeds of this underhand sale probably ended up with Mr Day.

'And if nothing comes of your plans, what are we going to do?'

'I have thought of that. So far I have been independent of my late husband's relatives and I know he has two great-nieces, Ada and Florence Kent, and we will throw ourselves on their mercy. There is also the Henriques family who I visited before we went; and I'm sure I can ask for help from them. You should never concern yourself that we will be destitute.

'It would be better if we were in London, where I can meet all my old friends.'

I remembered when we had come to London at the start of our Crimean adventure. Yes, the relatives she'd visited had been polite and helped her find lodgings but they hadn't taken her in to their homes. They also knew of her intention to travel to the Crimea, and had not helped her with that plan, either. I suspected they were relieved to hear it, not wanting such a determined and strange relative in their midst. I was sure that was what they had thought, although Mammy would never have accepted it, if I had told her.

Perhaps I am being unduly cynical and I know that's the first time I've used that word in this story, but only time will tell if I am right. How would we fare now, when we had no prospect of going anywhere? Would they be so welcoming?

Again I had to wait while she travelled to London on the train from Aldershot to make her visits to her family, and wait with trepidation, as I had done so many times before.

Her visits were successful – partly. A relative – I never discovered which one as she became quite reticent about her relationship with these people – found rooms for us close to Covent Garden. Although I was worried about the cost, I have to admit I was glad to be back in the large city which was bustling and, now I had more confidence, I was happy to go out on my own. I would watch the flower sellers plying their trade and look at the glittering theatres with their pretty posters outside to tempt customers to see their performances.

As I wandered through the crowds, or sat on the top of an omnibus as it rumbled its slow way along the Strand, I was always looking out for my Robert even though in my heart I thought him dead. I did meet up with some of my former acquaintances but I was very discreet, particularly as sometimes they were with their wives or lady friends. I would give a slight nod and, if it was acknowledged, would approach them. Quite often the men would guilelessly explain to their loved ones how I had been Mother Seacole's right hand woman when she was ministering to them in the battlefield. I suppose they took one look at my dark face and, not noticing my slender figure - but with a voluptuousness where it was needed – couldn't see me as a threat to their relationship, particularly as most of them held tightly to the arm of their man, now that he had returned to them. Sometimes it was sad to see that they were holding on to them because of the man's injuries. It was hard to walk without a leg. I also made sure I hid my expression in my large bonnet and ribbons which I had always favoured.

Of course, if the man did not acknowledge me, I accepted that, and walked on, sad that my kindnesses to them in the Crimea were now forgotten.

Mammy and I would meet in the evenings and she would tell me who she had met that day. Sometimes William Russell would visit and they would laugh over the times in the Crimea, sharing a glass or two of porter. Although Mammy rarely got drunk, she quite often became what I would describe as *merry*.

'You'll never guess what happened today, as I wandered up Whitehall after trying to see one of my friends at the Reform

Club – of course they would not let me in and I should have known that, Ratia.'

I interrupted her, because recently Mammy had taken to rambling a little, or going off the point and I wanted to know what had happened, in the hope that it would put funds into our empty purses.

'What happened, Mammy?'

'Oh, yes, we will forget about these clubs and their rules, shall we not? As I passed the guards outside Whitehall, they both nodded and smiled and I swear ordered their horses to toss their manes for me. It was very pleasing.'

I knew she always had a great imagination and I put it down to that, or a sort of desperation that she wanted to prove to me that she was still loved by all. I humoured her because of our relationship which was one of mutual respect now.

I had begun to think our life had settled a little and her visits to her friends were solving her money problems. So when the summons came it was like a bolt out of the blue.

Chapter 25: Dock leaf to cure the sting

The letter arrived when she was out and I put it on the little tray in the hall of our lodgings for her to open when she came in, but even the envelope frightened me, with its buff colour and official seal on the reverse. I heard her arrive as the day closed in, and she entered the back room where I was sitting, tapping the envelope with one hand.

'I wonder what this is? It's official – perhaps those medals I have are now confirmed and ratified.' She smiled as she said it. Some of her officer friends had presented her with a quartet of miniature medals, the same that a man who had been in the Crimea, and fought in the four different battles, would have received through the Army, and Mammy wore them proudly to any special event.

She sat down and, as usual, I went to the kettle to warm her with tea. As it boiled, I heard a cry from her and rushed to the room, thinking she had fallen or hurt herself, it was so despairing.

She was pressing her chest and held out the letter to me, her hand shaking. I took it from her slowly, fearing the worst.

It was more of a formal document than a letter and I read the main part.

JOSHUA EVANS, Esq., one of Her Majesty's Court Commissioners authorized to act under a Petition for adjudication of Bankruptcy, filed on the 27th day of October, 1856, against Mary Seacole and Thomas Day the younger, of No. 1, Tavistock Street, Covent Garden, and of No. 17, Ratcliffe Terrace, Goswell Road, both in the county of Middlesex, and late of Spring-hill and Balaklava, both in the Crimea, Provision Merchants, Traders, Dealers and Chapmen, will sit on the 8th day of January next, at one of the clock in the afternoon precisely, at the Court of Bankruptcy, in Basinghall Street, in the city of London, in order to Audit the Accounts of the

Assignees of the estate and effects of the said bankrupt, under the said Petition, pursuant to the Acts of Parliament made and now in force relating to bankrupts.

I didn't know what to say. Despite the convoluted language, I understood. My mistress was to be made bankrupt. I was horrified, and it was obvious Mammy was too. She had put her head in her hands before a great sob erupted from her and she started to wail and cry so that I was afraid our neighbours may think a murder was taking place.

'Oh, no, oh, no, how can it be? After all their promises, and assurances.'

She looked up at me, and explained, through choking sobs so that I had to guess half of what she was saying. 'I've been visiting them, the vintners and the provision wholesalers, explaining our predicament and they were all so kind to me, so kind, they assured me they would wait for better times for me.

'I know,' A great sob shook her so she stopped for several minutes. 'I know that they refused me any more credit and I have to admit that some of them recently were becoming brusque and downright rude to me, but I could understand that, and forgave them.'

I looked at the papers that accompanied this, and said, 'It is only Mr Gordon Ponsonby who has petitioned, and none of the others. Who is he?'

'Oh, no, he is the master mariner who brought over the remains of our buildings. I know you managed somehow to negotiate us away but you didn't think I was going to leave our goods behind, did you? He agreed a sum of £56 but said it could wait until we were settled. He did, he did, why would he go back on his word now?'

How could I tell her that it was some six months plus since we had returned and even I thought that a man might lose patience after that time when he was owed such a sum, but to tell her such obvious facts, would not have helped Mammy now so I let her carry on wailing. I always wondered how she had managed to get her tin planks, the wooden frames and preserves back.

'I thought my good name would go before me but it is not to be.'

All I could do was listen and coax her to try to eat and drink a little, to keep up her spirits. It was some time before the sobs had subsided and she was quiet for some time, staring into the caverns of the fire, as if she might find a solution there. I sat opposite, finding some sewing to do, which always calmed me. I waited for her to say something. She didn't, so I thought I must, because I wasn't sure, from those legal words, what it all meant.

'Mammy, Does it mean we'll be put into prison?'

I was terrified of what this new turn of events would mean as I had read a story about this very matter only recently in a monthly magazine that I had found. In it there was a serial about a man who had lived in such a prison for some twenty years with his young daughter; it was called *Little Dorrit*. It described how people in the prison, Marshalsea, starved if they did not have anyone to help them, and they could not get out until they had paid all their debts.

Even though it sounded a horrific place, I knew that, if Mammy went, I would go too, I would never abandon her. All I could do was read that story through and through to find some hope in it. Mammy shook her head. 'I don't know, dear girl, never having been in this position.' She put her head in her hands again, and I thought she would start the sobbing again. Instead, she stood up and walked towards me, and put her arms round my shoulders so that I had to put my sewing down.

'I am so sorry to put you through this, Ratia. You have been so loyal and now I fear we must part, if I am to go to prison.'

'No, Mammy, I will be there with you, how can I leave you? I think I'll be able to be with you and leave when I want because I will not be....' I could not say it, *a bankrupt,* so I stopped speaking, but it was also because I would start crying as well.

She sat down beside me and the old determined look came over her face again.

'We are going to find out what this means, because not knowing is far worse than facing the demons we know. Tomorrow morning, first thing, I will visit Willie Russell at *The Times* and ask for his advice.'

As usual the next morning she dressed in her finest clothes, and this time she wore an outfit she had made in navy blue that looked very military, with a flared skirt with a castellated edge in dark red and she wore it with a bonnet edged with the same navy blue, red and bright yellow, all the colours accentuated by the brightest white fichu we could find. I had to admit she looked smart, business-like and indomitable.

While she was out I thought I would make myself useful by bringing our accounts up to date, and I have to admit that I managed to show that she was owed money from some reputable officers, so that if anyone inspected Mammy's books it did not look as if she was totally without some money that she could collect. I managed this with a few more of my savings that had come my way. It was convenient that we lived near Covent Garden and Mammy was out for most days. I could rely on a few visitors myself during the afternoon, from my old customers from the Crimea and they were always handsomely generous with the gifts of money they left me. In truth, I believe that this was not because of the favours I allowed them, but because they, like me, loved their Mother Seacole, and thought this was a way of helping her.

When she returned it was obvious she'd had good news.

'It's not as bad as I first thought.' She explained as she stashed her umbrella in the stand, and drew off her gloves.

'Willie tells me that I will be examined in court, with Thomas by my side of course, and the court will appoint someone called an 'assignee' from the people who have petitioned for the bankruptcy to look into my finances, and then, if they find we can pay them all, which I hope will be the case, we will be discharged; that is the word he used, and all will be forgotten.'

'But prison, Mammy, will we have to go to prison before that happens?'

'Child, in truth, having had a few jars with Willie, I am in such a good mood I truly forgot the best news! No, because I am a tradeswoman – that is how Willie said the law looks on what I do – I will not be thrown into jail, but allowed to be free – and so will you. What good news.'

All smiles again, she was, and I admit that it was a mighty burden from my shoulders.

'Shall we look at the books now? I can prepare them for this assignee person.'

'No, let's go and celebrate. It's a lovely evening. If we take a walk along the Strand to Trafalgar Square we're sure to meet someone we know and we can have a good supper with them.'

And it was a mild evening for autumn in this country, and I could not feel guilty about spending a little money when I knew I'd done my best for Mammy.

It was still embarrassing when she was ordered to go to a bankruptcy court to be 'examined' and, even worse, *make a full discovery and disclosure of their estate and effects; when and where the creditors are to come prepared to prove their debts, and at the first sitting to choose assignees.* That was what she read out to me from the information she had received from Mr Russell.

'This does not mean a medical examination, you understand,' she explained 'I will be questioned about my way of using money and will have to tell them how I have been brought so low. Surely they will understand how I lost my livelihood when the Army decamped from the Crimea.'

She sounded doleful as she said this, but immediately changed tack, and smiled.

'I shall dress in my best and wear those medals that the

soldiers made for me after the Surrey Gardens celebration. I shall wear them proudly and the judge will see that I have served my country well, and truly hope he will be understanding and give me and Mr Day a chance to get ourselves out of this terrible trouble.'

I went with her mainly because I just could not sit at home and wait for her to return, not knowimg whether she would return or be imprisoned immediately. Even though she said she would not be, I could not quite believe it. I packed a few things in a large bag, just in case, that was how doubting I was.

'If you are to be sent to prison, I will go with you, you know that.'

She then hugged me, a rare privilege, and looked me straight in the face. 'Ratia, you are so true, it is like gold to have you with me.' Just by doing that, she confirmed my belief in her.

It was a bit of a let-down, the hearing. Mammy and Mr Day's names were called and they approached a raised platform, in front of the commissioner for bankruptcy, a Mr Evans. He was stern and ordered her and Mr Day to stand, to be questioned. He then asked the solicitor to step forward and say his piece. Mr George, one of the partners in the firm King and George, who Mammy had seen just before the hearing, stood up.

He cleared his throat and looped his thumbs into his braces and puffed his substantial stomach forward. He took a deep breath and spoke sonorously, as if he was at a funeral.

'Mrs Seacole and Mr Day are provision merchants, your honour, who spent their own money going to the Crimea and setting up a provisions shop and restaurant – called The British Hotel – while Mr Day also dealt in horses, selling them to the cavalry men out there who had their own horses shot from under them by the Russians.'

I was just getting interested in the way he described our way of life when the judge leaned forward and interrupted, 'Yes,

yes, Mr George, but we need to come to the main point of this hearing, that Mrs Seacole, here, and Mr Day, standing next to her – take your hands out of your pockets, sir – are either bankrupt or they are not.'

I had to smile to myself at the way Mr Day rapidly took his hands out of his pockets but did not then know where to put them. Poor Mr George looked deflated but he wound himself up again and explained to Mr Evans, 'Mr Day and Mrs Seacole owe money to all and sundry and the master mariner Gordon Ponsonby who shipped their British hotel back to England…'

'Pardon? How did that happen?'

'Well your honour, it was a makeshift place made of corrugated iron….'

Mammy leant forward, 'Excuse me, it was not a makeshift place, we made it very comfortable for our poor boys so they had respite from the terrible fighting they had to endure.'

'Silence, Madam, you should only speak in my court when I allow you to.'

'How can I explain things to you then, sir?'

'You call me *your honour* and it is court practice for the solicitor to speak on your behalf, so you cannot speak.'

Mammy sighed heavily and looked around at the public gallery and some of the men called out, 'Shame, shame for our Mother Seacole.'

'Silence in court,' intoned Mr Evans in a particularly authoritarian manner. 'Go on Mr George, before we have a riot in my court.'

Mr George harrumphed again before he started, and I began to dislike him intensely. 'The defendants claim that they are owed funds that will cover these debts but at present it is not possible to quantify…'

He got no further than that when the judge interrupted.

'I order they are bankrupt and appoint Mr Patrick Johnson to be their assignee to act for the petitioners in order to collect these debts, and make an account and report back to the court in one month's time. Go away now and I suggest you both co-operate with Mr Johnson and give him as much information as you can. Dismissed. Next case.'

Everyone sat there stunned, except for Mammy and Mr Day who both leaned forward as if they hadn't heard correctly. All the retired soldiers who were listening in the public gallery also stood and leaned forward. They started muttering but the judge said, 'Silence, clear the court.'

Her supporters in the gallery shuffled out, still muttering and I could hear some of them say, 'Pity poor Mother Seacole.'

My one thought was that Mammy had not been imprisoned. Although she assured me that she would not be, I had been doubtful and put it down to her constant optimism. But it was true, he had said she was dismissed, and we could carry on with our day to day living, and try to get out of this mess, as I knew Mammy would do. Then Mammy bowed and said a loud thank you to Mr Evans, who looked at her closely before I saw a little smile break his stern face.

Outside, in the courtyard near the Guildhall, soldiers crowded around Mammy and she was inclined to celebrate afterwards with some of the men she knew but I suggested we go home and try to find the papers that Mr Johnson needed to search for those who owed us money and collect the debts. I did not know who he was but I trusted that he had more authority than either Mr Day or Mammy to winkle money out of all those generals, lieutenant-generals, major-generals, colonels and lieutenant-colonels, majors and captains who owed her money, and force them to pay something.

This included a particularly nasty journalist called William Knight of the *Morning Herald* who owed Mammy over two hundred pounds which I was pretty sure he could never afford to repay, even when Mammy was allowing him credit in The British Hotel.

However, I had managed to prove from the accounts books that I had so carefully kept and from the information I'd gleaned from him that he could certainly repay twenty eight pounds nine and sixpence. I also handed over the papers relating to Captain St Clair.

Mr Johnson came to see me one day and asked me to help him read my books. He seemed an inoffensive little clerk so I did not show him I was a little offended and although I offered him coffee, I maintained my reserve.

'Why? I thought my accounts were very clear. What's wrong?'

He smiled at me, and that smile seemed to say, *we're not at loggerheads, I am here to help and I need your help.* He sighed, and opened up my neatly kept books and turned over the pages until he came to Captain St Clair's account.

'Look, here, the name, is it right? Are you sure you have written it correctly?'

Now there was one thing I always did, that came from Mammy's training when she was teaching me to read and write. She'd told me, 'Spelling correctly is important, you can use a dictionary, or ask people how they spell their names. It can be insulting if you get a name wrong. Just remember that the name *Smith* can be spelt many ways'. She had then asked me to write down how many ways I could think of but I could only get two. She then listed them; *Smith, Smythe, Smithe, Smyth*. I remember being astounded at this and so had made a point of asking people how they spelt their names, or, even better, I would ask them to write their names at the top of the account I kept for them.

So now I studied the open page and found that the handwriting of the name was not mine.

'That is the correct spelling, Sir, and I know because it is not my handwriting.' I explained to him my practice, and added, 'That's Captain St Clair's handwriting.'

He sighed again and I was sure he muttered, *oh dear* under his breath. I guessed what was amiss and would not rest until he told me, so I asked, 'You cannot find him, can you?'

He looked at me sharply and I changed my opinion of him. This man may hide behind a veneer of fussy officialdom, but he was also inquisitive and I felt that he would find all the debtors and make it all good for Mammy.

'I don't quite know how to tell your mistress, but not only can I not find him, I am now hearing the name everywhere, as someone who owes thousands to many. He is nothing but a common thief. There is no record of any such Captain in the British Army.'

My worst fears were once again proved; he had indeed, been a fraudster.

'Is there a way you cannot mention this to my mistress? She is such a kind old soul, she was quite taken in by him and she is already despairing enough.'

He patted my arm in a fatherly way, and agreed. 'You're a good girl to your mistress and I hope I can help you both to sort this out and I will merely say that he is one of those among the bad debts that cannot be traced. Thank you for your help.'

After that meeting I was glad to leave it all in the hands of Mr Johnson and just try to help Mammy keep up her spirits.

Because of my excellent record keeping and with a bit of help from Mammy who discovered where all her boys lived or, if not, what clubs they used in London, it was not more than a month later that there was another hearing.

Mammy was to be examined again. The public gallery was again full of her supporters. She had deliberately dressed in her dress with the jacket that looked like a guards' uniform of red with yellow buttons and her bonnet was bedecked with more ribbons than usual. I had suggested she wear sombre colours to show the examiner that she was serious about her parlous state but she refused.

'Don't be silly, Ratia, I have to make an impression that I am still an important and positive person. If I dress as you suggest, all will think I am in mourning for a close relative and they will certainly get the wrong idea then.'

So there was great cheering in the court when she stepped up to listen to the report of Mr Johnson. He said, 'I would ask that Mr Day be examined.'

That man came forward, and he too had decided to dress for the occasion with a brightly checked suit of waistcoat, jacket and tight trousers. I thought he looked gaudy and untrustworthy but then I'd always thought that and I wouldn't change my opinion now.

'Now, I want you to tell the court in your own words how you think this venture failed.'

'Well, sir...'

The clerk of the court jumped up and barked. 'Please address your remarks to the examiner and call him *your honour.*'

He turned slightly to face the examiner and started again. 'Well sir, sorry, your honour, I cannot remark on my partner's activity but I lost at least twenty shillings on horses in the Crimea, because they were either lost or lame. I trusted my partner to ensure there was good security but I couldn't be there all the time. It is true that when the Army left the area, we were left high and dry with a great deal of stock that we could not sell.'

Mammy listened to him and for the first time I could see a twitch over her left eye, as if she was burning to say something but was holding it in.

'Thank you, sir, I am sure the assignee will take that into account. What would you say, Mr Johnson?'

I have investigated the books and there are some good debts that I can recover. Mrs Seacole has asked in the meantime that you allow her three guineas a week to support herself, your honour, and Mr Day, two guineas.'

'Three guineas, sir? For the lady? That seems far too high.'

One of the creditors, I discovered it was that Mr Gordon Ponsonby, who was sitting at the front of the group, and, listening keenly had spoken and the commissioner looked sternly at him. 'Sir, please do not speak unless you are spoken to.'

He then turned to my mistress and said, 'That does seems unreasonably high, Madam, do you have anything to say?'

'I have my washing to pay.'

I could tell by the way she said it that it was the first thing that had come into her head and that she was indeed most stressed out, but she caused great laughter amongst the crowd near me and she, ever the performer, looked up and bowed, as if to acknowledge that she had made a great joke.

'Two guineas a week; that is all I will allow. Examination complete for now. Return in two months' time for the final hearing.'

He stood up and everyone in the court also stood and waited for him to bow and walk slowly out, and then the crowd dispersed. I ran down the stairs to meet Mammy, who was sitting outside, surrounded by common soldiers, who were commiserating with her.

When we were walking home, I said to her, 'Mammy, don't worry about paying me, as long as I have food and lodging for the time being, that's all I need. We must get the laundry done, that's important for both of us.'

She laughed but it was a quiet laugh, not like her usual loud guffaw, and it was so tinged with sadness, I had to turn my face away so she couldn't see the tears forming.

'Ratia, two guineas a week will be enough, we'll manage. There will still be some over for me to visit my boys and also my relations. But I feel so sorry for Mr Day who has been castigated and also has to live on the same amount; it is not easy for a man.'

I couldn't believe my ears, but then I sighed. Didn't I know my mistress by now?

It was a sad winter for us and it was about this time that Mammy, encouraged by some Irish soldiers and their wives with whom she met from time to time, started attending the

Catholic Church but I did not go with her after the first time. I found that the incense made me sneeze, all the kneeling made my legs hurt and the service lasted forever. In any event, it was a sombre sort of singing, not like the joyful sound we had made in my Jamaican church, which made you stand and sway, and clap. What I didn't realise until later was that my mistress was supporting the poor Irish who were castigated in this country for practising the 'popish religion' and I discovered that many ordinary English people considered such practise as being unpatriotic and almost treasonous, despite the Irish willingly going to war for their Queen.

Chapter 26: Preserves and guava jelly

Mammy was out a lot but came home happy and triumphant most times. She was tireless in her efforts to raise money and she told me that Lord Rokeby, with whom she had become very friendly and was one of the highest in the land, had come good and had promised to help. We'd known him well in the Crimea because he'd led the First Division and he spent many an evening quietly watching and listening and conversing with his fellow officers.

She also mentioned a Count Gleichen who I discovered was a cousin of Queen Victoria. When she first casually mentioned him, as if he were a close friend, I doubted it, but it was true. Then I remembered she'd helped to make him a net to keep out the mosquitoes so now he was repaying that kindness by being a true friend. I should always remember that Mammy did not lie, she embellished, but always there was that element of truth in it.

When we returned for the third hearing, it was a cold January day in 1857, but it did not deter her supporters who packed the gallery.

Mr Johnson spoke and I was very pleased with the way he presented matters.

'Mrs Seacole is a lady who, as you can see from the public gallery, has a great deal of support from the Army and it is true what she says that she helped many of the sick and wounded in terrible conditions and under enemy fire. I have examined her books which have been impeccably kept. There is one large doubtful debt of £260 from the journalist William Knight, of the Morning Herald which can be repaid to the tune of the twenty eight pounds certain, and the rest of his debt is considered bad.'

I rejoiced at the way he had mentioned this man as, not only had he taken advantage of Mammy, he had not mentioned her in his reports and it seemed to me that he was taking everyone 'for a ride'. So now the whole world would know that he did not pay his debts in full.

'Apart from this, there are about one hundred good debtors including generals, colonels, majors, captains, lieutenants and other officers who served in the Crimea. In addition to this, I hear from Mrs Seacole that she holds security upon two cases of saddlery to the value of thirty four pounds, one and sixpence.

'And finally, the famous Mr William Russell of *The Times* is good for five shillings and ninepence.

'I would add that this is not like the Crystal Palace Frauds that are also in the Bankruptcy Courts at this time, which was caused by out and out lies, but Mrs Seacole's debts have been caused by the collapse of the British Hotel in the Crimea, as a direct result of the end of the war.'

He carried on, intoning as if he was saying a prayer, but I was surprised at Mr Russell saying he owed something as that was not in my books, and I really wanted to say thank you to him for supporting Mammy.

Mr Johnson was still speaking. 'And I find that she can pay all her debts in full so I would ask that she be discharged from bankruptcy, along with Mr Day, as a class A bankrupt.'

He finished speaking and sat down. Before anyone else could speak, Mammy spoke loudly, 'Your honour, could I have my ticket of leave now?'

The Commissioner haughtily asked, 'Whatever do you mean, Madam?'

I could see he was eyeing her as if she was a specimen.

'Sorry, your honour, I find this place uncongenial. I mean my certificate of discharge. I understand that my friends in the Army are planning to support me with a collection and the soldiers will not pay their subscriptions until I am released. I've no intention to garrotte anyone but I would like my ticket of leave for the reason stated.'

I was truly surprised at this, I'd not heard of any subscriptions being collected and I hope this was not one of her desires and hopes that would go wrong in the future.

But she was not to be discharged just yet.

They asked that a Mr Robson be interrogated and he confirmed that he owed, and would pay up, for the purchases he'd made in the Crimea. I remembered him, he purchased lavender water and jockey perfume, being an effete type of gentleman. I never really thought he would pay up either but today was a day full of surprises.

One of them was that Mammy did not get her certificate of discharge on that day, because the Commissioner ordered us to return in three weeks' time, 'So you had better wait, Madam,' he said by way of dismissing us.

Those three weeks were hard for Mammy because she was desperate to start new projects. I asked her about the collection that was mentioned and, for once, she was reticent.

'I have learned through this process that I must not rely on promises – from others, not you, dear girl – so I will say nothing until I know it will happen. I am sure you will be part of it all if it takes place. If it doesn't then I will not have disappointed you by raising hopes that may be dashed.'

When the three weeks were up, the last hearing was somewhat of a disappointment. There were no speeches, just confirmation that she would be given her certificate, Class A, and it would be stamped and sent to her.

'What does Class A mean, Mammy?' I asked as we walked back to our lodgings, passing St Paul's. It was a sunny day so we sat in the little cemetery in its precincts, behind that great cathedral, for once enjoying the greenery and open space, now that the terrible ordeal was over.

'Yes, Mr Johnson has explained that, and I am very pleased to hear it. It means that there is no blame fixed on me or Mr Day, as the reason for the bankruptcy had nothing to do with anything that we did, it was just a misfortune that could have happened to anyone, and we have proved ourselves by being able to make good most of our debts. It means, Ratia that we can start to trade again very soon.'

'But not with Mr Day, I hope? Perhaps big ventures are too much for you now, Mammy, and we should just try to make jams and jellies, pickles and pies, that we used to make, and sell them at stalls that don't cost too much? Your preserves and guava jelly were always the most popular.'

Mammy stood up and started walking around the cathedral graveyard and round the great building, saying nothing until we stood in the great plaza before the entrance. I kept pace with her, and waited. I could see she was thinking and I thought she was going to be angry at my suggestion.

'You know, Ratia, I think you may be right. I am tired out now, I will admit. The Crimea took its toll on me, and this last terrible blow has made me realise I am no longer young. But how long will you stay with me, to support me with your wisdom?'

I took her arm, and smiled, 'I have no intention of leaving you, ever.'

Chapter 27: Claret, water, lemon peel, sugar, and nutmeg

The Class A certificate arrived in early February and it was only then that Mammy showed me an exchange of letters in *The Times* and once again, I was surprised at the turn of events.

Of course, I'd seen the witty poem in the Christmas edition of *Punch called 'A Stir for Seacole'* which was twelve verses of praise for her.

It began:
> Dame Seacole was a kindly old soul
> And a kindly old soul was she:
> You might call for your pot, you might call for your pipe
> In her tent on 'The Col' so free.

This was chanted to the nursery rhyme tune of 'Old King Cole' which Mr Russell demonstrated to me as he joined in our Christmas cheer, when we shared the claret cup I made out of claret, water, lemon peel, sugar, nutmeg and ice, the way Mammy had taught me.

We laughed and laughed as he recited it because he was a good mimic. I had never heard the old nursery rhyme before as we did not have such rhymes in Jamaica, just our rhythmic hymns or working songs so it was doubly fun for me, to hear these childish stories that English children were told, apparently before the candles were extinguished and they were tucked up in bed.

The last verse went like this:
> And now the good soul is 'in the hole',
> What red-coat in the land,
> But to set her on her legs again
> Will not lend a willing hand?'

Of course through our laughter, it never occurred to me that this might be the start of a great swell of sympathy for my

Mammy that would end with something so surprising, I would never have guessed it could happen.

But the first serious letter, that was published and which she did not show me until later, was written just a short while after her second examination so she had known about the proposals since January. But I remembered what she had said, she didn't want to rely on anything again until it was truly happening.

The first letter was written under a pseudonym, *Da Meritis*, which Mammy said Mr Russell had told her was Latin for 'a friend of merit' and I wondered if it was Mr Russell himself who had written it. I couldn't believe that a famous newspaper like *The Times* would accept anonymous letters. After all, it could have been Mary Seacole herself who had written it. I knew her well and although I truly believe it was not her, I wouldn't put it past her.

It read:

Sir, That good old soul whose generous hospitality has warmed up many a gallant spirit on the chilly heights of Balaklava has now in her turn been caught in the worst storm of all – the gale of adversity.

Where are the Crimeans? Have a few months erased from their memories those many acts of comfort and kindness which made the name of the old mother venerated throughout the camp?

It mentioned Florence Nightingale as being worshipped and ended by offering a donation of £20 - £20 - just imagine, more than I earned from Mammy in several years – and urging others to contribute too:

This is a favourable opportunity of showing an appreciation.....of Mrs Seacole.'

This was the beginning of an exchange of letters that became ever more favourable to the idea of a collection – some suggesting that Cox's should be the agents – as in many Army cases – and others saying that the money should go to Mammy herself. I didn't agree with that and thought what a good idea it would be for Mammy to have funds she could call on without having to worry about investing those funds or –

which I thought more likely – finding a way to spend all of them in new ventures that would inevitably fail. She needed someone to guide her but I didn't have the knowledge to know what to do with large amounts of money although I was good at building up savings from the little coin that was given to me from time to time.

Mammy explained that the collection could not have gone ahead while she was a bankrupt because it would just go to Mr Johnson to pay more of her debts and it would not encourage him to pursue those generals and captains whose purses were proving difficult to prise open and release the funds that they had promised and quite correctly owed. That was why she had been so desperate to get her clearance from bankruptcy.

One of those letters even referred to our time in Jamaica in 1850 and 1853 when we had worked with the Army surgeons with the outbreak of cholera and yellow fever. It was really true that Mammy's fame had spread and her whole life acknowledged.

But a greater surprise was in store for us. It started with the letters but grew and grew until she burst in one day and, before she had even taken off her bonnet, called out to me.

'Ratia, oh my dear, you'll never guess what the latest mad scheme is, and no, it was not me this time. I have met a wonderful man called Louis Jullien, and we must have him come for tea. He has been approached by my dear boys and he is going to organise a concert to raise funds for us at the Surrey Gardens. A concert! I must get a new outfit made and we can go shopping and I insist on a new bonnet...'

She collapsed into a chair and started to laugh, the old raucous laugh. 'Oh, what a great time will be had. And Ratia, I insist you also have a new outfit and accompany me. It's to be at the end of July so it will be warm and be light until late in the evening.'

Was she fantasising again? July was over two months' away. I put the kettle on, always my defence to give me time to catch my thoughts and work out how to reply to her. She came up to me and, as heavy as she was, swirled me around in a mock waltz and laughed again and exclaimed, 'We'll dance the night away listening to wonderful music and the military bands.'

Monsieur Jullien came to tea and I liked him immediately because he reminded me of Monsieur Soyer, a courteous man who was also business-like but I could see why he got on well with Mammy; he too was full of grandiose ideas. He gave ever more outlandish descriptions of how the concert would be organised.

He waved his arms in the air and made a large circle and explained, 'We'll have elephants and tigers. We'll string great banners across the hall, proclaiming 'Mother Seacole is wonderful' and there'll be one hundred bands, no, a thousand bands, and the combined choral societies of London.'

He didn't stop as I handed him a cup of tea and I worried in case he spilt it, as he still waved his hands in the air. 'The concert hall is ideal for it as it holds twelve thousand people – just think of that, Madam, and we can charge more for those who go into the hall but also charge for those who want to promenade in the gardens and listen to the different bands in the open air.'

I couldn't imagine a hall that held so many people and wondered if he was fantasising but said nothing.

And so he continued, until my head began to spin with Mammy laughing and clapping her hands as if the concert was already being performed. But when I was on my own and quiet, I began to wonder; was he so much like Mammy that he was being over ambitious and this hare-brained scheme would not work? How could he persuade the regimental bands to perform?

While this was going on Mammy was out a lot, as usual, and quite often came home looking strained and spent the evening quietly, without telling me what she had been doing all day. So it was a strange time, with some evenings she could be found, chatting away about her boys and their doings in raising funds for her, reading me other letters in the papers, and showing me her picture in *Punch*. On other evenings, she would sit dozing, her breathing heavy and noisy, like a person who had asthma, with the newspaper slipping from her lap. It seemed that both *Punch* and *The Times* loved Mary Seacole and were always mentioning her and her Crimean exploits and all that involved her now she was in London.

One day she came in and said, 'Tonight we're going out to celebrate and I don't care how much money we haven't got, Ratia. We're going to taste champagne and eat at the best chop house in the City, which I know is a bit of a walk, but we'll build up an appetite.'

'But why, when I have a perfectly good steak pie awaiting us on the range?'

'Steak pie, Ratia? Tonight? No, we're both worth far more than a steak pie.'

I knew something was in the air, and couldn't refuse her, so I dressed and, making sure we had the umbrella, because I was always ready for rain in this country, accompanied her.

As we left our lodgings and walked away from Covent Garden, I thought I would try to find out why she was in such a good mood. She had a mischievous streak in her though and I knew that she would not tell me if I asked directly.

'Have you seen Willy Russell today?'

'I may have because I've invited him to the chop house – and Ratia, when we get there, I will make an announcement so you will find out then.'

With that I had to be content, so I occupied myself by watching the passers-by and looking into the shops and avoiding the beggars, some of them obviously poor soldiers, with terrible injuries, although Mammy usually stopped and chatted to them before giving them some coin.

Because of this, we arrived late at the chop house in Fleet Street and it was full, with many men who perched against the bar in the tiny space downstairs, but Mammy marched through these men and led me up two flights of rickety stairs covered in sawdust, until we reached a closed door which had the word 'private' engraved on the frosted glass on the door. She pushed it open and as soon as she entered, there was a cheer, for most of her military friends, as well as Willie, and Alexis Soyer were gathered, and stood up as she came.

'Welcome, welcome, my boys. Tonight we're going to have a grand dinner at my expense, to celebrate a special event, but first, let's all take some champagne to toast the success of my latest venture.'

My heart sank, what had she been planning now? And where would the money come from? Since she had been discharged from the bankruptcy, we had depended upon handouts from the subscriptions that had come in, but Lord Rokeby, who was in charge, had warned me that this was drying up and cautioned me to keep an eye on Mammy's spending. None of her guests seemed worried about her ability to pay but then they did not truly know her situation like I did. *They didn't have to live with the consequences or try to sort out the mess.* I sipped the champagne nervously. Of course I'd tasted it before but it was not something I had taken to.

Then Mary raised her glass.

'Before the food comes, I want to make my announcement, so you all know why we're gathered and why I want to thank you all for your support. This is to let you know that I have written of my life and the book is to be published by James Blackwood in July – just before the benefit concert.'

There was a great gasp from all of us, with me nearly falling over with the shock. A kindly Captain caught me and held me upright as Mary continued, 'Yes, I have been helped by a great editor to get the book finished in time and it is called *'Wonderful Adventures of Mrs Seacole in Many Lands.'*

'Where can we buy it – we want a copy,' were the responses from the gathering.

I was truly puzzled, and wondered when she had written it because although she had taught me to read and write I knew that she didn't like writing and rarely wrote letters home. She could write when she wanted to, but she never kept a diary and was not one to put her thoughts down on paper, instead, she would insist on *doing.* To see her puzzle over a business letter was a picture, although when it was complete, it was quite literate. She would be sucking on the quill pen for longer than she would write, and that is why she liked the way I carried out the dealings with invoices and payments.

But I had no chance to ask her until we had got home, dropped by Lord Rokeby in his carriage. I had noticed how he'd quietly left the gathering and approached the head waiter and a large note had passed hands. He'd whipped us away then and Mammy had not even worried about paying the bill.

As Mammy struggled into the coach and I followed her, with Lord Rokeby behind me, I turned and whispered, 'Thank you sir, I noticed you paid the bill.'

He nodded in acknowledgement but then put his finger to his lips. He was a most affable man with a long nose and large eyes, and his mouth always seemed to have a little smile waiting at the corners, even though he was old. He and Mammy were very comfortable together.

When we had been dropped she said to me, 'I'm very pleased for the Honourable Henry, as I am allowed to call him, as he has just acquired a fine post as Major General commanding the Brigade of Guards. *He* is not a useless old veteran put out to pasture.'

'Mammy, you're not useless and you're not old. An old person could not write their own story, could they? They wouldn't have the energy.' I wasn't sure if that was true, but it was said to comfort her. 'Come on, I'll make you a cup of tea to wash down all the wine you've drunk while you tell me how you came to write that book.'

I was lighting the lamp as I said it and turned to her and I wasn't sure if it was the reflection of the light or whether there really was that old twinkle in her eye. She did not tell immediately but, when her hands were wrapped around her cup, with the saucer on the table, she smiled at me.

'Very well, I'll tell you, but you must keep it a secret. You know I've been out a lot and it is true I've been seeing my friends but it's not all been pleasure. I met with a Mr Stewart and he agreed to be my editor. After he'd seen my first few efforts he took me to one side and said, "My dear, you must work harder than this, or else the book will not be finished in my lifetime, let alone yours." You know I can't think what to write and sentences do not form easily on the page, although I know I'm good at talking.'

She said this without a trace of irony and I could only agree with her.

'So he made a suggestion. Willy knows how to write quickly and uses a form of shorthand when he takes notes to make his reports to *The Times*, so it was agreed that I would tell him my story, he would take it down and then transcribe it. I must say it has been a great pleasure to tell him of our older adventures and fill him in with our time at the Crimea when he was not with us.

'But I warn you, Ratia, that if you read it, you must forgive me for a little licence, here and there. I rather fear I have been bad at mentioning you at my side, now I come to think of it. My only excuse is that you are so familiar to me that I rather take you for granted.'

I must have looked most upset. I certainly felt it, but she hastened to correct herself. 'That is meant as a compliment, my dear, for I feel as if you are so much a part of my life that I do not notice you. I am always looking out for other people so don't see those close to me like you.'

I didn't answer her, but realized it *was* a form of compliment. She hardly bothered with her relations as long as she knew they were safe and in comfort or if she thought they could help her in her many projects. It was only when she heard they were in trouble that she flew to them to help.

I moved to clear away the tea things for I suddenly felt exhausted.

'Well, I'll have to read the book to see what our lives have been all about.'

It made her laugh and that laugh made me happy, so what else was there to worry about?

Chapter 28: Kind nursing and attention

I was soon worried again.

'Look at this, Ratia, our boys are being mobilised to India. There's a terrible story here about a mutiny. Women raped, children murdered and our men cannot stop the tide of Indian anger. There will be terrible bloodshed.'

I feared what was coming.

'We ought to go, we can be of help, don't you think? They need our kind nursing and attention. I cannot stay here when I know we're needed there.'

'Let me look at the report,' I asked, playing for time.

It was true; the Indian soldiers had turned on their English masters and were massacring the population, both British, Indian, Muslim and Hindu. Anybody who was pro-British, as I was shocked to hear.

'How long would it take us to get there?'

Mammy went to the globe and turned it. I watched fascinated, as she pointed out where the country was situated. India looked twice the distance than that we had travelled to the Crimea, with a lot of sea in between.

'Would it not be all over by the time we arrived?' I ventured. Mammy said nothing.

'And we have the concert to think about.'

Still she said nothing.

'And I think we ought to consider what would happen if we arranged supplies, and how we would pay for them, and if they arrived after the war was over, what then would we do?'

I think it had to be said, even though I was certain Mammy would explode, as I reminded her of her bankruptcy and her anger at the waste of supplies in our last days in the Crimea.

But she did not explode. She spun the globe again, tracing the distance from England to India. The island we were living in looked so tiny, I wondered how Englishmen had managed to travel to all parts of the world and gain so much Empire, and how they managed to rule the vast land that was India. She slowed the globe as her finger reached the tip of Africa, and I thought I knew what she was thinking. It could take us weeks to reach there, was there another way? Her finger traced the line back, hesitated and then went through the straits of Gibraltar and I watched mesmerised as the digit reached Egypt.

'We could get here and go overland, and reach the Arabian Sea. That might be quicker.'

I could see I was not getting through to her. The old glow was upon her that she seemed to emanate, when she was ready to travel again. Could I refuse to go with her this time? I would try one more idea. If I could not persuade her, perhaps others could.

'Why don't you talk this over with Lord Rokeby? After all, he's done so much for us so far, he would have inside knowledge about what the government is planning and could advise you further.' Then I tried a trump card, 'Surely, now you are so feted, the government might even sponsor you.'

With the knowledge I had acquired from her previous attempts to get the British government to help her to travel to the Crimea, I was almost certain – and I prayed I was right – that she would be rebuffed again.

She stopped spinning the globe and reached for her bag and gloves. 'You're right, as ever, I will approach the Secretary of state for War, Lord Panmure, and see what can be done.'

I waited in our apartment, and walked up and down in a tizzy of trepidation. I found that my hands were clasped tightly in prayer. I was desperate for her to be rebuffed, no matter how upset she would be. Surely a woman who was nearly sixty and her servant could not be expected to travel all that way and go through what we had endured in the Crimea? Someone had to make Mammy see this.

She returned late in the night and I could see by the way her shoulders slumped that she had not been successful. She didn't have to tell me. One part of me was sad for her and I reached for the all comforting kettle and tea caddy, but as the steam came from the kettle, I felt a moment of triumph and relief.

Eventually she confirmed my supposition. 'You are right, Ratia. You know what the Minister told me? That I'm *too precious* to be allowed to go so far, and that I must stay here. I then visited some of my most influential friends but nobody I met today thought it was a good idea for us to go.

'For one thing, they reminded me that I had nursed all in the Crimea, not concerning myself with their nationality and then mentioned something that I found totally abhorrent. In India, they have something called the caste system and no Indian of a higher caste would let me nurse them. I would only be allowed to nurse the English soldiers even if I went, and some of the Indians out there would consider me to be of a lower caste than them, just by my colour and because I would heal those of a lower caste. So, we are to stay in England, useless.'

'Mammy, you are never useless. Perhaps we can organise a healing clinic of some sort, here, in England.'

'All I ask Ratia, is that I be of use to my fellow men. If I am not doing, time drags and I find depression hugging my shoulders and forcing me down into darkness.'

Oh poor Mammy, I didn't know what to say. But I knew, from the many hours I sat and waited for her, after my duties were done, what she meant; I could occupy myself for a while, but the four walls around me would seem to grow smaller and the darkness of evening would wrap itself around me. I would mourn for my lost Robert and feel that life was hopeless. Until Mammy returned of course and then, busying myself with her needs, the darkness in my soul dissipated. But I could never burden her with these woes of mine, she had enough of her own. At least I did not have to worry about her setting off again on her travels.

Chapter 29: Cloves

But the next morning her optimistic nature had set in train ideas, and my heart sank.

She waved her spoon in the air as she ate the porridge I'd placed before her and expounded. 'Once we have had the concert I will use the money raised, to go to India without sponsorship. We did it once before and we can do it again.'

I sighed, and said nothing, knowing that the concert was some weeks away so I would think about what we would do when the time came.

After I'd put that to the back of my mind, I stopped worrying. I didn't have time, as I was eternally busy in a whirlwind of activity preparing new clothes, meeting old friends and spreading the word about the book and the concert.

For a start we moved from Tavistock Square to a smaller and cheaper place in Soho although Mammy stood out for an upstairs room and refused to take the attic which would have been cheaper. Our quarters were cramped but dry and warm, and I thought that anyone who had spent time in the rains of Panama and the mud of the Crimea, like we had, would think this pure luxury. I crushed cloves to perfume the air in our new quarters and to disinfect it.

I knew that the plans for the concert were forging ahead and for once it was me that spotted the huge advertisement in the *Illustrated London News* – although I suspect that Mammy already knew about it and was just humouring me, when I stuck it under her nose as soon as she entered our rooms.

A fund had been set up, under the auspices of Lord Rokeby, and everyone was busy inviting all and sundry to contribute. I was proud of the many pennies and shillings I managed to winkle out of my soldiers, but I knew that his Lordship and

Mammy for that matter, were talking hundreds of pounds being given.

The advertisement was so impressive, it was well worth keeping and I have a copy of it today in my memory trunk, along with the letter from the poor mother of the youngster who died in Mammy's arms back in Jamaica, and other important documents.

It was so grand, starting with a banner listing those who were patrons, headed by His Royal Highness the General Commanding-in-Chief – the Duke of Cambridge no less.

'He's a cousin of the Queen, you know,' explained Mammy and I was so impressed that I nearly stopped reading. When I continued I saw the list went on and on and contained the names of the Dukes of Wellington, of Newcastle and the Marchioness of Ely and of Winchester. In addition, there was the Earl of Westmoreland, the Countess of Westmoreland and the Earl of Euston.

I knew where Euston was and imagined this Earl living among the steam and noise of the trains that came and went but Mammy laughed at this when I mentioned it to her.

'No my dear, it's just a name they choose, because they have some connection with the place, but I must admit it reads like a veritable map of the country does it not? Look at the atlas; from the north to the west to the east and the south, all the lords and ladies of the land are listed there.'

That was of course another of her exaggerations but it was said that even Queen Victoria and Florence Nightingale supported the fund and the concert.

I read the description of the event, and realised that Monsieur Jullien had exaggerated only slightly, although there were to be no elephants or tigers.

'And look, Mammy, no less than eleven military bands are going to appear and it's going to last four days, and in the famous Royal Surrey Gardens. I can't quite believe it.'

I was staring at her I know, with wonder on my face, but she smiled a quiet smile of satisfaction.

'This would not have happened if I had come back from the Crimea a rich woman, Ratia. It is because these men know I have sacrificed myself to help them and give them nourishment and succour when they most needed it.'

'Yes, I can see that now, although I always know you are kind. You have captured their hearts – and their purses, for once.'

'I don't like that tone, my girl, it sounds cynical. Lord Rokeby will look after the money for us, and ensure all pay their dues, based on what we have done for them.'

I said no more but I kept on reading the advertisement which stated:

These bands will be supported by M Jullien's renowned Orchestra, strengthened by leading performers from the Philharmonic Society, Her Majesty's Theatre, and The Royal Italian Opera. The Royal Surrey Choral Society will also lend its aid, assisted by deputations from the principal Choral Societies in the country.'

All those royal societies – and I'd never heard an Italian Opera so I truly hoped I could go. Then I became perturbed and wondered if I would be included in the guests, because sometimes Mammy did overlook me and she had not mentioned me being included again since that night of the dinner when she announced the publication of her book.

The days became warmer and the concert was fast approaching and Mammy still did not say anything to confirm that I would be one of the party. I felt shy about broaching it, as if it was taken for granted that I would go, but I just couldn't be sure.

The matter came to a head when she was again talking about the outfits she would wear – slightly different every night but with a military air about them.

'Should I think about what I should wear?' I asked, as she placed the dress she intended to wear on the first evening against her body and studied herself in the small mirror we had in our lodgings.

She looked really surprised. 'But of course Ratia, I thought it was taken for granted that you would be one of my party, but don't you want to come? You sound rather diffident.'

I sat down on the one chair in the room and looked up at her but she was still preening herself in the unconscious way she had.

'Of course I want to come, but you haven't actually said whether...'

She interrupted me, with a sort of anger that I knew was feigned.

'My dear girl, do you really expect a written invitation to something that so obviously involves you? Whatever are you thinking?'

Then she turned to me and nodded, rapidly changing her tune.

'Yes, I do take you for granted, don't I? I just assumed you were following me all the time, the same as when we were in the Crimea, with the essential equipment that you handed to me at just the right moment – there you will be, by my side, at the concert, to hold my umbrella or shawl, as I parade amongst my boys.'

She came near, and held my hand in both hers, and said, with a sort of sadness.

'I'm sorry, Ratia, if I assume, but you are so much a part of my life, that I give as little thought to you as I do to myself. You must know that. I am repeating myself, but you must appreciate how much I care for you and rely on you. You must understand that by now.'

Then she gave that great guffaw, and stroked my face, 'Come on, we're going out *now* to find some pretty material for a gown for you. I insist we find a bonnet that does not cover your pretty face, because you have grown into a woman of stature and yes, you are pretty.'

I thought, there's always a first for everything and to be called *pretty* was a first. I swelled with pride and suddenly I looked in the mirror and thought, *well, I'm not so ugly and perhaps I am pretty to some people.* Then, with a tinge of pain, I remembered that Robert had found me pretty. Oh, even as I was delighted about my invitation to the great party, there was a sadness about my losing him, deep in my heart. I was sure that I would never see him again.

Chapter 30: Porter and pies

The six copies of her book that she could have free came from Blackwood's the printers a few weeks' before the concert. Mammy ripped open the brown parcel and as she did so, the closely packed books fell on the floor. I quickly picked one up and looked at the cover. I was astonished. I'd seen a rough drawing that Mammy kept of herself drawn by someone called Mr Simpson which I thought made her look bitter. But the portraitist had captured her here on the front cover – in her military-styled dress, and her ribbons flowing from her bonnet. She had that determined and dignified look and held herself in such a way that you could see she meant business. The only disappointment was that she wasn't shown wearing her medals.

'Oh, Mammy, can I read this now? Can I start this afternoon?'

She laughed, turning the book over and over in her hand so she could see the back and the spine. I think she was a little overawed by it as well.

She nodded, and I took the book to my room, suddenly shy to read it in front of her. What did I think of it? I read it quickly, because I knew what it was about, and Willy Russell had really captured Mammy. The way she spoke and told stories. The way she was at once self-effacing but proud of what she had achieved.

I didn't mind that she only mentioned me once, when we started our journeys together travelling to Cruces, and then she called me by my real name, *Mary,* not the name she had given me. I was pleased that she remembered how hard it had been for me to sleep in the bottom of the boat, under her hammock, as I truly believe that was the worst experience of my life, or so I thought when I saw it related in black and white.

Inside there was a picture of our British Hotel, with Monsieur Soyer at the door, dressed as dapper as he always was, and I wondered what had happened to him. Had Mammy remembered their bantering in the Crimea, when they had said they would open a restaurant together, and make it the best in London? I thought one day I might ask her about this, but for the moment, with the book and the impending concert, I thought both of us had enough on our minds. I hadn't seen him since the day of the dinner in the chop house when she had announced the writing of the book.

By the time the first day of the great event arrived I had of course read it through, and also the newspaper reviews. Mammy received a letter from the printers to say that it was selling well and she should receive royalties after one year. I asked her what this meant and she explained that in her contract she had been allowed a percentage of the sale proceeds of the book, and this was called royalties although she had received a lump sum as well.

As she explained this, I felt a certain uplift to my spirits as it looked as if Mammy would have regular income for the rest of her life, and I began to look forward to the concerts.

The Monday came at last and we left our Soho garret, as we'd jokingly called it between ourselves, to find our way to Kennington. Mammy said we would arrive in a dignified manner by taking a hansom cab because it was too far to walk.

'And we don't want to arrive dusty and tired out, do we?'

When we arrived at the gated entrance to Surrey Gardens I had to agree with her that it would have been too far to walk, along the north side of the Thames, across Westminster Bridge, and along the Embankment south of the river, where we had a good view of the shell of new Houses of Parliament which were still being built.

Mammy moaned about this. 'You know, Ratia, they started that in 1840 and look at it, still a building site. Would you believe that our great empire, stretching around the globe, would have such a disastrous construction? We could build something like that much quicker.'

I was inclined to agree with her but we were turning away from the river now and I was too excited to see the place where our great concert was going to be to worry about a partially-built government office.

The large gates were open but there were crowds of people milling around so when we dismounted I hoped we could mingle and find our seats without much fuss. Of course, it was not to be. Several soldiers, splendidly attired in their dress uniforms, recognised Mammy. We were soon surrounded by thousands of well-wishers and it was hard to push our way up the paths towards the hall itself.

Along the way there were bandstands and the military bands were already playing, their sounds competing with each other in a true cacophony. There were stalls selling pies and porter and mutton chops and fruit, and the rich smells blended together so that I couldn't tell what else there was.

When I first glimpsed the hall, I was astonished by its size. It had four towers at each corner and three rows of terraces so it towered above us. But I was not prepared for the sumptuousness of the interior and I was quite simply speechless, so it was good that Mammy was in her element, waving and smiling and greeting all she knew.

She was led to the main box, right opposite the stage, where Lord Rokeby greeted us. Everyone cheered as Mammy stood up at the front of the box and I thought this was what it would be like if the Queen herself was gracing the hall with her presence.

I looked around at the beribboned decorations. Mammy whispered to me as she saw me staring, 'They've decorated it with flags representing England, France, Sardinia and Turkey – and look, there's a huge representation of me.'

Everyone was chattering noisily and the din echoed around the large hall but suddenly there was a hush Monsieur Jullien appeared on the stage, looking quite dwarfed, announcing the first performance.

One of the turns was the opera company and they sang songs from a new opera called *La Fille du Regiment*. I couldn't understand a word, although the music made me sad and happy at the same time. Lord Paget, who was one of Mammy's trustees and who was sitting in front of me, turned as I sighed.

He whispered, 'Do you understand the words?'

I shook my head and the kind man took pity on me, and explained, as the crowd cheered and clapped at the end of the turn, that the opera was about 'the daughter of the regiment' so it was thought to be most appropriate, having resonances of Mammy's time in the Crimea. In the opera, he explained, a girl had been adopted by a regiment, but in Mammy's case, the whole army had adopted her. I thanked him and told him I thought the music was sublime and most appropriate.

'I could sit and listen to it all night.'

He laughed and said, 'There is much more to go yet, and I'm sure you will love it all.'

In the interval Monsieur Jullien joined us and he was very excited.

'We had so many people booking tickets that we increased the fee for tonight from one shilling to five shillings and we're still sold out.'

He took Mammy's hand and kissed it in a theatrical way and praised her. 'You are the most popular lady in London tonight, I would say even more so than the Queen. Just look at the crowds.'

From our vantage point we watched the soldiers who milled around. Many wore their red uniforms so it was like a sea of crimson, with little room between them. As newcomers arrived there would be enthusiastic greetings with backslappings and handshakes, then the crowd would part to help them to find a place to sit. There would be waves and clapping, and every now and then a spontaneous cheer would erupt. Even in the interval there was a mass of noise as a great chorus filled the air, and I discovered that the music was by Handel, and called the Hallelujah Chorus; everyone was singing and standing to attention as it echoed around the room.

After the interval I heard some more opera, from a man called Mozart and then there was an orchestral piece from a man called Beethoven. I'd never heard of these composers and I was transported into a totally new world where the music was loud and rich and deep.

At the end, it was difficult to get away as crowds surrounded us and Mammy asked one of them to find a hansom cab to take us home. Half a dozen young soldiers, who couldn't possibly have been in the Crimea, ran off in all directions and soon a cab was with us. We were helped into it and everyone cheered and clapped as we were driven away.

I sat back in the cab, exhausted. I don't think I had ever been so happy in my life. The music I'd heard echoed in my ears and made me want to hear more, and left me with a sort of longing that was sublime. Mammy didn't say much either and I guessed she was totally content. When we arrived at our doorstep, Mammy leant forward to pay the driver but he refused.

'No, Ma-am, indeed not. I know who you are and I thank you for what you did for our boys. I've seen your picture in *Punch* and I'll dine out on the story of picking up such a famous person.'

Mammy accepted the free ride graciously.

I didn't think the next night would be so good but it was and for each of the other nights too, with Mammy waving and the crowds cheering even though the eleven regimental bands were reduced to six for the last evenings.

As we left on the final evening, Mammy said, 'We're sure to have made so much money from these concerts I can well afford to finance my trip and go to my boys in India now.'

I had put this idea of hers to the back of my mind but the

whole excitement and happiness of the last four days dissipated and the worry started. Would it happen? And would I have the strength to refuse to go and make my own way in life without Mammy?

Chapter 31: Peppermint tea

Lord Rokeby visited us a few days later and was beaming.

'Now my dear, I have some very pleasant news. The committee has studied the accounts and we have made £228 for you. It will be invested but you must tell us if you would like us to buy a property for you to live in or whether it is better for us to invest it in good Government stocks so that you are guaranteed an income.'

I waited, I knew what her answer would be. But would Lord Rokeby let her spend this money in the way she wanted?

'Dear Lord Rokeby, if you know me well, you must know that I need to be useful and would have this money to get to India to help the poor soldiers there. I've already seen the Minister of War and he hasn't said no to me going, but I dare say he will not sponsor me. '

This wasn't quite true. She'd been told she was too precious to go, I quite clearly remember her telling me that when she'd returned, but I knew I couldn't contradict her and I just hoped that her plans would not be allowed.

Lord Rokeby said nothing but looked down at his hat which rested on his knees.

'Well, let's see when the money is available. At the moment Monsieur Jullien has not yet received the takings from the Surrey Gardens' directors who claim they are still collating it. I have to confess I was a little worried at what they are saying but we must trust to Jullien, must we not?'

I did not like the sound of this at all. To raise Mammy's hopes with a definite figure raised, and then say it hadn't been raised: what did this mean? Was it Lord Rokeby's way of delaying matters so that Mammy gave up on the idea of going to India?

He did not stay long but when he had gone, Mammy put on

her shawl even though it was a warm day and said, 'I'm going to see Monsieur Jullien to find out what is happening. If I can push for the money, we'll be able to leave as soon as possible.'

'Can I come with you? I've cleaned up and I can buy some shopping on the way back.'

She smiled as she agreed.

We found Monsieur Jullien at home and he ushered us into his drawing room which was full of papers, theatre bills, posters, invoices and scraps of material piled high, I supposed to try out for costumes. The walls were plastered with posters advertising old and forthcoming events.

'Madam Seacole,' he kissed her hand, 'How lovely to see you. What can I do for you?'

'I will be frank, my dear sir. Lord Rokeby told me there is some difficulty over getting the money from my concerts. Now I revere all those who have put their hands in their pockets and please don't think I'm greedy in coming here to find out when I can have the money. It is just that I have an important use for it and would want it as soon as possible to set out on another venture to help my poor boys.'

Monsieur Jullien looked embarrassed. He jumped up from his large leather chair and walked towards the window, where he fiddled with the curtain tassels.

'Madam, I rather fear that the Surrey Gardens are going to cheat on us and I am tempted to sue them for bankruptcy. Would you join me in this as a creditor, as we have to give proofs of what they owe?'

Mammy said nothing but the look on her face became fierce.

'What do you know?'

He turned and opened his arms in a gesture of openness.

'I have to confess I was so involved in organising a spectacle that we could all be proud of that I did not pay attention to what was happening in the venue itself. I now discover that several directors had resigned even before the concert because they were concerned about the finances of the company and it would appear there has been some fraud or mismanagement.'

Mammy gripped her bag. 'Yes, I will join in with you if you believe that's the only way we can get the money out of them.'

So a writ was served on the company and there were hearings in the very court where Mammy had appeared as a debtor, but this time she was a creditor. We watched the same procedure from the 'other side of the courtroom'.

A Mr James Coppock stood where Mammy had stood and on examination confirmed he was a director of the Surrey Gardens Company. I did not like his high handed manner, so unlike Mammy. She had been polite in her own way, although she did not know how to address the judge. Once she had found out, she had answered clearly and in the proper manner, confident in her own ability to pay every penny she owed. This Mr Coppock on the other hand, stood nonchalantly, as if he was leaning on the bar of The British Hotel. When he started speaking, he gesticulated with a wide-armed shrug, showing his disdain for the whole procedure.

He explained arrogantly, 'I do not understand why I'm here. This matter has been cleared up already as I've sent a cheque to Cox's, who I understand are the agents for Mrs Seacole. She should make enquiries of them, not take out writs against perfectly respectable English gentlemen.'

It was the way he said it, implying that Mammy was not a gentlewoman. I could see her half rise in her seat, but Monsieur Jullien gently placed his hand on her arm and when she looked at him, surprised, he shook his head, and whispered to her.

'Very well, case adjourned until October,' said the judge.

I could see Mammy about to protest – that was three months away, but again Monsieur Jullien took her arm and helped her to stand and steered her out of the court.

For once, she took notice of someone else and I joined them in the square outside. She shook hands with Monsieur Jullien and said, 'I do hope that he can pay you soon, but I will let you know when I receive my cheque. Please let me know if I can do anything further for you.'

'Madam, I am just pleased that you are not out of pocket after all the effort that your kind friends took to raise funds for you.'

We turned away, and made our way to Cox's that very morning, walking as fast as we could to Whitehall, where the company had their offices in Craig's Court.

'Can't we take an omnibus, Mammy? It's quite a way from the City.'

'Yes, you're right, Ratia, we can afford to take a bus in such circumstances. The sooner I get there and find out if that cheque has been paid in the better. I didn't like that man's attitude one little bit and I would not be surprised to find he was lying, even though I don't like the thought of an English *gentleman* lying on oath before a judge.'

I smiled grimly at Mammy's assessment of the man.

When we reached the agents, Mammy was greeted by the clerks like a long lost hero and they even gave me an affable nod, to acknowledge that I'd been Mammy's companion for many years.

We were sat down and offered a drink. Mammy asked for peppermint tea and I was surprised and worried about her. This was a drink we gave to calm the stomach and I watched her closely and I could see that the day was telling on her.

When she was sipping her drink the clerk asked, 'Now, what can we do for you?'

Mammy explained. 'We've just come from the bankruptcy court at Basinghall Street where a Mr Coppock, one of the directors of the Surrey Halls, where a concert was held...'

The clerk, a little man with thick glasses interrupted her, 'Indeed, Mother Seacole, I visited the concert on three occasions although on the last night I could only afford the gardens. What a wonder! Amazing music and very well organised.'

Mammy acknowledged the comment with a little smile and

then continued, 'He assured the court that he had deposited a cheque with you this morning in settlement of the funds owed to me, in the sum of two hundred and twenty eight pounds and I am come to make sure, and find out when I can draw on it.'

The clerk reached for a heavy ledger in the in-tray by his side and flicked through the pages until he came to the latest page which had some writing on it but the right hand page was still blank. He scanned the latest entries with his forefinger moving along the lines and stopped at an entry that was a few lines from the bottom.

'Yes, here we have it. The cheque has been paid in this morning.'

Mammy was jubilant, and said, 'Oh, wonderful. Perhaps we can discuss using that to purchase supplies?'

He looked up at her and added, 'Of course, we can't pay out until the cheque has cleared.'

'But I need the money soon. I'm planning to go to India to help my poor boys. How long will it take?'

'We like to make sure. I would say ten days.'

Mammy put her cup down and leaned forward. 'Ten days? Did you say ten days?'

He nodded, and added, 'We're extra careful with cheques from those in the bankruptcy courts, you understand.'

'Will you give me credit against that cheque?'

He slowly shook his head. I wondered if he'd been primed by some of her friends who I knew were reluctant to see her making such a long trip at her age. Some of them had been calling her, *old lady,* which she greeted with a dignified acceptance although I was sure she did not see herself as old. I could see that many did think of her as old now.

'Never mind, there's no harm in looking. Can we make an order, of the stock that I'll need to take and put them to one side, and see how we can book a passage to India?'

I came forward then in an effort to dissuade her. 'Mammy,

you've had enough excitement today and you look tired. We should await Cox's confirming the cheque has cleared, and then we can look at the supplies we need, don't you think?'

She glanced at me, and it was a sharp glance, as if to say, *do you know something I don't know?*

I didn't elaborate, and she stood up and said, 'Very well, I can see that we are dependent upon others. I'll come back in ten days' time.'

I took her arm and the clerk opened the door for us and bowed as we left and I realised he really did have a deep respect for Mammy.

We didn't have to wait ten days to see if the cheque was good. In a week's time Mammy opened the letter from Cox's with the bad news.

I was right – the cheque bounced. Mammy immediately dressed to go out.

'I'm going in search of my influential friends and when I return I'll tell you what happens, but I trust that dreadful man will be brought to book. He blatantly lied in court.'

'Mammy, think about it, he didn't lie – he said he'd sent a cheque to Cox's and he had; he just hasn't got the backing to make it good.'

She stopped in her tracks, putting her umbrella over her arm.

'Ratia that may be so, but it is not helpful to say so.'

While she was out I decided to look at our finances but stopped when I realised it was not good. We really needed the money raised from the concert to live, let alone travelling halfway across the globe to help wounded soldiers. The royalties from her book wouldn't come in until next year and my savings had dwindled.

I did not have long to dwell on my worries before Mammy returned. She burst in so excited, my heart sank. From her demeanour I would have guessed that she had raised thousands for her India scheme, but the truth was that her visits had been successful in another way, by confirming her worth to the English nobles she knew, even if it was unsuccessful in raising actual money.

'I can only describe the Duke of Cambridge as apoplectic when he heard. He sat down and wrote to the Prime Minister, Lord Palmerston, then and there and you'll never guess? Even as we were taking tea, a reply came back, by the same messenger. He has sent a directive to that Coppock man that he must pay me immediately. What do you think of that, Ratia?'

I was impressed, but I still wanted to see the actual money before I would be happy about the matter.

October came, the hearing came, and went and no money was forthcoming. Instead an investigation of the finances of the Surrey Gardens' directors was ordered. It was not good, there were hardly any available funds and many debts, and Mammy said despairingly, 'I truly believe we will never see the money and I feel sorry for all those who came and contributed, what a terrible, terrible waste.'

Then she changed tack. 'The news from India is not good, Ratia, there are such heavy casualties and there are only some noble ladies coping with the nursing. I must get there.'

She sat around the house for long periods now, writing letters in that laborious way she had. 'Now that the concert money is not forthcoming, I'll shall write to see if I can get sponsorship and not wait any longer.'

While she was doing this, she received another blow to her plans.

'Look at this, Ratia, a letter from Mr Day, not even the good manners to come and tell me personally. He has decided to leave the country and is going to the Antipodes, where he believes there are opportunities. Oh, how sad, I'll not have his support now in my India venture.'

I reached for the kettle, trying to hide my jubilation. I know he was a distant relative of hers, but my dislike of him had never wavered and I was truly glad that he had gone and left us to our own devices. His flattery would have swayed Mammy into some foolishness, I was sure. Now that worry was gone.

November was a long and awful month with Mammy meeting her friends and moaning about the lack of movement in the bankruptcy proceedings. It was not until four days before Christmas when we discovered the awful truth. The company's creditors, of which there were many, would receive twenty-five per cent of what they were entitled to. There was uproar in the court as this was announced but Mammy, for once, sat there, her face set as if in stone. I knew she was facing the idea that her plans to go to India would have to wait. How could she and I travel so far, with supplies, and enough to set up a little building, with only fifty-seven pounds? I couldn't believe that such a small sum had been raised from those wonderful concerts, and I will believe to my dying day that Mr Coppock and his cronies were crooks and somewhere they and their families had hidden wealth which should really belong to Mammy, Monsieur Jullien and all the other creditors.

To add salt into the wound, the money was not paid out for another three months and the only bright star we had was that her book, the *Wonderful Adventures of Mrs Seacole in Many Lands* was reprinted so there was going to be more money coming in from the sales eventually.

I had learned to be frugal and cook with the leanest of victuals in the Crimea and this stood us in good stead now. Money was always tight but it was made worse by Mammy being so profligate – she would say generous – with any cash that did reach our doors. I had to exercise discretion and I suppose a little bit of dishonesty to make sure that when funds did arrive I could siphon some off for the leaner times. I hope I will be forgiven for taking the odd shilling from the housekeeping and squirreling it away, and I was helped by Mammy's lack of interest in figures. But she was sometimes surprisingly astute and would say, 'I can't believe two bottles of porter and those vegetables would cost so much, Ratia, did you go to the market or to the Queen's grocer?'

It was said as a sort of joke, as she always tempered a rebuke or perceived misdemeanour with a gentle humour, and I felt guilty but I continued to do it, but with greater care.

Mammy spent a lot of time with Lord Rokeby and her other cronies at this time but I knew she was not planning the trip to India, and I was pleased that she seemed to have settled down and relaxed a bit. But it didn't last long.

'I've seen Monsieur Soyer and he's proposing that we run a stall together in a benefit bazaar at the Wellington Barracks. It's a really good cause, Ratia, and you must be there as well. It's to raise funds for the wives and families of soldiers to relieve the dreadful distress of the families while the troops are being sent out east. I understand that Lord Palmerston has now realised the seriousness of the mutiny in India and is sending out thousands of troops. If I can't be there, then I shall be useful on the home front.'

She handed me the leaflet advertising the bazaar and carried on talking. 'The barracks are just behind Buckingham Palace so we might be lucky and have a visit from the Queen herself.'

I read the brochure. There were to be gifts donated by many titled ladies, such as personally embroidered handkerchiefs or paintings. It was to last three days and I doubted if Mammy had the energy to stand all day for each of the days. She was tired now and often slept in the evenings.

'And while we're manning the stall I can talk over plans with Monsieur Soyer to see if we can run that restaurant together. We talked about it so much in the Crimea. That would be a good venture, what do you think, Ratia?'

'We'll see what he says, shall we, Mammy? Don't raise your hopes, we've had so many setbacks I'm almost beginning to think nothing will go right again.'

Mammy guffawed. 'You should learn to see good in everything my girl, and you'll see how good life is. Look, we have a chance to meet some of our old boys again at this bazaar and help others as well. The weather is warming and we won't have to stay in the cold so long during the day. I must admit it does wear me down, to always be wrapped in so many shawls.'

The bazaar was held under a huge marquee which covered the parade ground, now desolate as the troops were long gone to India, the marquee being decorated with flags hanging down at each of the tent poles holding up the great structure. I enjoyed helping out and seeing some of our former Crimean stalwarts, who were too old to go to war, but I enjoyed it more seeing Mammy reinvigorated, being her old self, smiling and serving customers and persuading some to buy when they were reluctant. All her old skills came back to her easily.

When there was a lull, usually about lunchtime, she and Monsieur Soyer sat on camp chairs at the back of our little stall area and talked together of the old times. They spent a deal of time congratulating each other on their feats in the Crimea but I said nothing, just smiled to myself, knowing it gave them both pleasure to remember that they had been *useful*.

Every now and then, I heard them talk about plans for the restaurant they would run.

'We can use your Caribbean chicken to set off my soups,' suggested Alexis, and Mammy would answer, 'I loved your ice cream,' and he would riposte, 'And what about your milkless rice pudding. A triumph, Mary, a triumph.'

'And we should order the best wines and champagne to go with the good food.'

They never really got further than talking about the recipes as if to be able to plan to rent a building, furnish it, and open it to the public would be too much. Although one day I heard Mammy suggest, 'We should call it the British and French Hotel.' Alexis laughed and answered, 'I think we should put the French first, Madam, and call it the French and British Hotel,' but when I turned to look at them to see how Mammy took this, I could see he was teasing her.

We were not only visited by the old common soldiers, but generals and Majors and Major-generals and all the other officers came and they wore their dress uniforms, so that the public could see that Mammy's stall was important and worth visiting. One of those who came was Count Gleichen and he greeted Mammy like a long lost friend. The ordinary people who flocked around noted this, because he bore a striking resemblance to his cousin Bertie, and was well known for being a relative of the Queen, so we managed to sell even more of the little gifts that had been donated than any other stall.

'I feel so happy, Ratia, that we're doing something for our poor boys and their families. It is sad that no provision is made for the wives and children when their men are away. We must make our healing skills known to them and help them with our herbal remedies when we can.'

From that day, we were constantly visited by poor women, every one of them thin and badly clothed, holding children who were usually malnourished and I became used to always having a pot of soup on the range and fresh bread in the oven. I also kept my old clothes and would sometimes cut them up to make little jackets and trousers or thick skirts for the children.

Apart from these visitors, the days seemed quiet after the excitement of the bazaar, and we both felt a little let down, not least because the weather became oppressively hot. You might think that ladies from the Caribbean would be able to wallow in the heat but this was different. In Jamaica, the sun beat down and bathed flowers that emitted wonderful perfumes, and it was dry and life enhancing, with the cool breeze from the Blue Mountains above Kingston, and the sea competing to cool your skin. We had waterfalls that sprayed the air and the surrounding thick forests could be cool because of the thick growth, and to walk along the paths was a joy. Here, in London, it was a cloying and damp heat that wrapped itself around you and made your underskirts stick to your legs so it was difficult to walk. I was constantly rinsing out our chemises and fichus which became black with the dust and dirt that blew around us because there was no water to keep it down. To walk along the Strand or Kingsway was to be choking in the dust that whirled from the coach wheels lumbering past and the stench from the horse droppings and the workers made our chests tight. I held up a lavender-soaked handkerchief to my nose to try to block out the odours but it was to little avail.

Both Mammy and I would hide away in our rooms with the curtains pulled to, in an effort to keep cool. Mammy suffered more than me, as her legs swelled and she found it painful to walk more than a few yards.

It was as if we were in a vacuum of swelteringness waiting for something to happen.

And then we heard the news. There were two items that were unrelated but both of them upset Mammy so much that she lay on the chaise longue and cried all afternoon.

The first item was that peace was declared in July in India, so Mammy would definitely not be needed now, even if she could have raised the funds, which I knew she would never be able to do. This was because Lord Rokeby, with the wisdom of his position, had insisted that any funds raised should be placed into a trust and the trustees would be himself and other great personages, and they would make sure Mammy's money would be invested so that she had enough to live on, but not to 'get into debt again,' as he kindly put it to her. I was surprised that Mammy graciously accepted the situation, but she later admitted to me, 'I'm sure that if you and I want to set off home or travel elsewhere to be of use to our men, they will not refuse us, otherwise they cannot be our friends.'

Going home, that was an idea that she had seeded in my brain, partly because I yearned for the dry heat of Jamaica, but also because we felt as if we were both useless, here in England.

The second piece of news was different but more tragic as

far as I was concerned, because a well-liked and generous person was no longer. Yes, I'd seen many good men die of battle and disease and closed many an eye and prayed over their lifeless bodies, but this somehow was different. Perhaps it was because it was so unexpected and it occurred when there was no war or disease.

It was the 5 August, three months after the bazaar, that Mammy's friend, Alexis Soyer died.

Mammy was disbelieving, as was I.

'He couldn't die, a man so full of life, how could it happen? He was so much younger than me. Oh, how sad.' She collapsed on the chaise longue and curled into a ball and her wailing was frightening to behold. At one point, she looked up and dried her eyes and said, quite rationally, 'We'll never have our restaurant now, Ratia.'

After that, as if the awfulness of life without Monsieur Soyer engulfed her again, she started to sob into her already soaking handkerchief.

Of course we went to the funeral, following the black coach containing his family with a large entourage behind it, to the new Catholic cemetery at Kensal Green in Harrow Road, a long journey which seemed to last forever, after the funeral mass in the Catholic Church.

After the awful ceremony of *dust to dust, ashes to ashes*, at the grave edge, we walked slowly away from the crowds, unnoticed, and Mammy said, 'Let's inspect this cemetery, Ratia, it is so peaceful here and the graves look so new, it is like a very heaven in microcosm.'

As we walked between the graves on the dried-up grass and the withered flowers – flowers that might have been a day old, I thought, but withered with the terrible heat we endured – Mammy leaned on me, as if the weight of our loss made her weak. After a while she whispered to me, 'This is where I would like to be buried. I thought it might be back in Jamaica, but no, this is the place.'

'You should specify what you want, then, Mammy, because who will bury you? All your close relatives are in Jamaica.'

She stood up straight, and said, 'No, I have my husband's family and some of them keep in touch as you know. And then there is the Henriques clan, who are distant cousins, and now we have a little more time, I must look them up.'

I was concerned at what she said.

'Don't you need me here, anymore, Mammy? Shall I leave you with your relatives?'

'Of course I want you here, Ratia, you know that. Please don't abandon me now I have more leisure. Although I truly hope that we may still find something to do to make ourselves useful, or else our lives won't be worth it, will they?'

Chapter 32: Incense

It was a dull few months which I called 'the Roman Catholic months'. She never explained to me, as was her way, but I could see she was thinking of her own mortality. She started attending the Catholic Church and would return, smelling of incense, and would sit quietly, her hands in her lap, and sometimes muttering to herself, as if praying.

As we sat companionably one day, when the nights were drawing in and I could feel the chill of autumn creeping around my feet, she suddenly said, 'You know, Ratia, I keep thinking of my family in Jamaica. I know I don't write often enough but there are youngsters coming along that I haven't even seen. I think it's time we paid a visit.'

In fact this was not unexpected, as I'd been sowing the seeds for some time, mentioning that our money did not really cover the cost of food in London. I'd asked around at my military and navy friends and would often tell Mammy, as if in gossip, the difference between the cost of mangoes in Jamaica, one of her favourite fruits and hard to come by in London, and the apples and pears I was forced to buy because they were plentiful here.

Mammy would laugh, and agree. 'You're quite right Ratia, when we can pick mangoes off the trees in our gardens, and we can't even get the ackee fruit here, to make our breakfasts, our island home seems like heaven compared to here. And how you find the spices to make our Jamaican dishes, I just don't know. Yes, we should return, at least for a while.'

As it grew chill in the evening, I'd refuse to light the fire blaming the expense of coal. Instead I would cosset Mammy in more and more shawls so that she looked like a woolly ball as they bulked out her already rounded shape. We took to wearing thick cotton bonnets indoors to keep out the cold around our necks and ears. Despite the fact that I was that much younger than her, I still felt the cold.

And when she visited friends, I made sure it was a house visit and not to an expensive chop house or wine shop, so that no money would be used.

Mammy did not like these penny-pinching ways and when she found out that I refused to open the door to the poor widows and others who came for succour, and I stopped making nourishing soups for them, she was really annoyed. Again, I had to point out that our funds, which came from the trust set up by Lord Rokeby and the royalties from her book, had to be used carefully.

I had explained it was because I wanted to care for her and, instead of arguing with me, she accepted it, or seemed to, but now that she had voiced the idea of going back to Jamaica, I realised she had been mulling over her options. She was not stupid, I knew that. There was one drawback to the idea - money.

'We need not worry about that, my trustees will help. You remember Lord Rokeby saying that we could ask for funds if we needed it and this is a necessity which I'm sure he'll understand. You want to go home, as well, don't you?'

See, she had realised what I was up to. She was right. I yearned for the warmth of my home, not only from the sun but from my family. The years had flown by and I couldn't believe that I had been away for over five years.

My parents were getting older and my siblings – I know, I've never mentioned them much before, but this is Mammy's story really so they should not figure in this tale – had written saying that my parents were ailing. I had an older brother and I'd always relied on him to care of them, but there were younger ones who I hardly remembered before I tore off with Mammy all those years ago, and now I felt as if I ought to meet them and get to know them, as they had babies of their own. Like Mammy, I realised I was not getting any younger and I had resigned myself to never finding Robert and had not found anyone else, so the idea of having my own children seemed so remote that I could not contemplate it. I had to look to the future and get to know the younger generation to work out who would care for me in my old age. Does that sound so bad?

So I helped Mammy to dress as she set out to meet with her trustees.

I had no doubt that she would return with good news. When Mammy was determined, nothing could stop her, and I knew she was determined to go. And of course, it was so.

'Yes, they have granted me the funds to take passage, and take you Ratia, as I explained you could not be left behind. We leave in three weeks' time.'

Three weeks! Typical of Mammy that she had not let the grass grow under her feet; she'd gone straight from the meeting with her trustees to the shipping agents.

'And we're travelling in style, Lord Rokeby insisted on it. We have a suite, you and I, Ratia, with our own rooms and a small sitting room. What do you say to that?'

'I'd better start packing,' I answered, and couldn't help a rueful smile knowing that we were going because our money was running out. Instead of choosing a cheap passage, and hoarding some of the money to set herself up when she arrived, Mammy would blow the whole amount granted to her on luxury.

As I packed, and Mammy wrote letters to warn of her coming, not only to her relatives but to the garrison commanders of the British stations on the island, I extracted my carefully hoarded savings. It was in English sterling of course, and I remembered when I'd come to England how valued such money was, and knew that many impoverished gentlemen travelled to Jamaica because the cost of living was cheaper there. I wondered if I had enough to set myself up in my own country, and stop this travelling life? I would have to wait and see.

I enjoyed the journey home, as Mammy met up with many of her acquaintances, of course, and I began to wonder whether there was anywhere in the world she could go where she was not known, and feted. We were treated well, and there was many a night when I had to put my mistress to bed, as she was the worse for champagne and other drinks that had been plied on her by those who wanted to show their appreciation of the way she'd treated them in the past. It was also a wonder that, as we travelled close to home, the weather improved. I had forgotten that the sky could be blue for days on end, with wispy clouds that dissolved by lunchtime, and I found myself divesting my mistress and myself of ever more shawls and undergarments. I even finished up with a loose short-sleeve blouse, and without a fichu, showing my lower arms and décolletage, in an effort to keep cool. It was a shock to me to find that, as our island came into view, I found myself fanning myself and wishing that it was cooler. I realised that we can never be satisfied.

As we approached the harbour, Mammy leant over the rails and started waving excitedly. I thought she had seen Louisa and tried vainly to spot her in the sea of faces, even though I didn't think I'd recognise her after all these years. But it wasn't the sight of family members that Mammy was looking at.

'I do swear, Ratia that the whole island has come out to greet us. Look at the crowds.'

It was true. Bunting adorned the warehouses and flags waved in the breeze and thousands of our people had little flags and were frantically waving and cheering. Was this really for Mammy? We hadn't heard of any famous army man travelling with us. As Mammy waved, the crowd's cheering was so raucous that it was drowning the sound of a military band that was vainly trying to play a welcoming tune. I couldn't even see Bravo's the ice factory's large sign, for all the decorations. If I had any doubts, I spotted the huge banner 'Welcome home, Mrs Seacole.'

'And look, even the soldiers have come in their finery.'

I could see them now, marching in their stiff way, their bright red tunics standing out from the other colours in the crowd. They came towards where we were docking, and formed a double long row. There was a shout from their Sergeant-major and they halted and stomped in that one-legged way they have, and then stiffly turned to face each other. An even greater cheer went up from the crowd as they withdrew their swords from their scabbards and raised them. I'd never seen anything like it before.

'My, my, a guard of honour, look how they raise their swords to form an arch. Oh, and Ratia, look, they're rolling out a red carpet now.'

And they were.

'It can only be for me, Ratia, because we never heard of anyone else so important.'

I hid a smile, as she untied her bonnet and waved it in the air, and another great burst of cheering rose from the crowd. I was so proud that all this *was* for my Mammy. *My Mistress,* who I'd served so faithfully.

The captain approached us as the ship finally docked at its resting place and invited us to step away from the deck and follow him. He explained, 'I understand the mayor, Mr Jordan, has organised all this as he knows of your fame. Once it is safe, I will escort you and introduce him.'

'Oh, I know Edward Jordan of old, and heard he'd been made mayor. What is the world coming to when a journalist can become such an important person, hey, Ratia?'

She turned to me and her great laugh could be heard over the crowd and I knew she was in her element. I followed behind quietly, hoping that I would not be caught up in all of the celebrations because all I wanted to do was to visit my parents and be in the bosom of my family. I really felt I was an old maid now, I realised, ruefully, not liking all the noise.

But it had to be got through and we waited at the top of the gangplank until the music ended and then Mammy was escorted by the captain while the chief engineer held my arm and squeezed it to comfort me. I tried to dignify my walk as I followed Mammy but did not wave at the crowds like she did.

When we were safe on land, she was led to a daïs where she shook hands with Mr Jordan and he held his hands high to halt the adulation of the crowd.

'Ladies and Gentlemen, it is my great pleasure to welcome Mrs Mary Seacole – our mother, as she is known – back to Jamaica, her true home. We all know she is famous in our mother country, Great Britain, for her medical work and nourishing support of that country's army and navy in war. We are all so very proud of what she has achieved. So, from all of us, I welcome you back and know that your fellow Jamaicans join in the pride of your fame.'

He shook hands with her and she bowed her head, truly in humility because I could see a tear in the corner of her eye, which only occurred when she was really emotional.

'We are now going to the town hall to a private reception and thank you all for coming.'

He lifted his hands again and then dropped them and there was a great sigh from the crowd and then they all started talking again, calling out 'Mother Seacole, welcome back, Mother Seacole.'

But he had turned away and was disappearing round the back of the daïs, gently guiding my mistress. I ran forward to keep with my mistress, as I was scared to join that great crowd of my people. Some of the officials tried to stop me but I called out, 'Mammy, Mammy,' and she heard me and said something to Mr Jordan and he nodded and waved me through.

We were led into the town hall and there I recognised Louisa, sitting stiffly on a high back chair, all the world as if she was waiting to visit a doctor or government official. Mammy saw her and rushed over to her and pulled her into her arms and gave her a great bear hug. I'd reached them by this time and heard her talking soothingly to her younger sister.

'Dear Louisa, this must be too much for you, oh, I'm so glad to be home. So glad, so glad.' As she repeated this mantra, she patted her sister's back but Louisa hesitated to return the hug and her arms seemed to hang limply by her side. I was perturbed by this. If Louisa was not happy about her older sister's return, would she refuse to take us in?

It was all a blur after that, what with drinks being served and us being led to a table, laden with high mountains of rich food, and assisted to take plates and fill them. There were piles of the mangoes we had dreamed about, with melons and bananas and Jamaican apples. Hot dishes of chicken curried in coconut, of goat and braised fishes on beds of rice steamed and there were plates of yams and sweet potatoes. I ate a little but did not know who to talk to as Mammy was in the centre of a crowd of local worthies and military men from the Up-Park Camp who had been invited.

Could I slip away, I wondered? It would be impossible, and another thought occurred to me. If Mammy was given too many brim-full glasses of champagne how would she manage? Would Louisa help her to bed?

I sat beside Louisa, who had taken a large plate of food but was sitting eating it on her own. She smiled at me, and, through mouthfuls, asked, 'Now what will you do, Ratia? You sure are grown into a pretty woman. Too grand now I suspect to work for me?'

I wasn't quite sure how to take this. 'I'll try to stay with Mrs Seacole for a while and see if she needs me, but if I need work, I don't mind coming to you, Miss Louisa.'

You see, I had learnt to keep my options open but, knowing Mammy, I thought I would not have to work for her sister. After I had finished my small plate I edged through the crowd and stayed by my mistress's side, keeping quiet and watching all the festivities. A band played but nobody listened to the music, everyone circled around Mammy, trying to get nearer to her. She recognised some of the military men and greeted them like the long-lost friends they were and I knew she was loving every minute of the party.

It had to end eventually and I noticed the crowd becoming thinner and I caught Louisa's eye. She looked away, as if she didn't want to acknowledge me, but I sidled up to her.

'I hope we can take Mammy back to Blundells tonight? I know she appears bright and energetic, but she will need to rest; I am sure this has been too much for her.'

Louisa looked surprised at the way I spoke to her but glanced at where her sister was leaning heavily on a military officer, looking up into his face, and laughing.

She replied seriously, 'She's aged, but she's still got that spark. I can't believe she'll rest. But yes, of course she must come back, and you too. I can see she may need a lady's maid.'

It was said without irony but I could detect a little bitterness in the way she spoke and I worried for our future. Louisa was not happy to see her sister return.

Chapter 33: Simples and sympathy

I was right. And who could blame her? She'd been in charge of the business for so long she must have assumed that the place was hers, and she ruled it the way she wanted. I thought it might be sensible to make myself scarce and let Mammy, with her good sense, work out a way to settle down with her sister.

The next morning, after a sleepless night because the old sofa I slept on was lumpy, I decided to leave early to visit my family. Mammy immediately agreed.

'Of course you must go, I have a lot to do. I can see that Kingston has deteriorated since we were last here but more importantly, there is much to do in the hotel to bring it up to standard.'

I thought I might warn her. 'Mammy, be careful. Louisa's had the running of the place for all the time you've been away, and might not like you taking over.'

'This is my home as well as hers. Surely, a little help from me would be welcome.'

'Mammy, I know you don't always listen to others, but I repeat, be careful. Nobody who's been in charge likes to be told they're doing it wrong, do they?'

She'd already started to spruce up her room, moving trinkets away from the sun and pumping up cushions. I tried once more, 'Mammy, how would you like it if someone came into your hotel and started telling you what to do?'

She looked at me then, that old sharp look that I hadn't seen for some time. She put the cushion down and sat on it, as if the stuffing had gone out of her, rather than the cushion.

'You may be right. Off you go, and I'll look after myself for a few days. If I need you, I'll call you.'

So I left her, with a deal of perturbation, to go to my family. They lived in a shanty suburb of Kingston and the road outside was dusty, with half-dressed children playing and skinny chickens rooting in the dust for insects. I found both my parents toothless, with thin hair and bent backs, living in the back room of my brother, Tom's house with his family. Now I was older, I felt a need to know about their youth and the hard work on the plantation, but it was no good asking them about their slave days, for they drooled through toothless mouths and smiled at me as if they remembered me. It was with a mounting awareness that I realised they did not.

My brother Tom was called from work by his wife, Ester, who was all smiles. 'Oh, your brother has told me so much about his little sister who has travelled the world, and we treasured every letter we received and asked the minister to read it to us, over and over. Look.'

She went to the drawer of her dresser and took out a tattered thin bundle of correspondence, grey and wrapped around with red silk. I liked her immediately and felt guilty that the bundle was so small.

When Tom came in, he welcomed me like a stranger.

'Mary, how are you? I have to say I don't recognise you.'

I stood a moment, wondering who he was referring to. I'd forgotten my own name!

'Tom, my, you've grown into a muscular giant of a man.'

I remembered him only a little because he was out at work and living his own life when I had left.

'My name's no longer Tom; I was baptised into the Baptist church when I married Ester here, who used to be called Tasiyah. We were baptised with new names and became Isiah and Ester to recognise our membership of God's church.'

I laughed. 'And I've been known as Horatia, or Ratia, for short, for all the time I've been away, so I'm happy to use your chosen names and you'll have to call me Ratia, as I wouldn't recognise anyone calling me Mary, now.'

Isiah was serious for a moment, and answered, 'Mary is a good name, but Ratia it is.'

Then he came towards me and gave me a bear hug, not awkward at all.

'We're sure happy you've returned and the children are so looking forward to meeting you. You will stay with us?'

I was happy to confirm I would and when the children came home, Denzal, Cordell, Beccalah, which I discovered was the pet derivative of Rebeccah, and Ben, I was introduced, in a comically formal manner, they all lining up in front of me and Isiah touching each on the shoulder as he gave their names. At first, they were all awkward. I even noticed that Beccalah played with a plait and twisted her foot inward as I had done as a child, but I soon put them at their ease and I spent the next few days looking after them while Ester worked around the house. I discovered that my siblings had done well, the same as Isiah, who worked as a carpenter. He earned enough to raise and educate the children, as well as look after our parents, and the younger ones were all away on the island, working in trades.

'We are all blessed since we joined the Baptist church,' he explained. 'They are practical people and recognised that, if we were to have a chance to succeed, we needed skills and found apprenticeships for us, God bless them. I now give ten per cent of my woodwork skills to keep our church in good order.'

He told me that both he and his wife could now read, as well. 'We can read our bible together,' he added.

But this is not the story of my family but of Mammy Seacole so I will gloss over the joy of getting to know my siblings and their families, and return to her, which I did after a week.

The reason I returned was that I'd heard there were queues of people at Blundells, all asking for Mammy to help them one way or another but my brother told me something even more disturbing.

'Hortense, the kitchen maid is a cousin of Ester's and she says there's almighty rows between your mistress and her sister. Hortense says that Mammy keeps interfering in the kitchen and cooking up her brews and spending money they don't have.'

I sighed. 'I'll have to go. Maybe I can help there.'

He grinned and agreed. 'I'll walk up there with you, perhaps you can introduce me to Mother Seacole.'

I laughed. 'You know, she's just an ordinary person really, just doing a job.'

He loped by my side, and stood in front of me, looking at me closely. 'Oh yes, so why do you feel such loyalty to her?'

'Because she's been good to me. She taught me to read and write.'

'There you are then. Just the way I feel about our church. I know she's special and I'd like to shake her hand.'

When we reached Blundells, it was still early morning and all seemed calm. There was Mammy sitting in a rocking chair on the veranda, chopping up vegetables. By her side were cloth bags and a pestle and mortar. I recognised what she'd been doing; preparing her special herbs and medicines. She looked up as we reached the steps and her face lit up.

'Ratia! How are you?'

I nodded to show I was well, and introduced my brother. She smiled at him and stood to shake his hand.

'You know, sir, I could not have done what I've done without your sister. She has been a great support and, dare I say it, friend and companion.'

I could feel that old blush under my skin but I was so pleased and my brother looked at me, pride in his stance.

'Yes, we sure have missed her. Although I understand she was a naughty and rebellious child. But she is a grown lady now, like you Ma-am, and I thank you for that.'

Mammy looked at me then as if surprised, but the great laugh came, 'Yes, you know, I do believe she is *a lady* and she's certainly in charge of me now, what do you say to that?'

I protested, but both of them were enjoying the mutual admiration so I let it go.

'Mammy, have you had tea? Shall I get you some?'

She sat down and leaned back, 'No, not for the moment. I'll finish this and then we'll go inside to sort some matters. It was sure good to meet you, sir.'

My brother was dismissed and I sat down on the steps, helping myself to the pestle and mortar and choosing some leaves to crush and grind.

'You know, Ratia, you were right. I have to be careful here.' She said it quietly, as if she didn't want to admit it.

'But what I will do is make myself useful and I'm sure things will settle down. I've spoken to Louisa about you and told her how good you are, but she remembers what you were like as a child and that opinion has not changed. She thinks that you're a flighty thing that will only cause trouble, but I assured her you'd matured, so we will have to talk to her and you must be discreet and prove your worth.'

I nodded. I'd known Louisa wouldn't be good news. She didn't have the unconditional love and generosity in her that Mammy had, which had endeared her to everyone. Perhaps her life had been hard, trying to run the hotel on her own.

It wasn't long before I discovered why she resented Mammy being there.

It was in the kitchen that the argument started, when they were skirting around each other preparing the dinner for a greater number of guests than was usual and I was helping young Hortense with the vegetables.

'I think it's because I'm here, Louisa, they all want to see me.'

'Oh, don't be so big-headed. It's the season, it's my oxtail soup, it's the beef I braise, that they like.' She pushed past Mammy's bulk, and added, 'Why should everything revolve around you?'

Mammy sat down, seemingly winded by the barbed comment. After a deep breath, she answered, 'Louisa, you sure sound bitter. Sit down, let us share some tea and we can talk about this. I don't mean to sound my own trumpet.' I coughed as I put the kettle on, hoping that if I did this, Louisa would join her sister, but instead she snapped, 'That's right, a good English cup of tea will solve everything. We must get this dinner prepared before we rest.'

'Miss Louisa, we can do this, while the kettle's boiling. You and your sister go into the parlour and I'll bring you some tea.'

To my surprise, she stared at me, and I thought for a minute she was going to snap back, but her mouth tightened into a thin line, as if she was forcing herself not to answer a servant. But she stopped staring at me, turned and walked out of the kitchen and Mammy muttered, 'Thanks, Ratia,' and followed her.

I laid the tray, carefully, with napkins and cut up some of the ginger cake that I'd made that morning. I tapped on the closed door as I thought there would be some delicacy in interrupting these two women.

They were sitting opposite each other, one plump and kindly, the other tall and upright, without any spare flesh at all. They said nothing as I put down the tray and I left the room, leaving the door ajar and leant against the wall in the hall where I could see through the gap.

There was the chink of cups and tea being served and I could feel the tension even from outside the room. It felt worse than any of the battles that we'd fought – they had been all out in the open and obvious. This was unknown and insidious.

Mammy spoke first. 'I'm sorry you resent me coming back, Louisa, but I own part of this business, and we must learn to work together. You know that. But what is eating you up? Why are you so angry?'

Again, the chink of cups and no answer. Then the bitterness came out in a sort of wail. 'Why did you leave Edward to die in that God forsaken country? Why didn't you stay and heal him?'

'What?'

Mammy's exclamation showed that she was genuinely surprised and so was I.

'And now I have his woman here, in a hut down the road, with his son to feed. *She* told me what you'd done.'

'I'm sorry, what was I supposed to have done?'

'You left him to die. You could have stayed and she saw how you cured all the others there. If you'd stayed…'

'But Louisa, I kept asking him to come with me, and he wouldn't. My enterprises were failing, I wasn't making any money, and nor was he at the end. I swear this is true.'

'Well she sees it differently. And she is a burden to me.'

Mammy didn't answer immediately and then she said, in a pondering sort of way, 'I have noticed that people perceive of actions in different ways. For instance, one country will say they have been attacked when the attacking country will say they are rescuing the people from bondage. It is impossible to reconcile. This lady may truly believe that is what I did but my understanding is different. How can we reconcile this?'

There was no answer from Louisa, and I could imagine her being very surprised at the way Mammy had answered her. Mammy spoke again.

'Would it help if I met this woman, and tried to assist with her son?'

I didn't hear any more because I heard a scraping near me and noticed that Hortense was watching me, her white eyes standing our from her dark face, so I headed towards her and asked her imperiously what she was doing hanging about. She scuttled back into the kitchen, not answering me, not having the nerve to ask me the same thing, so I asked her how long she'd been there.

'I don't know, Ma-am, not long.' she said, with a sort of bow. She had thick hair tied in many bunches with scraps of old cloth and I noticed she played with one of them as she answered. I recognised myself in her and smiled. 'Hortense, that's a good name. My name is Horatia, and I used to be the skivvy here, like you, but now I'm a companion. We're related you know.' And I named my brother's wife. The girl brightened and nodded, and I thought I would give her some encouragement. 'If you're a good girl like me, you'll maybe grow into a companion one day.'

We understood each other; we were servants but curious about our masters. So we became friends, Hortense and I.

I went with my mistress to visit Ann, the woman that Edward had loved and refused to leave. She was a small, bronze woman with the almond-shaped eyes, thick lips and long nose of a native of the Americas. She greeted Mammy with dignity and led us into the small room she lived in. There were rolls of mattresses tidy in a corner and a low table in the middle of the room with hardly any space to move around it. She gestured for us to sit on the mattress rolls for there were no chairs.

Mammy said, 'Sorry, I'm not being rude but I'd rather stand. If I sit that low I won't be able to get up again.' She smiled as she said it and the woman shrugged and also remained standing.

'I've come to see if you need any help. I understand my sister has assisted you but if there is anything I can do, you must let me know.'

The woman said nothing and I could not work out what she felt. Her face remained still. It reminded me of the natives we had seen in Panama, who had always seemed impassive, despite watching us, crouched down and wrapped in their blankets against the incessant rain, their eyes half-closed.

'You must know that I am a doctress and can help if anyone is ill, so you can always call on me in that way.'

The woman nodded now but remained impassive.

I could tell Mammy was becoming exasperated. She did not like silent people, it frightened her. She was used to loud conversation and laughter, to straight talking. That's why she liked the army and navy men who could be counted on to talk once they had a taken a grog of rum or a pint of beer.

'There must be something I can do to help, I can't offer you a larger home but perhaps I can help your boy in some way?'

I saw the woman move, infinitesimally, and realised Mammy had hit on something.

'Perhaps I can help to educate him? So he can find a good profession when he is older?'

She spoke at last, with a thick accent. 'Yes, that would be good. He could go to the Catholic school, but he's not baptised. I never had the nerve to approach the priest.'

At last, I could see how Mammy could help and so did she.

'Of course, I am happy to sponsor him in that way and will make sure he gets to school. What is his name?'

'I named him Edward, after his father. He agreed. He was good to me, your brother, he wouldn't leave me.'

Mammy looked away and for once I thought she had regrets, but, like the good soul she was, she agreed with Edward's woman.

'Yes, he was a good man.'

I didn't countenance all this Catholic mumbo-jumbo that Mammy was involved in, my family had now become ardent Baptists, and I liked the straightforward way of worshipping, with joyful singing and clapping. I'd learned from my brothers that the Baptist ministers had been more than practical in helping my people, not only in training them so they had good jobs but helping them in negotiating land from the plantation owners. They helped those who bought the land to earn a living from the land. I didn't think the Catholics did anything like that, although I have to admit I didn't know.

Mammy was as good as her word and visited the Catholic priest and it was all arranged. So on a warm day in July, Edward Ambleton, aged ten now, was baptised with the name Edward Ambleton Seacoll, just to show he had the same name as the famous doctress, although I found out later that they'd spelt Mammy's name wrong when registering the baptism. He started to attend the school nearby. He was a good looking lad and keen. He was also courteous and I begin to admire his mother for that, for, as he passed by, if we were sitting on the veranda, he would stop and ask us how we were and tell us naughty stories of the teachers, which made Mammy roar with laughter.

He was so unlike the other boy from England that Mammy had also sponsored, a few months' before, who was on the legitimate side of her family, Christopher Henricks Seacole. Once the ceremony was over, he returned to the bosom of his family and hardly ever visited. He was related to the Henriques who lived in England but I never did fathom Mammy's extended family, and I think she too was probably vague about how they were all related. When we first met him, a few months after his baptism, Christopher was thirteen, and had the bloom of his first growth of beard on his face, so Mammy excused him by saying, 'It's a shame he's not a child anymore, for then he would have loved to sit and listen to our old women's stories. But a youngster of that age is building his own life, Ratia, and has no time for us old ones. Give him time, and when he has his own family, he'll want to introduce them to us and ask us to tell the little one of our exploits, you wait and see.'

I think she was right, because my nieces and nephews always clamoured for me to tell them the story of the wicked American who tried to cheat us and how I stopped him by counting the eggshells under the table. They also enjoyed the tale of how we built a hotel with our bare hands. I might have exaggerated a bit here and there but it was such a joy to see their upturned faces and open mouths. As I told these stories, I couldn't quite believe what I had experienced and felt that I had at last come home and was at peace.

Chapter 34: Camomile tea compresses

I revelled in looking after Mammy and helping her on the odd visit to sick people, chatting to her, and being with my family.

Christmas came and went and, after Mammy went to the Catholic Church and I went to the Baptist chapel to celebrate on Christmas Day, we all joined in the Jonkanoo, with Mammy helping her nephew Edward to make a grotesque mask so he could join in the dancing on Boxing Day. I found rags and old tin drums and made colourful costumes for the children in our family and was surprised when all the adults came out in grotesque costumes as well. I'd been away so long I'd forgotten how exciting and colourful this festival was, and that it wasn't just for children. I sat with Mammy on the veranda of New Blundells House and watched as the parade passed by, with whistles and tin drums making such a cacophony that we had to cover our ears. I could feel my foot tapping but thought I was now too matronly to join in the wild cavorting.

A few months later Carnival was celebrated in a similar manner but in the meantime all was calm.

It was during this time that I met someone and finally forgot about my Robert. Phineas was a friend of my brother's, although he did not worship at the Baptist chapel. He ran a grocery shop in the high town of Kingston and was a widower who had no children. I found myself going to his store more and more and he would put a chair out for me at the counter, and listen as I told him my stories. He was a light brown Creole whose mother had been a Jew lady. He was lithe from humping the sacks of malt and cereals and grain that he sold by the pound.

I wasn't surprised when he suggested we go to the Baptist minister and ask to be married. I agreed at once. Ours was a relationship based on friendship and understanding. His mixed parentage gave him an understanding of others so that he was tolerant and kindly but he was also inquisitive about the rest of the world, and indulged me by listening to my experiences.

After we had spoken to the Baptist minister, he did surprise me by saying he would like to get married in the synagogue as well and I was happy to do that for him.

'But I warn you, if Mammy needs me, I'll be there.'

He kissed me on the nose, kindly, and smiled as he said, 'Mrs Seacole helped my parents in the yellow fever epidemic so if she needs you, you go. I know you'll come back to me.'

As he said it, I thought again, is there anyone anywhere who doesn't have something to thank Mammy for?

When I assured Mammy that I would still be able to help her she was thoughtful at first, and insisted on meeting Phineas. So I took her to his shop and while they sat and talked, I busied myself serving customers which I really enjoyed. It reminded me of the days in the British Hotel at Spring Hill, and I knew I was doing the right thing by marrying Phineas.

So I had my wedding and then settled down to serving in the shop in the mornings and when it got too hot in the afternoons I would visit Mammy, or my nieces and nephews, with church on Sundays. Phineas explained that Friday night suppers were a special time for his family, when they all met so we invited Mammy and my family on Fridays and it was with pride that I lit candles and offered wine to my guests around my own dining room table. *I could get used to this life,* I thought, and did not worry about Mammy so much.

Or perhaps it was because Mammy never mentioned what was going on inside the hotel. I rarely visited the kitchen or the living quarters, now that I was a married woman. I was just pleased to bask in the warmth of the shaded veranda, helping Mammy to roll bandages, or mix herbs, or just quietly reminiscing with her. I knew I was a great help to her because, although she would never admit it, her eyesight was getting bad. I would venture into the kitchen when Louisa was not around and make her a camomile tea compress which she found soothed her eyes. They were not so bad that she couldn't see long distance, but she squinted at close things and, one day when I saw her moving the newspaper from one side to another, holding it close and then a long way away, I volunteered to read it for her and she smiled and agreed.

'That would be a good idea, as they seem to be making these newspapers with ever smaller print.'

I could see she was being ironic and I didn't answer, but started to read the main stories on the front page and carried on until I had finished the last item.

One of the items of news that she was particularly pleased to hear about was that her old friend, Edward Jordan, received a knighthood.

'Fancy, the first Black Jamaican to be so feted. Ratia, what wonderful news.'

But after saying that, she seemed to sink into a reverie and I stopped reading, thinking she was dozing, but she waved me to continue. I wondered if she was pondering that, despite those four small medals she had been given by her friends, she had never been publicly rewarded for all she had done in the Crimea. I didn't ever mention it and I was sure that Mammy would not let it rankle with her for too long, but hearing of another Jamaican being so lauded must have made her reflect.

'Maybe one day our people will govern this island without the help of Britain. I'm sure they are capable of it, what do you think?'

I shrugged. I'd never been interested in politics but Mammy always kept a keen watch on what was going on, even though she kept a foot in both camps. What I mean by that is she visited Mr Jordan and his friends, and even became friendly with our Baptist deacon, Paul Bogle, but at the same time, she was a welcome visitor to the British Governor Edward Eyre. She never discriminated either between rich and poor, or between the Jamaican locals and the British 'overlords'.

So our days settled down into a dull routine of visits, preparing remedies, and resting, all of which I enjoyed but, if there wasn't some healing emergency that Mammy was called to, in a few days she would begin to get restless.

She came seeking me once and I introduced her to the members of my family she had not yet met, who all embarrassed me by bowing to her. My sister-in-law, who was a quiet sensible woman, even tried a curtsey, but Mammy laughed, and put them at their ease.

I could see though she was bursting to tell me something so I said I'd walk back to the hotel with her.

When we were out of earshot, she took my arm and told me. 'I've been invited to meet the Queen of Hawaii. What do you think of that?'

Before I could answer she added, 'And you'll have to help me, and quickly, to make a new outfit. With my eyes, I couldn't do the fine needlework anymore. I'd like to wear something that will reflect our time in the Crimea, with a Scottish theme to reflect my Scottish ancestry. We could cut up that old dress I wore at the farewell ceremony at Balaklava and use if for the trimmings. I see the dress being in deep blue, with the scarlet and blue tartan to add the colour.'

I entered into the spirit. 'And we have some of that fine lace left. Shall I make a very wide fichu, all in white, with cuffs of the same material?'

'Ratia, you always know my mind. Yes, that would be most acceptable, I believe.'

'And I can trim your bonnet with white lace, with ribbons of blue and red to match the colour of the dress.'

'Of course, that would be perfect.'

'So, how long have we got?'

'Oh, plenty of time. The ball is to be in two weeks' time.'

'A ball? My, you never told me that. I thought you would just be introduced to her.'

'And a grand banquet as well.' Mammy was positively shining.

'Well, we'd better start today.'

'Oh, there's plenty of time. Come let's have a small drink at this little stall before we go back to Blundells. I find it convenient to be out in the mornings when Louisa is at her busiest.'

I did not usually encourage Mammy in her drinking, but I thought there was a cause for celebration and I could read a whole lot of trouble in the way she casually mentioned some of the domestic arrangements back at the hotel, but Mammy said nothing more.

In the next few weeks, we sewed on the veranda of New Blundells House and as we sat companionably together, I could hear the bustle of domestic work going on inside. Hortense came out and offered us a cooling drink.

'I've just made some lemonade if you'd like it? The mistress is out at the moment and she won't notice if I water the rest of it down.'

I looked at Mammy. She graciously accepted and kept on with the cutting and matching bits of material. The lemonade was brought and I thanked the girl, and was proud of the way she served us with dignity and poise. When I could see she had got to the kitchen I said, 'Mammy? Can you not tell me?'

She looked at me, that old sharp look despite the eyes being a creamy colour, 'Oh, it's just a case of too many cooks. I try to be diplomatic and keep out of the way, for I am mindful that I am dependent on my sister for the roof over my head.'

She stopped speaking and I said nothing. Then she added, as she sighed, 'If only she would let me help her, but she says I'm old and slow. Old and slow, Ratia, it's such a hurtful thing to say to me.

'But I do help, when there's illness and she can't take that away from me.'

'Mammy, you should accept what she says in the nature of

it. Perhaps it is time for you to rest and let others do the work.'

'But Ratia, if I can't be useful, what is my worth? I only ever wanted to be useful.'

Yes, I'd heard that refrain so many times before and I'd also seen her thwarted in her need *to be useful*, like when she never managed to get to India. And I'd sympathised. But this time, I really did believe that her usefulness, except for the odd activity which didn't tax her too much, was over. But of course I would never say that to her.

How wrong I was.

I helped her to dress on the night of the banquet and ball. A carriage was sent from the governor's house and I waved her off but did not feel like staying although I really wanted to wait for her to return, even if it was to get her to bed. The atmosphere in that hotel cut through me and made it very clear that I could not sit around, imbibing tea or lemonade with Hortense. I would return tomorrow afternoon to sit on the veranda and hear all about it.

That evening, I sat in the porch with Phineas and we watched the fireworks that were let off over the governor's house, a surprise to me but very welcome and I thought of Mammy enjoying herself at such an event, as I knew she would be in her element.

I couldn't wait to meet with her and the next day, after I'd helped my husband and also my sister-in-law with the little ones and my parents, settling them in their bath chairs in the shade of the trees in the garden, I walked down the hill into East Street to New Blundells House. It was a warm day but there was a welcome breeze from the harbour which I could see at the bottom of the road. Most people were inside but when I reached the hotel, there was Mammy dozing on the veranda, and I guessed she'd had a good time.

I sat on the chair near her, as quietly as I could, and picked up the newspaper folded on the floor beside her, where it had fallen from her lap. She still tried to read for herself but I knew it always sent her to sleep. I was as quiet as I could be, but my presence eventually penetrated and she lifted her head with a jerk, and opened her eyes. When she saw me, she excused herself, 'Ratia, is it you? I must have dropped off. What time is it?'

'Don't you worry about the time. It's early afternoon, but you probably needed a sleep. Are you going to tell me all about it?'

She was immediately alert and sat upright, her old charismatic self, ready to tell a story. She smoothed down the plain skirt that she wore, and then placed her hands in her lap, one on top of the other, and took a deep breath.

'The governor was not there, and I had to be the hostess, so I tried to be as dignified as I could. The Queen is very attractive, with large dark eyes, but there was a sadness about her which I found out later was based on true tragedy. She is similar to Queen Victoria, as she has lost her husband, and has also known the death of a child. She told me all this, quietly over dinner.

'But let me tell you about it from the beginning. When I arrived, they took me to a chamber where there were refreshments and I was briefed – that was what the secretary called it – about how to address the Hawaiian Queen. He also gave me some hints on how to keep the conversation flowing. You know Ratia, I don't need such hints to keep talking.' She was laughing as she said this, that old loud chuckle, 'But it was helpful because the Queen was very dignified and I realised that I should not just talk about any old subject.

'The governor's house has a wonderful wide staircase and I felt dwarfed as I descended into a huge hall, with a chandelier so large, and so glittering with candles, that the place looked as if it was lit by daylight. It helped that there were many mirrors, so that the candlelight was reflected a hundred times.

'So, when the Queen arrived she was escorted to me and introduced, and we both half curtseyed to each other, although mine was lower than hers, which is the correct protocol as I was told.'

I guessed Mammy had not liked being told how to act, but then had taken it all in good part and I was sure carried out her duties admirably.

'We got on famously after the first few introductions and as we were being served at the banquet, which was ten courses, we became quite intimate in our conversation and when I discovered her recent loss, I sympathised with her and told her about my own dear husband and how I had spent my widowhood, being useful.

'I told her about my work with cholera and yellow fever and she was most interested. I knew it was not feigned, and she informed me she had in fact persuaded her husband to open a hospital in Hawaii for her poor people who suffered badly from smallpox and other diseases. She was very proud of her country, and says that it is more lush than Jamaica with wonderful waterfalls and clean waters in the forests, but I told her we too had beautiful waterfalls and we laughed together and agreed that we could both be proud of our own countries, and we would not disagree.

'But I tell you Ratia, this high society is a peculiar thing. When we laughed, the whole assembly laughed; when we stood, they stood and we had to go into the ballroom before the music would start. Of course neither of us danced but we sat on a daïs to one side, not far from the orchestra, where we could enjoy the dancing of the crowds.

'And to top it all we were then invited to sit outside, on a large balcony and a grand firework display then erupted.'

'I know, I saw them from my place.'

Mammy nodded, and said, 'I'm glad that the ordinary people managed to enjoy some of it. I don't really feel comfortable with such high and mighty people, who don't do any work, not like my dear boys in the Army and Navy. They're dignified because they have a purpose in life. I know some of them are nobility, like Count Gleichem, but he too was useful. It seems that these royal people are unable to relax and enjoy a good laugh, as if they have boards stuck down the back of their clothes.'

'Perhaps they should come and work among the ordinary people?'

We laughed and Mammy did not realise I was being serious. I have to confess that the sermons I heard on Sundays from our Baptist minister made me think like that. He insisted that everyone was equal in the eyes of God and that on the judgement day all would be judged the same, no matter how poor or wealthy they had been in life. He often quoted the verse which said that it was harder for a rich man to go to heaven then for a camel to get through the eye of a needle, and I loved that description because I'd seen camels, and they were such funny creatures anyway that the idea of them being pushed through the eye of a needle made me laugh.

'I think some of us are born to work, like worker bees, and some are born to be graceful and always keep their hands clean,' she answered after a while.

Maybe I wouldn't tell her about those sermons I'd heard.

It was about this time that my sister-in-law Ester came to me to see if I could influence my brother, because she was so worried about what he was up to. He had been creeping out at night to attend political meetings and there were rumours flying around that a rebellion was being planned.

'Can you have a word with him? He respects you.'

I wondered that my older brother looked up to his much younger sister but realised it was so; my travelling had matured me beyond my years.

'It's the clandestine way he leaves the house that I don't like. He goes to meetings and comes home somehow different. I don't agree with the way those meetings are pushing ordinary people into thinking they are *uppity.*'

That was the phrase she'd used. I agreed to speak to him.

When I spoke to Isiah, I said, 'You know, Ester is worried about you going to meetings at night. What are they about?'

He explained quite calmly. 'The plantation owners are hanging on to their land, even though some of it is not being used anymore. Haven't you noticed that there's not so much sugar cane being grown?'

I shook my head. I liked Kingston and rarely left it, and even when Mammy visited her Black River relations, I stayed behind.

'You should go for trips with that Mother Seacole, and find out for yourself. It is true that in the north, some of the plantation owners have sold their land to our kind and they have taken to growing bananas, and are doing well. Our Baptist ministers are helping others to negotiate to buy more land but those dog-in-the-manger owners won't sell, even though they go around in rags because they're not getting the money they used to get when we were all slaves.

'I tell you, girl, something is going to happen soon, I can feel it. The meetings are getting more and more rumbustious and one of our congregation threatened to go and take a gun to force the sale he wanted.'

'But you're not wanting to buy? You're a carpenter.'

'No, I don't want to buy, I saw what working on the land did to our poor parents, just look at them. Worn out before their time, and even if I were to willingly labour in the fields for my own profit, it would wear me out too. But I have got to support our friends and neighbours in the church, haven't I?'

I said nothing but it worried me, this undercurrent of discontent. I'd never seen it before. I'd been born too late for the slaves' uprising and being given their freedom, but I knew there'd been riots and killings back then. Surely it wasn't going to happen again?

One day when I was sitting with Mammy, a group of men passed by New Blundells House, holding up placards which read, *'fair sales to buyers'* or *'join us for a fair share of the land'* and similar slogans. My heart sank. If they were coming into our town, so far from the country, they must be getting really angry.

Mammy could see the slogans, and asked, 'Ratia, what is all that about?'

I explained what my brother had told me.

'Perhaps I can help,' she said, half rising, 'If I go to the governor, perhaps he can do something about it.'

I knew she was friendly with Mr Eyre, and he was all powerful, on our island, but I asked, 'What can he do about it? If the white owners won't sell, he can't make them, can he?'

'I don't know Ratia,' she answered as she picked up her bag from the floor under her seat, 'but it will give me something to do to try. Do you want to come with me?'

I hesitated only a second, and then nodded. I felt protective of her and didn't know if she would be safe in that angry crowd, especially if they saw her just walking into the governor's residence like the friend she was. I guessed they might feel she was on the wrong side.

We walked together to the residence and were allowed in and soon shown into the governor's office, and I marvelled at the ease of this, compared to the difficult time Mammy had had in London in the government offices there.

He came round from his huge desk and invited us to sit and ordered some tea.

'Now, first I have to thank you personally for being so good with Queen Emma, as we can call her. I seem to remember that her official names were so long and unpronounceable that my secretary had to practice for two or three days. But I have good reports of the event and you did well.'

Mammy bowed in thanks but said nothing.

I wanted to shout at him, *of course she did well, this lady knows how to conduct herself,* but as is my way, I kept quiet.

'Now, what do I owe this visit, and with your lady's maid as well?'

'If you don't mind, can I ask my companion here, whose name is Horatia, to explain what is happening? And we need your help.'

I protested. 'Me? Oh, Mammy, please, no, it's not for me...'

'Ratia, just speak ordinary, and explain to this gentleman what you told me.'

I hesitated, because despite being with Mammy for years, I still distrusted these men in authority. After a pause, I told him that some of the ex-slaves wanted to better themselves but couldn't, and how the Baptist ministers were helping them.

The man listened, stroking his beard and I noticed that his hair was still dark, and quite thick, but that his beard was greying. He had a serious look about him, which I thought was because he had a high forehead and a long nose. He nodded in encouragement, as I hesitated on one or two occasions but when I'd finished, he said to Mammy.

'Very well explained. I'll try to do something, but will have to consider what is for the best. While I sympathise with those who wish to better themselves by purchasing land, laws don't get passed just by thinking about them and it may take some time. Certainly it is unfair if the people have the money to pay the right price and the owners are refusing to sell to them just because they're black and ex-slaves. That is not good.'

I felt pleased with his answer, and when we were on our way home, I asked Mammy if she thought something would be done.

'He's a good man, but I believe he has to get instructions from England so, as he says, it may take some time to change the law.'

But the law wasn't changed quickly enough for some people on our island and it was a few months after that meeting that we heard the terrible news that a demonstration outside the court house in St-Thomas-in-the-East, near Morant Bay – some thirty miles east of Kingston – had developed into a riot which was dispersed by our own militia firing into the crowd. I'd always been warned as a child about the Maroons as being dangerous outlaws who would kidnap me if I wasn't a good child, and the rebellion was in their lands and although I read the news out to Mammy, I had no idea that it affected me.

'Many killed,' I read out to Mammy from the Gleaner newspaper and as I spoke, my heart flipped. I knew my brother had spoken about going to a peaceful demonstration, if he could get there easily to support people he knew, and I hadn't seen him that morning. I prayed he did not have the means to travel so far, over hilly countryside. Or would he have taken a boat?

'But on which side? Surely our soldiers wouldn't shoot at innocent people?' Mammy had leaned towards me as if anxiety made her want to jump up and be away.

I read on. Yes, they had been ordered to fire on unarmed men, and had fired indiscriminately into the crowd. I dropped the paper in fear.

'Oh, Mammy I must get home, to check on my family, please, I'll return with more news. But I'm worried sick.'

She looked at me sharply as I jumped up.

'Ratia, surely your family are law abiding and wouldn't take part in something like this?'

'I surely hope not, Mammy, but as I told that governor, the Baptist ministers were helping us and I know my brother looks up to what they advise, and if they'd encouraged their congregation to go to that meeting he might have gone. I just don't know.'

Mammy also stood up. 'I'll come with you, to make sure. And then I'll go down to the docks and see if we can't get a passage to the Bay to help the wounded. It might be too late, but I have to be there.'

I wanted to walk much faster than Mammy was capable of but felt I had to be polite and measure my pace with hers until she noted my impatience, and urged, 'You go on, girl, and I'll follow. I can see how anxious you are.'

With that I almost ran up East Street and into the suburbs where our homestead was. I dashed up the hill and ran into the kitchen where my sister-in-law was to be found, wringing her hands and swaying in a hard-back chair. Before I was through the door, she called, 'Is that you, Isiah?'

I had to disabuse her and she jumped up and clung to me. 'He said he was going but I tried to delay him, forcing him to eat breakfast before he went. Oh, I hope he didn't get there. Everyone's talking about it and George Gordon is talking about it in the house in Kingston and there's uproar'.

'Why did they demonstrate? What was it all about?'

'Oh, that Bogle man took forty-five of them from where they lived in Stony Gut to meet the governor, who said he would see them, but he then refused to even listen and when they returned home, they were upset and angry. Then that Bogle man suggested they form an orderly demonstration – we all knew about it but I pleaded and pleaded.'

Mammy came in and heard this. 'Come, sit down and we'll make you a special drink. You mustn't worry about your husband until we know more. He'll be alive, or if the Lord so wishes it, he'll be in heaven. We can't do anything about it but be brave and stay calm. Ratia tells me you have children and you must think about them now.'

As she spoke she busied herself at the range and I could see her crushing some rosemary and sage from her bag and, when the pot had boiled, she pushed these in. I knew this would form a calming potion and encouraged my sister-in-law to drink.

Once we had calmed her, Mammy explained what we would do to find out more.

'The only way is to be there and I will ensure we get there as quickly as we can and see for ourselves.'

Ester was quieted, so I found a bag and packed it quickly, Ester nodding in agreement as I raided her cupboard for what we'd need, and followed Mammy who was talking to a stranger. She told me, 'I've found out more from the passers-by and it's serious.

'Many are wounded and twenty-eight are dead. Terrible, terrible news and I'm surprised that Governor Eyre allowed it. I only hope it was a mistake, for the whole island will rise up now.'

She was breathing heavily as she waddled along and I had to pace myself with her, and knew it was hard for her to talk and move at the same time.

'We have to get there and help those who are wounded, although my sympathies lie with our boys who are carrying out orders. It's not right though to fire on unarmed men.'

We arrived back at New Blundells House and it wasn't long before Mammy came out with her carpet bag packed and her herbal box in the other hand. We hurried down to the harbour, Mammy panting and slowing so I took the box from her, she releasing it gratefully, but I still left her behind. As I waited for her, I wondered at myself. Did I really want to be involved again with nursing the wounded in a battle area, because that was what it sounded like, but as soon as she appeared, I knew where I had to be; by her side.

As soon as the ferrymen saw Mammy, they were keen to take her. She had been feted by all since she had been on the island, and this was more evidence that she was a famous heroine who would travel where there was trouble.

It took all the rest of the day to reach Morant Bay and it was not hard to find the wounded who, on hearing that Mother Seacole had arrived, came to her with their cuts and bruises and bullet wounds. We worked by oil-lamp throughout the night to see to their injuries.

I asked for my brother but nobody knew about him and each person I asked said they would ask around so when the next morning came, exhausted, I fell into a fitful sleep. I dreamt that he came to me as an angel to thank me.

We stayed several days and we were there when the

governor carried out a terrible act and I could never believe it, especially as I'd met him and he promised he would help. Instead, he captured our deacon, Paul Bogle, who I had seen preaching, and in front of a great crowd, he hanged him, claiming he was the ringleader. I didn't attend but was told of the execution.

It got worse. Paul Bogle had been helped by a Governor that Mammy knew and it was she who told me what was happening.

'They're bringing George William Gordon here, who's in the House of Assembly and he's been accused of incitement. I know it can't be true, he's a good man.'

'If he's in Kingston, where's there's a court, why are they bringing him here? Surely we can all go back to Kingston and he can be dealt with there?'

Mammy sighed. 'You know, Ratia, you're good at the sums, and I know your letters are better than mine now, but when it comes to the ways of men, you don't understand enough.'

I wanted to protest. After all, I read the newspapers to her, so I did know the names of all these people and what they got up to but I had to admit that I didn't take that much interest in why, as it made my head spin.

'All right, Ratia, and this is truly serious. The governor-general has declared martial law in Morant Bay, which means that there is no proper court in this district, and he can decide how to punish the ringleaders. That's how he managed to hang Paul Bogle without a trial. He's done it to stop the rioting and that means he can convict anyone without a proper trial, it's almost like going back to the old days when the blackies were slaves – their masters would just whip them if they so much as muttered against them.'

I had a spark of initiative then. 'And there's no martial law in Kingston?'

'Right. You understand now.'

All the time we witnessed the goings-on I worried about my

brother but the only thing that consoled me was that no-one had heard of him in these parts and I garnered enough knowledge about the events to realise that, if his name was not known, then it was likely he wasn't here in Morant Bay.

Mammy and I ministered to those who were still suffering and Mammy tried to see Governor Edward Eyre, based on old times' sake but she was fobbed off with the explanation that he was too busy.

That evening, I found her with her head in her hands, and rocking, she was that upset.

'Ratia, what is happening to our country? I fear for tomorrow, because I've heard that Mr Gordon is going to be tried by a court martial and that means he is being tried for a military offence, as I well know, and for even the slightest of offences, the death penalty is imposed. I cannot believe – I will not believe – that this is happening.'

We spent a sleepless night, on the floor of a kind woman's living room after we had treated her husband for a bayonet wound in the side and he was still alive.

The next morning there was a sort of roar that woke us and we quickly joined the crowd that was gathering in the square. None of us were allowed inside the court house but it wasn't long before someone ran out and shouted, 'He's been convicted! It's the death sentence.' There was a great cry and people surged forward but suddenly there was a thick line of red where the local militia came running and formed a wall to stop us going anywhere. I hated to see our local men, dressed in the English red, standing against their own people. I hid behind Mammy and she stood in the middle of the crowd and watched. Such was her fame that the people around her gave her space and guided others away from her.

We heard the shattering of many rifles going off in the back of the courthouse and we all knew that Mr Gordon had been summarily executed.

The whole day was one of nightmare for me and Mammy as

we fled the angry crowd, to save our lives, as the militia marched forward, their guns at the ready.

'We make for the harbour and get back to Kingston, quickly,' gasped Mammy as we hid down a side road. 'There's too much anger here and I don't want to risk your life as well as mine.'

There'd been mutterings in the crowd sometimes that Mammy had been friends with Mr Eyre, and how they knew that, I don't know. It might have been because Mammy was so used to being open with her acquaintances and thought nothing of boasting about knowing the highest in the land. But I could see that the crowd was not sane and could turn against anyone who they thought was against them, even though some of them protested that Mammy was helping them. It was as if the world had gone mad and no-one knew who was friend or foe.

I felt guilty too, and thought about this as we sailed back along the coast. Was it my fault for telling Mr Eyre how Mr Bogle had helped my people? Was that why he had him hanged? I would never know, but it made me go hot every now and then for the rest of my life, thinking about it.

Arriving back at Kingston you would think nothing had happened. All was calm and when I eventually arrived home there was Isiah, sitting in the kitchen.

I ran to him and threw myself into his arms, and he was considerably surprised.

'I've been seeking you at Morant Bay, I thought you'd been one of the killed.'

'No, I know seventy-eight were killed in the end, but thank God, I was not there to witness it.' He said as he dislodged my arms from his neck. As I sat down, he explained that although he'd tried to get to the demonstration he had been thwarted by lack of money and an important carpentry job he'd had to finish. I discovered later that it was Phineas who had been instrumental in this, by asking a friend to force Isiah to finish a job of repairing a dangerous veranda before he would release him, and then not paying him until he could get to his bank to withdraw the fee.

A few days later and the whole affair was over but we discovered that after the first 'official' executions, over four hundred other demonstrators had been captured and summarily executed, and the rest of our congregation were so cowed that nobody dared mention it again.

A short while after this, Mr Eyre was called back to England and removed from his post, and I was pleased to hear that he was heavily criticized. It hit Mammy badly and I could tell Mammy was thinking of leaving again.

'Where do I belong, Ratia?' she asked me one day. 'I cannot condone what has happened but I must always believe in my father's country and its justice. This must have happened because Mr Eyre is a wicked man, but I dined in his house and carried out his wishes and I liked him. I truly believed he would help to solve the problem with the land.

'And our boys, the local militia. All I can accept is that they carried out their duties to the end, no matter how wrong their orders were.'

It was about this time that Louisa came out on to the veranda on several occasions and asked questions like, 'Are you both comfortable here? Need anything?'

It was the way she said it, in a bitter, enquiring way and I looked at Mammy for guidance but she smiled sweetly and answered her sister kindly.

When we were shopping and away from the house, I took courage and asked, 'I thought matters had settled down between you and Louisa. What's the matter?'

Mammy didn't answer at once and it was as if, unusually for her, she was measuring her words. 'I am perfectly happy with her, and she carries out her duties as a hotel keeper admirably but she does not have the continuous number of guests that we used to have in my mother's day and when I ran it.

'I've tried to suggest that she tempers her strict ways, and be a little gentle, but it's not in her nature. I sit on the veranda and try to be an ambassador for the hotel, but, Ratia, I hesitate to say this, and I would not want you to ever repeat it in my lifetime, I think she resents her older sister. And she does not have my generosity of spirit when it comes to hospitality. I admit she has made several references to my expenditure.'

Mammy said this in such a sad manner that I patted her arm and diverted her by suggesting we enter the millinery that we were passing to look over their variety of ribbons, and she immediately brightened.

I thought it was time to write to her old patrons in London, who might be able to help

.

Chapter 35: Jelly and sweetmeats

I hoped Mammy never found out what I'd written, as I'm sure she would be mortified.

This is the letter I wrote to Lord Rokeby:

Dear Lord Rokeby

I hope you will forgive the liberty I take in writing direct to you, but you were complimentary to me when I had the pleasure of meeting with you as Mrs Seacole's companion and we colluded in ensuring her good care when she was in London.

You could well have read about the awful events that happened in our island a few months ago and my mistress is deeply distressed by all that occurred, always wanting to see the good in people, but not knowing the rights or wrongs of it.

Since then she has been sorely troubled by some of her country-people's reaction to her. They know that she is totally supportive of the British way of life, and the Army, and they would see that as a betrayal of her own people, many of whom were killed in the uprising. This is so, even though she carried out her duties as a doctress among the rioters.

This is not her only trouble, although she would never admit to it. She has been living under sufferance at her sister's hotel, The New Blundells Hotel – which you may have heard of it as your famous author Anthony Trollope stayed there a few years' ago and highly praised it – and it is becoming irksome to her.

As you know my mistress is a gentlewoman and has always enjoyed the little luxuries that such a status bequeaths on her and the supply of these are resented by her sister, only because they stretch her sister's purse.

I write this knowing you have my mistress's best interests at heart and do hope that some attention could be given to the matter of helping her, at the very least, to set up her own establishment here in Jamaica. Please destroy this letter if you think I am being presumptuous and there is no possibility that my request can be considered.'

I read the letter three times, and corrected it twice, before I was satisfied with it. I didn't mention this to Phineas as I thought Mammy's affairs were mine and nobody else need know. I took it down to the post ship and gave it personally to Captain Cooper, the Royal Mail Company Captain who we knew, and pressed on him the secrecy and urgency of the letter. As I walked back up home, I recalled how I had done something similar all those years ago when that poor doctor died.

I waited in great trepidation for the result of my letter. I prayed and prayed that Lord Rokeby would not write direct to my mistress to inform her of her companion's presumption. That would be the worst that could happen. If he ignored it, so be it.

But, as in other times, dear Lord Rokeby responded in the best way possible.

We discovered that advertisements and letters had been placed in the British newspapers – which of course we did not see for some weeks afterwards – to raise funds for her 'to carry out a scheme to ensure for Mrs Seacole in her declining years, the means of obtaining remunerative employment, whereby competence or financial self-sufficiency would be secured.'

Not only that, but the notice went on to say,

The Committee feel the more emboldened to solicit aid to carry out this good work, from the circumstance of THE QUEEN having been graciously pleased to express her approbation of Mrs Seacole's services, and HER MAJESTY's kind interest in her future welfare.'

But before we read these notices, a large cheque was delivered to Mammy with a letter from Cox's agents on the island. It was accompanied by a letter which read:

Dear Mrs Seacole

It has come to our notice that you do not have an establishment of your own where you can practise as you should do, in your chosen profession of doctress and healer.

We, the undersigned have therefore raised funds and hereby enclose the cheque totalling the amount raised, in order that you can purchase a property of your own and have some funds to set yourself up once again in the manner that you are accustomed.

We would ask that you keep us informed of your welfare and hope that, in your declining years, you are more than comfortable.'

I knew nothing about this of course until the afternoon when I visited Mammy, who, as I approached, raised herself from her seat and, leaning on the balustrade of the veranda, waved the cheque at me as I approached. She called loudly to me, and others turned to look at her, and smiled at her excitement.

'Ratia, Ratia, come quickly, oh good news, wonderful news. We are in funds!'

When I saw the size of the cheque I was stunned. It was more than enough to purchase a property and have some over to furnish it and buy equipment, herbs and medicines to really set us up. Mammy did not delay. We went out that afternoon, and Mammy knew where she was going. We headed down to the harbour and walked a block along Water Lane, and turned right into Duke Street.

'Up here, Ratia, there's a plot of land at the top, just right for us. I noticed it when I came back the other day.'

She led me along Duke Street until its junction with East Queen Street, where there were few houses. It was not far from Blundells and I wondered whether it would be sensible to move farther away, but Mammy was so enthusiastic, I let her show me the plot, and, once we had inspected it, and noticed it was on a slight incline, we went to the agents whose name was on a board outside.

Mammy drove a hard bargain and purchased the land for less than the asking price.

'Now I have the money and I want your brother Isiah to build our house. Ratia, can you ask him to call on me tomorrow?'

What a happy time that was, watching her own house growing and my brother eagerly building it, with the carved wood of the veranda that Mammy asked for, and the rounded balusters on the stairs, with carved patterns, and a special wood panelled room with cupboards that she would use as a consulting room. It was built in the traditional way, around a central garden and Mammy talked of planting herbs and fast growing trees of coconut, mango and banana so we would be well provided with fruit and the shade these trees provided.

Ester brought the children one Sunday morning, after chapel, and they ran in and out of the building, and the gaps where the windows were still to be fitted; along the walkways on the upper floors, laughing and playing mothers and fathers in the make-believe kitchen, and Mammy sat on an old rocker that we'd brought over, watching the activity with a gentle smile on her face. I thought she was truly content at last.

When she moved in, she had a grand party for my family and hers, and the Henriques' families came over from Black River and I still didn't like that lad Christopher who thought he was the little gentleman, and stood on the veranda smoking, his hands in the pockets of his light grey suit, ignoring my nephews who were gazing up at him and tugging at his coat tails, trying to get him to play with them. Louisa came too and spent the time gossiping in the corner with the Henriques women, and I realised they thought they were a cut above us. Mammy noticed it too and tried to introduce different members of my family, but apart from a handshake, they went back to their gossiping.

I called to Mammy, 'Mistress, come and look at my naughty niece, whose fingers are all sticky with the jelly, and she's wiped it all over her face.'

She came to us, smiling and I occupied her with the little ones, offering sweetmeats to her so she could spoil them, until she forgot that she had been trying to get everyone mixed together and we all managed well enough.

I was grateful that Mr Day, from our Crimean disaster, did not come, as he was still in the Antipodes and I hoped never to see him again.

After that, word seemed to get out that Mammy was entertaining as in the old days, and many of the old guard, who I remembered, such as Naval Captain Cooper, came and hugged her and thanked her for saving his life. He raised an eyebrow at me and smiled but did not otherwise acknowledge me, and I was grateful for that, because I would not want Mammy to know that I'd posted that letter which resulted in our present good fortune.

As always, just as I thought our life was settled and we would never need to worry about money or go travelling again, the world interfered with my dreams. I was reading to Mammy one afternoon, and as I read the front page news, which was several weeks' old, she leant forward in that way I dreaded and I knew that something had fired her enthusiasm.

'An appeal has been made for people with medical skills to help the injured in the war that has been raging between France and Prussia. Our medical men realise that to assist those injured in battle is not a partisan issue and all those with such skills, both doctors and nurses, should on humanitarian grounds go to the front to minister to those wounded.'

My heart sank as I read. I could almost foretell what her response would be, and I was right.

'We have to go, Ratia, with our skills, they can't refuse us. And we have the money for the passage.'

I knew it was no good protesting. I left to pack my bag and explain to Phineas that I had to go. He was kind enough to give his blessing, and also agreed to look after Mammy's property while we were away, saying he would find a tenant among his colleagues who would be good to pay rent. That way, there would be some funds available for Mammy when we returned. You see, I knew that, not only would he understand, he was ever practical and a good businessman

Chapter 36: Dandelion and burdock tincture

'How I wish I could thank the Queen personally, Ratia, but I know how hard it is to get an audience with her, still grieving for her Albert.'

I couldn't believe that Mammy would even consider that the Queen would grant her an audience, but I suppose she had achieved so much with the great and good in the army and navy, and had friends among the aristocracy, that this seemed a natural extension of her thinking.

'First, we have to concentrate on our aim to help the soldiers, Mammy.'

'Yes, you're right.'

So, as soon as we were in London, she started to petition all those she knew and this time she wrote to Lord Verney, the Member of Parliament who she heard was heading the organisation to recruit medical people, and explained about her doctoring skills.

He took some time to write back and never even offered to meet Mammy, and the letter was a firm refusal to even consider her. He had enough medical people and didn't need any more, so he said.

She went to see the Minister for War, to offer to go under her own steam, as she had done all those years before, but he said they were organising their own supplies and medical people.

She visited her old friends and bankers at Cox's and they explained that, this time, the Army had organised the supply systems much better and were even providing free food, drink and tobacco to the fighting men.

'This time, Mrs Seacole, they have learned lessons, perhaps from the way you dealt with matters in the Crimea, and you will be wasted if you go. War is getting professional and they don't need camp followers to help them now.'

It was explained to her kindly but she still felt affronted and I had to offer her some port and brandy before she could reconcile herself, and go to bed.

I ached for her, as I had in the days gone by. She was so kindly, always willing to help, *to be useful,* that my heart bled for her, in these rejections, even though I knew they were for the best. After all, she was nearly seventy, I guessed, although we never discussed her age, and she was frequently exhausted and would not really have been much help. I sat up, watching the embers of the fire die down from bright red, through orange to a dull blue and thought what I could do. I took up *Punch* to see if that would give me any inspiration and there I saw it.

Her old friend, Count Gleichen, had turned sculptor and there was a satirical picture of him with a bust of his cousin, Queen Victoria, which looked very good.

Supposing I suggested to him that he ask Mammy to sit for him? She would enjoy that, talking over old times.

Once again, I prepared my pen and wrote a letter. Which was promptly answered by the next post.

'I will take it as an honour if Mrs Seacole would sit for me and may I suggest Tuesday next at my studios for the first time?'

It was of course addressed to Mammy, with no reference to my missive, and she perked up as soon as she opened it, and read it aloud to me. I expressed suitable astonishment and urged her to attend. The next weeks were taken up by her sitting for Prince Victor, as she took to calling him, while old friends dropped in and kept her amused as she sat.

One day she came home in unusually high spirits and gave me the news.

'I was sitting for Prince Victor, and truth to tell I was becoming mighty weary with sitting still for so long, when a visitor was announced. Princess Alexandra, the wife of the Prince of Wales entered. She did not make a fuss of her royalty but sat quietly until Prince Victor stopped and turned to her. He graciously introduced us and ordered tea, and I had a welcome break from sitting.

'She is a kind soul but suffers greatly. You have to speak quite clearly to her and face her for her to hear you but she bears this affliction very well.

'Ratia, we liked it each other enormously and she has invited me to Marlborough House for tea. I feel this is the start of a friendship which I will treasure. You never know…'

She did not continue but I guessed what she was thinking. If she was a friend of the daughter-in-law of Queen Victoria, might she meet that great Queen on one of her visits?

This friendship made Mammy very happy, not just because she became familiar with a member of the royal household, but also because, as she explained, she could be *useful*. Princess Alexandra was not only deaf, she explained, but also suffered bouts of all sorts of aches and pains and often Mammy would go with her herbal box and mix potions for her and Alexandra would drop little notes round to our house in Upper George Street, thanking her kindly for the medicine.

One day we had another visit from Captain Cooper who loved Mammy for helping him in the Crimea, the same Captain who had carried my letters not only to the mother of that poor dead doctor but also to Lord Rokeby.

As they chatted about old times, Mammy suddenly exclaimed, 'I've had a brainwave. I would like you to bring back some mangoes, on ice, so I can present them to Princess Alexandra. She has never tasted them and it will do her good to have some good fruit, can you do that for me?'

He didn't hesitate. 'But of course, Mary, I will deliver them to you as soon as I dock.'

He was as true as his word and, some weeks' later, when, in truth I'd forgotten all about it, a knock came at the door and luckily Mammy was in. The fruit nestled in palm leaves in an old woven basket which I recognised from home, and, as soon as I handed it to her, Mammy rushed the basket of fruit to Marlborough House, but not before I managed to filch one. Oh, how it tasted of home, the rich juice flowing over my chin as I put the flesh, still in its thick skin, to my mouth and sucked at its interior, tearing the flesh from the oval stone in the middle with my teeth so that strands stuck in between my teeth. I'm sure my mistress wouldn't have minded if she'd known.

Mammy was very eager to tell me of her visits to the royal residence and when she returned, she told me, 'It was so good to see her biting into one and enjoying it so. I had to explain to her how to cut it, with her own little fruit knife, and everything was very intimate. You understand that this was not in the public reception room, but in her own private apartments, where we make ourselves quite comfortable. I don't even have to formally curtsey to her now, and we have a laugh together about the formal servants who come and go. She is kind to them though and very thoughtful.

'Between you and me, Ratia, she wants to be useful as I have been, and looks to me to guide her in her public works. She loves children and I've suggested she might want to take an interest in maternity hospitals for the poor, so that the little mites will have a healthy entrance into this world of ours.'

'What made you think of that, Mammy? We don't usually act as midwives, so why...?

'Oh, it was my priest, who preached on Sunday, 'suffer the little children to come unto me'. Ratia, he gave us a graphic description of how the poor have no help in their births and even though there is talk about nurses being trained, some of which ideas come from our dear friend Florence Nightingale, they are often attended upon by gin-soaked so-called midwives who do not have the training we have. If I was younger I would start a whole new career, but I fear I must now keep to the old ways that I know and understand.'

I noted that Mammy was calling Florence Nightingale a friend but I made no comment, realising it was one of her exaggerations, and merely answered, 'Mammy you deserve to rest now, and enjoy your friends and acquaintances.'

'Yes, I know. And my mind is turning to my demise, and making peace with my maker. But you do not mention relatives, Ratia, and they are becoming important to me now. It's so good to be round the corner from Amos.'

Amos Henriques! And his wife, Julia. They had had little time for us when we were trying to get to the Crimea, but asked for Mammy's help for their nephew, who was a Seacole, to be baptised into the Catholic Church in Jamaica. Amos was one of her mother's family and they were well spread in both Jamaica and England.

I had no time for them. They had never been forthcoming in helping us in what Mammy wanted to do in the past but once Mammy had become famous they were round her like hummingbirds at the nectar, constantly winging their way near her, especially when there were special public events.

One of those events was the public display of Count Gleichen's bust of my mistress at the Royal Academy at the annual exhibition. She mentioned she was going and they immediately said they would accompany her.

'Mammy, can you let me come as well? I'll keep in the background.'

'Ratia, you don't have to keep in the background, of course you can come, and as one of my guests. I'm sure Amos and Julia won't mind.'

So we set off, a party of four, to the Royal Academy, in Burlington House, Piccadilly and I felt overwhelmed by the grandeur of the courtyard and the building itself, although you would think I would be familiar with large imposing buildings by now. The stairs up to the exhibition rooms were wide and imposing, and many people flocked around as we entered. Then someone whispered, 'It's Mary Seacole'. Some of those gathered craned forward but Mammy swept on, bowing to right and left and it was as if the waters of the Red Sea opened for the Israelites as she walked slowly up the stairs and the company parted to allow her to enter the galleries. Amos had taken her arm and Julia stood on the other side of her and made it quite clear that I should follow. But then I saw Count Gleichen come out of the crowd and, after greeting Mammy and nodding to her companions, he edged around them and walked beside me and smiled, bowing slightly.

'Hello, young companion, how are you?' He spoke quietly, 'I am deeply indebted to you for suggesting such a sitter, and I am very pleased with the result. I remember how kind you were to all the soldiers and I watched as you gave them extra measures when no-one was watching. Come, I'll lead you to my exhibit, the bust of your mistress and you can tell me what you think of it.'

I hoped he wasn't alluding to what I thought no-one knew, about my goings on in the Crimea, and I looked at him closely. He had a slight smile on his face as he took my arm and we entered the exhibition hall which was huge and I just stood there, staring. Every wall was covered with paintings of all sizes and shapes as if the idea was to hide the flock wallpaper. It was huge with a glass ceiling which filtered light into the chamber. Mammy turned and laughed and extracted herself from Amos and returned to us.

'Victor, how are you? I'm pleased to see you looking after Ratia. So, where is it?'

He grinned and said, 'Follow me.'

Nobody bothered to introduce Amos and Julia, and I smiled to myself as they scuttled behind us, desperate to be seen to be part of our group.

He led us into a room which had many busts and sculptures in it and, in the middle, on a plinth, there it was. I couldn't believe the likeness, all in white. I walked all round it and admired the carving of the bosom of her dress and the huge pearls she wore.

Count Gleichen watched us, without smiling, and I guessed

he was anxious for our approval. I couldn't help it, but, before anyone else could speak, I said, 'You have really caught her likeness, it is wonderful.'

Mammy glanced at me and smiled. 'Yes, Victor, it really is wonderful and I'm mighty proud of you and your skills.'

Then there was a burst of applause from the crowds who had gathered around us and Mammy smiled and bowed at them. We stayed a while looking at the statue before we moved off, casually glancing at the other exhibits, and it was only then that Mammy recollected herself and introduced her cousins to Count Gleichen. With dignity he bowed to them but made no effort to make further conversation.

I realised then that those of us who had been in the Crimea had formed a special bond and those who had not been there, like the Henriques, could never comprehend the sufferings we had endured and could never be a part of our company. But I recalled that Amos had been in the Turkish Medical Corps so I wondered what sights he had seen and wondered if he was, truly, a modest man, by never mentioning his experiences. I had to admit that he was attentive towards Mammy now.

It was shortly after this that it was very obvious to others that Mammy's eyesight was failing. She did not like to be seen to be an invalid and began to go out less and less, and we spent many an hour while I read the newspapers and journals, such as *Punch* to her. She would sleep a lot too and, quite often, I would think she was getting forgetful and repeat things to her, until she snapped at me that her mind was quite good and I didn't need to keep on at her.

It was because of this I reminded her that she had not made a will. I knew she now had two properties in Jamaica. Phineas had done so well for her with rents, and looking after her other little savings that he had purchased a second property with the rents she had received from the Duke Street house and the second house was a little distance from it. It was only because she would sometimes come out with comments like, 'I really must leave Nelson's ring to Count Gleichen. He's been so good to me. They've all been so good to me' that I urged her to do something about it.

'I will, Ratia, all in good time,' she would say.

I was also in touch with her trustees and they were urging me to persuade her to write her will because she had what was called a power of appointment over the funds they had collected for her and over which they kept a watchful eye. They explained this to me and I understood the significance. I was now a trusted messenger or rather reporter of Mammy's situation, to the trustees. I rather fear I pressed her to see her lawyer and she would retort, 'Make a will? Ratia, I feel that, if I do, it would be like signing my own death warrant.'

I knew that many of my Jamaican relatives felt the same when they heard that their betters were making wills, although most of them never had anything to leave themselves. When a family had become successful, sometimes arguments over an estate became public property, because the courts would be involved. Now that some of the older successful planters who had once been slaves, had died, leaving large banana plantations, there were almighty arguments over who would inherit. Sons argued that daughters had married and moved away and they had worked the land for their parents; daughters argued that they should have some because they'd saved their parents money by moving out, and that the sons had always hung on the coat tails of their parents. I was glad to be out of it but knew that my family would never argue like that – because we didn't have any property to argue about.

When I had a letter from Ester telling me the gossip of the family, it contained the history of one of her distant relatives and I read this out to Mammy to warn her what might happen.

'Listen to this, Mammy, do you remember the family of Andersons, who moved over Cambridge way and bought all that land?'

She rested her head on one side, her brow creasing. It took

her some time to remember but then she answered. 'Yes, I remember, some of them died of the yellow fever in that terrible scourge we had, I recall.'

I nodded, and knew I had her attention, for she always liked to hear about those she had helped in the past. 'Their mother has died without a will and now the eldest son is frightening off his siblings and threatening them with a gun if they come onto the land. He says it's his because he's the eldest.'

Mammy shook her head, and looked sad. 'What a shame, how cruel.'

Then she stared into the fire and ignored me. I was guessing that she was thinking.

But it was Amos who finally persuaded her. She kept on saying she wished she could do something for his family and he told her not to worry, because they were comfortably off. It was the way he leaned forward and patted her on the arm, when he said it, that made me cringe.

He added, 'but if you want to make a will I know just the man. Horace, our friend, Horace Smith. His offices are in Craven Street, just off the Strand. Shall I make an appointment?'

Mammy agreed but with some reluctance. As the appointed day came nearer I could see she was getting herself in a dither.

'You know, Ratia, going to see a solicitor in these circumstances is worse than going into battle in the Crimea. He'll surely twist me with strange words and argue that I can't do what I want to do. What shall I wear?'

'Mammy, you've been in court before, it will be like that. And you've seen lawyers when you signed the leases and when you bought the Duke Street house. Wear what you wore to go to court. Look, why don't you try this blue military style outfit, the one you wore before? I could turn it here, and here, and make new lace cuffs and collar, instead of that old fichu.'

I held up the lace fichu, to show her that the lace was fraying and it looked grey, despite my efforts to whiten it.

She agreed, and we spent pleasant afternoons sewing but she did little of the close work, because of her eyes.

But before the appointment an unwelcome visitor called. Unwelcome as far as I was concerned, but not to Mammy, who greeted Thomas Day as if he was the prodigal son. She insisted they go out for a meal at her expense and he smirked at me as he left.

Later I discovered that he'd set himself up as a merchant in Gracechurch Street, right in the centre of the commercial part of the City. I truly hoped that he'd learnt some business sense and that Mammy wouldn't be inveigled into partnership with him again. I wondered if I ought to warn Lord Rokeby but I decided to wait and see what happened.

When the day came for the solicitor's appointment, Mammy insisted on a dandelion and burdock tincture, to calm her and by the time Amos Henriques arrived, she turned to me and said, 'I'm ready for the fray, I really am.' This told me that the tincture had not worked and she was still apprehensive. She squared her shoulders, took a deep breath and followed Amos to his carriage.

She was gone several hours and I began to worry about her. When she came in she was tired to death and I knew it wasn't right to question her.

After handing her a refreshing glass of port I left her to doze while I prepared the evening meal. I took a while over it and made our Jamaican chicken, with chillies and other spices, not to warm her, because it was a mild September evening, but to make her think of home comforts. Eventually she called to me, 'Ratia, what is that delicious aroma? I swear I was dreaming of my dear husband, and our meals together. I am famishing.'

I smiled as I brought in the steaming pot and ladled her some of the stew.

'The only regret I have, Mammy, is that our native food such as our sweet potato in this country.'

She laughed and took a forkful of moist chicken and nodded appreciatively.

'I know what you mean, Ratia, but a good Scotch broth and rice pudding to follow is just as good as our Jamaican dishes.'

When we had finished the meal, and were sitting comfortably together, she started the conversation. 'I suppose you want to know how it all went today?'

'Only if you want to tell me.'

'Well, Ratia, I think I do, because it's been mighty hard, as I knew it would be, but I have to say these lawyers are wily ones.'

'What do you mean?'

'I started giving him the list of people and sums I wanted to give them and he stopped me immediately when he saw the amounts.'

'What, because he thought they were too much or not enough?'

'Nothing like that, Ratia. It's to do with tax. There's something called Succession Duty and anything over twenty pounds means the poor person who is entitled to that money has to pay tax on it. Don't you think that's right mean?'

I'd never heard of anything like this so I kept quiet and let Mammy go on.

'Well. I'm playing a trick on the government and I'm not letting my friends and relatives pay tax. You wait and see, Ratia.'

She wasn't going to tell me who was getting what and I didn't care really. She'd paid me well and I always assumed she would leave her money to her relations; that was what it was all about as far as I was concerned.

'So is it done?'

'Ratia, you would not believe it but Amos and Mr Smith insisted on taking me to lunch and Mr Smith instructed his clerk to write up the will there and then. I protested, and said I couldn't countenance the poor man missing his lunch as well.

I suggested we return on another day, but they insisted. The poor clerk didn't say anything and just dipped his quill into his ink, hunched over his desk, pulled a large piece of parchment towards him and started writing.

Amos said there was nothing like the present and we could spend a few hours at our meal. So I was well and truly wined and dined and then taken back.'

'And was it ready?'

'It was and Mr Smith sat me down and Amos sat outside but the poor clerk, whose name was Boddy,' Mammy laughed at this and I laughed too, 'Poor Boddy had to stand up beside me while Mr Smith read the whole will to me. Ratia, it's nine pages long and it took him some time to read it. Then he insulted me by asking me if I understood it. Cheek!'

'And did you?'

She gave her old guffaw. 'It was couched in the most convoluted language but I kept interrupting him and made him explain. By the time he had finished, I understood he had made a good job of my wishes.'

'Then what happened?'

'He gave me that quill pen and I signed it and was about to walk out, totally exhausted, when Mr Smith told me to sit, as if I was a schoolchild trying to leave the classroom. Both he and Mr Boddy then signed it, with flourishes as if they thoroughly enjoyed it.

'I gave Mr Boddy seven and sixpence because I was sorry for him and to thank him for his efficiency.'

'But what happens now?'

'To be honest, I feel quite relieved it's all over. They keep the will and nothing happens until I breathe my last breath. I think I have done the right thing by everyone, and thank you Ratia, for making me do it. You were quite right. I do swear they thought I was going to die if I left that office without the will being signed. I'll show them Ratia, we'll travel some more, you'll see.'

It was dark now and the lamp was burning low, so I suggested we retire and no more was said and the making of the will was never referred to again.

Mammy enjoyed her life now, as if she had completed her life's work and could relax, visiting her friends and having small parties at home, where I helped and joined in.

'We're well and truly settled now, aren't we, Ratia? There's nothing else we could wish for.'

I didn't agree and as I sat there, I realised I was homesick and wanted to see my Phineas and my nieces and nephews. Several years had passed and it was unfair to leave my husband for so long, although he would write me long letters about his and Mammy's business affairs, and I could read between the lines for the affection he ad for me.

Could I leave Mammy? I knew I could not. She was getting old and slower, her bulk preventing her from rising from her chair without me assisting her and it became harder and harder for her to dress herself.

On one occasion I found her on the floor.

'I don't know what happened, Ratia. I must have blacked out.'

I knew if I left, I couldn't leave her on her own and it became quite onerous to look after her, partly because she was so independent she just would not stay in her chair and wait for me to help her. Instead, she would try to make a cup of tea and drop the cup, or pour the water onto the tray instead of in the teapot, because she could not see too well.

It was about this time that her husband's nieces became concerned and I have to admit it was helpful for me that they sat and watched Mammy while I went out to buy essentials. The Henriques also made frequent visits and I learned to like them, only because they were genuinely fond of my mistress and I could forgive anyone who showed her kindness.

Ada and Florence were the children of her late husband's younger sister and although they were in their thirties neither of them were married. They had been too young for us to get to know them when we had been in England before. And anyway, Mammy was never good at keeping up with her relations unless she thought they might be useful to her.

They told me about their grandfather, the old Mr Seacole who had lived in Prittlewell, near Westcliff, and claimed that he'd been man-midwife to Lady Hamilton, the consort of Nelson.

'We know a secret. Will you promise to keep it?'

I nodded. I was used to keeping secrets.

'Mr Seacole – Mary's husband, was truly the son of Nelson, but he was a sickly child and Lady Hamilton thought he did not survive, and that he was stillborn. Also our grandfather wanted a son so he took the boy. He thought it was for the best because Lady Hamilton was not married to Nelson and there was already a scandal surrounding their relationship.

'Later on, when Nelson returned, our grandfather introduced the boy to him and Nelson agreed to be godfather, not realising that he was really the father.'

'No! Is this all true?'

'Of course it is – your mistress was told the story when she married Edwin who was told when he was twenty-one and his true father was dead. By that time he was sickly and knew he could never follow in his father Nelson's footsteps so he was sent out to our relations in Jamaica, because his father – our grandfather - thought the warmth would do him good.'

I remember Mammy telling me some such tale, when we were on our way to England the first time, but I thought it was all made up by her. Now here were these two twittery spinsters telling me the family history.

I asked them, 'How do you know all this? Who told *you*?'

They looked at each other, not quite sure what to say and I began to wonder if they had made it up.

Ada said to Florence, 'Shall I tell her?'

Her sister nodded. Ada took a deep breath.

'When our grandfather was dying, we had the nursing of him and he was very troubled, tossing and turning at night, muttering and sweating. He kept saying, 'Lord, forgive me, I did it for the best,' or that was what we thought he said. I kept asking him to tell me what troubled him, hoping it would ease him. He kept on saying, 'Will I be forgiven? Will the Lord forgive me?' I discussed it with my sister and wondered whether we should call the vicar, but there is no confession in the Church of England, and we were worried about what dreadful thing he had done.'

Florence interrupted her. 'Yes, yes, but tell her if you're going to, she's probably guessed anyway.'

Ada gave her sister a look and then went on. 'I urged him to tell me and one night, when he was particularly in pain with the terrible illness that took him, he shouted, 'Nelson, forgive me.' He then fell into a deep sleep and I thought that was the end of it, but in the morning he woke, peaceful and quiet, as if all the pain had gone. I dared to remind him what he had said in the night and I asked him what he meant, and he then told me about taking the boy. He said he had done it for the best because Lady Hamilton was not married to Nelson and the bastard would have an unhappy life.

'I comforted him by saying that he had given Edwin a good childhood and educated him. By then we all knew that Lady Hamilton had died impoverished in France, so Edwin would, indeed, have had a terrible life with her, would he not? I kept on repeating this, that he was a good man, and had done the right thing. Eventually, he fell into a deep sleep and never recovered consciousness but his face was relaxed and I'm sure he was at peace.'

'My, that's quite something. You should tell Mammy what you know some time, although she will tell you she never had any doubts about what her late husband had told her.'

I watched Ada and Florence and they were good to Mammy and she began to rely on them more and more, which I did not mind. I'd received letters from Phineas and for the first time, he wrote he was missing me, and asking when I was coming home. It was time, and truth to tell, I too was missing him and the warmth of my relatives and Jamaica. I'd been in England five years by now although it did not seem like it, especially when there was so much happening around Mammy.

I spoke with those nieces one day and asked if they minded me going before I told Mammy. I knew their regret at my leaving was genuine.

'I am sure Aunt Seacole will not like it at all, but we promise we will care for her, as we cared for our grandfather.'

With this assurance I approached Mammy.

'Ratia, you always seem to be in whispered conversations with my nieces. I may not be able to see very well, but my hearing is good. What are you all talking about?'

That was something that had happened since her falls. She had become a little deaf, although she would not admit it to herself, and, because she thought people were whispering, it made her suspicious. I had to explain everything to her very carefully, in a clear voice. She'd never worried about the spending of money but recently, she would ask me how much I'd spent in the market or where I had acquired a piece of clothing.

'That's not my old blue dress you've cut up for yourself, is it Ratia?' she said to me one day. I had to get close to her to let her feel the material before she would believe that it was not. I always was honest with her, but sometimes she would give me a glazed look, and I knew she was puzzled and not knowing whether to believe me or not. It hurt, but I forgave her because I knew she was getting old. I now had to tell her the truth about what I was going to do. Of course I did, I couldn't just disappear. I tried to broach the subject sideways.

'Mammy, you like your nieces don't you?'

'Of course I do, they're very good to me and so are you. I know that.' Her eyes started watering, which was becoming a common sight now, as if anything to do with emotions affected her far more greatly than before.

'And Amos and Julia live round the corner and pop in, as do all your old comrades from the Crimea.'

'Yes, Ratia, those who are still alive.' And she sighed heavily.

'So you have plenty of support around you.'

She became suspicious. 'What are you trying to say, Ratia?'

I came out with it. 'Mammy I'm homesick, and Phineas is urging me to return to him. I want to go.'

'How can you desert me now? You don't know what you're saying.' She said it in what I called her suspicious voice and I knew it was her illness speaking. She half rose in her chair but fell back and put her hands to her head. She started swaying and I thought she might have one of the collapses which were becoming common.

I spoke calmly and reasoned with her, 'Mammy, you have Ada and Florence in constant attendance, and that is how it should be; your relatives helping you.'

'But they don't read to me like you do,' she said plaintively.

'I'll teach them how to do it. And I can also tell them to spot the items that you like, and describe the pictures to you.'

'But they don't know how to mix herbs like you do, as I taught you.'

'No, but Amos is a doctor and he can help them to care for you. I'll show them what tinctures you like and what will be good for you. It can all be organised, Mammy.'

She calmed a little. She no longer argued, but folded her hands in her lap. I knew that as a sign she was thinking, because sometimes, even in the midst of the suspicions, her mind would suddenly clear and she would be her old comfortable, kind self, but her hearty laugh was not often heard these days.

'Ratia, is this because Ada and Florence are here? Do you think they're usurpers?'

I patted her hands. 'It is because they're here that I feel I can leave you. I don't see them as usurpers, but two of the best people I can trust to care for you as I would. I feel totally content leaving you in their good hands. In a way, I feel as if I don't have any more help to give you, but you need your family around you now. Our story together is finished.'

She nodded and took my hand in hers and held it tight. She had come round to the idea, I could tell.

'I hope I am wise enough to know when things come to an end. You've served me well, Ratia and I am happy for you to go, knowing that I'll never see you again. I know I'm too old and frail to travel.'

I could see her eyes watering and mine also watered. We clasped each other in a great hug and stayed like that for some time, while all the memories of our life together flooded through me.

I left soon afterwards, with Ada and Florence seeing me off.

I heard, when I got to Jamaica, that she'd died of a massive stroke a few days after I'd gone, as if she knew, somehow, that her life's work was done.

Chapter 37: Finale

I hope I've told my mistress's story well – it's a bit like an eulogy that is read out at a funeral – I wanted people to see how kind and wonderful she was, despite her faults of self-advertising, and delusion when it came to managing money and being too trustful of others.

She left me the amount that she had described in her will which meant that I didn't have to pay any tax on it, being nineteen guineas. She described me as 'Mary, the wife of Phineas Bravo,' and that made me so proud. The name she gave me, *Ratia,* was for the time I spent with her, and she knew it. See, even at the end, she was mindful of other people and how to please them.

The rest of the will was quite something and set people's tongues wagging, because when you read it, it's all about her self-promotion and how she wanted to be seen in society, mentioning all the lords and ladies she knew, even in a small way, but, finally, leaving the rest of her estate to the relatives who she knew would need it – her sister and nieces and nephews in Jamaica.

I was surprised at how much she left, but the telling bit is that Lord Rokeby had the trust of her money and this was why she couldn't give it away or use it in wasteful ways during her lifetime, like helping the poor and homeless. As she got older she became more and more religious and wanted to give more and more away. She frequently offered me knick-knacks or extra money but I kept a very accurate book of our household expenditure and my wages so that the trustees could see that I was trustworthy and caring for my mistress in the best way.

She looked after her nephew Edward, by giving him the money to buy a house but I was pleased to see she never left anything to that Christopher even though he was a sort of godson. He never bothered about us and made his own way.

I always wondered if she knew about my extra activities in the Crimea and in Soho. She had said a few words every now and then which made me think she did know and while she would never condemn me, in her later life, because she believed that all should be forgiven, I was sure she could not condone that *activity*. But, if she knew, she obviously forgave me and generously gave me the same sum as some of her other Crimean cronies.

I made one more visit to England, with Phineas, because he had some business with his Jewish friends, and we visited her grave in Kensal Green, in the Roman Catholic part, and I was sad to see the humble grave stone, although it was simple and dignified. I only hope those relatives of hers will look after it and visit it from time to time. I hope others go to see it and it is kept clean from moss, and that the inscription will be always clear.

Anyway, she had been generous with my pay during her lifetime, and I did not have many expenses, especially as I grew into middle age, so Phineas and I have enough money to live comfortably with our families in Jamaica, help to care for my elderly parents, and, make provision for my nieces and nephews, just as Mammy had done.

References

SEACOLE, MARY, *Wonderful Adventures of Mrs Seacole in Many Lands*; (Black Classics, reprinted 1999 and Falling Wall Press (reprinted 1984 with some notes)

ROBINSON, JANE, *Mary Seacole*, (Constable, 2005)

PAXMAN, JEREMY, *The Victorians*, (BBC Books, 1998)

ANONYMOUS, *Camp and Field* (published "under the direction of the Committee of General Literature and Education, appointed by the Society for Promoting Christian Knowledge")

Many articles in the Crimean War Research Society's journals, and the input from members of the Crimean War Research Society (CWRS).

Also thanks to the Registrar in Jamaica, the Jamaican Library in Kingston, the University of the West Indies and Rocky, our driver, who all provided valuable background information.

Historical note

I have used real people where I have been able to verify them but I have made up some names where Mary Seacole, in her book, uses initials, and my friends and researchers from the CWRS have not been able to find a person that would match her description. For instance, The Mackworth-Smith family are totally fictitious based on Mary's contention that she had a letter from the mother of a doctor who died in her arms, called 'M-S'. I've also made up some of the names of military men that she met as she travelled to the Crimea, again where Mary uses initials, although some of them are easily identifiable.

Apart from that, most of the characters were real people who knew and supported Mary Seacole.

Mary did travel to all the places described but I would stress that Horatia is my own fictional creation, although Mary Seacole mentions a young servant called Mary who travelled to the Panama with her on that journey so I have 'allowed' that 'Mary' to continue her adventures with Mrs Seacole.

Goldenford Publishers Ltd
Guildford
info@goldenford.co.uk
www.goldenford.co.uk